*A Generative Thought*

*A Generative Thought*

# An Introduction to the Works of Luigi Giussani

EDITED BY ELISA BUZZI

McGill-Queen's University Press
Montreal & Kingston · London · Ithaca

© McGill-Queen's University Press 2003
ISBN 0-7735-2612-9 (cloth)
ISBN 0-7735-2631-5 (paper)

Legal deposit fourth quarter 2003
Bibliothèque nationale du Québec

Special acknowledgment is due Professor John McCarthy
of the Catholic University of America, Washington, DC,
and Ms Amanda Murphy for their friendly and helpful
suggestions.

**National Library of Canada Cataloguing in Publication**

A generative thought: an introduction to the works
of Luigi Giussani/edited by Elisa Buzzi.
Includes bibliographical references and index.
ISBN 0-7735-2612-9 (bnd)
ISBN 0-7735-2631-5 (pbk)
1. Giussani, Luigi. 2. Theologians – Italy. 3. Religious
educators – Italy. 4. Catholic Church – Clergy.
5. Theology. I. Buzzi, Elisa
BX4705.G5564G45 2003    230'.2'092    C2003-902404-0

Typeset in Sabon 10/12
by Caractéra inc., Quebec City

# Contents

Foreword   vii
IAN KER

Introduction   ix
ELISA BUZZI

PART ONE   PASSION FOR HUMAN DESTINY   1

1   A Style of Thought   3
ANGELO SCOLA

2   Christianity: A Fact in History   34
REMI BRAGUE

3   The Spirituality of Luigi Giussani   40
LORENZO ALBACETE

PART TWO   FAITH REASONABLY
COMMUNICATED   49

4   Living the Real Intensely   51
MICHAEL WALDSTEIN

5   The Religious Sense   58
J. FRANCIS STAFFORD

6   An Extraordinary Educator   73
MARC OUELLET

7   For Man   79
    JORGE MARIO BERGOGLIO

8   The Religious Sense and American Culture   84
    DAVID L. SCHINDLER

    PART THREE   THE CHRISTIAN EVENT:
    LIFE IN THE CHURCH   103

9   Mystery Incarnate   105
    JOHN O'CONNOR

10  The Christian: Subject of a New Culture   113
    JAVIER PRADES

11  Toward Human Flourishing   128
    RALPH DEL COLLE

12  Against the Theological Prejudices of the Age   133
    RODNEY HOWSARE

13  The Only Point of View   143
    CARLO CAFFARRA

    PART FOUR   AT HOME WITH TRUTH:
    ECUMENICAL PERSPECTIVES   147

14  Ecumenical by Its Nature   149
    NIKOLAUS LOBKOWICZ

15  A Presence That Can Be Touched   156
    GILBERT MEILAENDER

16  Common Root and Christian Claim   161
    NEIL GILLMAN

17  Abraham and Liberty   167
    RAVAN FARHÂDI

18  Intercultural Dialogue   173
    SHINGEN TAKAGI

19  The Religious Sense and Modern Man   177
    DAVID J. HOROWITZ

20  Educating in Reason   182
    GIORGIO FELICIANI

    Contributors   187

    Sources of Contributions   189

    Profile of Luigi Giussani   193

    Selected Works by Luigi Giussani   197

# Foreword

In his address to the ecclesial movements and new communities at Pentecost 1998, Pope John Paul II referred to the key text in the Second Vatican Council's constitution on the Church, *Lumen Gentium*, where the council asserts: "It is not only through the sacraments and the ministrations of the Church that the Holy Spirit makes holy the People [of God], leads them and enriches them with his virtues. Allotting his gifts according as he wills (cf. 1 Cor 12:11), he also distributes special graces among the faithful of every rank ... he makes them fit and ready to undertake various tasks and offices for the renewal and building up of the Church."[1] The Pope commented on this text with extraordinary enthusiasm: "Whenever the Spirit intervenes, he leaves people astonished. He brings about events of amazing newness; he radically changes persons and history. This was the unforgettable experience of the Second Vatican Ecumenical Council during which, under the guidance of the same Spirit, the Church rediscovered the charismatic dimension as one of her constitutive elements." And the Pope concluded, "It is from this providential rediscovery of the Church's charismatic dimension that, before and after the Council, a remarkable pattern of growth has been established for ecclesial movements and new communities." With a reference to Pope John XXIII's dream of a new Pentecost for the Church, John Paul called the movements "one of the most significant fruits of that springtime in the Church which was foretold by the Second Vatican Council ... they are the response, given by the Holy Spirit, to this critical challenge at the end of the millennium."[2]

The ecclesial movements, which have a common ecclesiological character, have different charisms. In the Pope's words, "charisms are communicative and give rise to that 'spiritual affinity among persons' and to that friendship in Christ which is the origin of 'movements.'"[3] That definition would seem to apply in a very specific way to the movement called Communion and Liberation, which has the idea of friendship as an essential part of its charism, in a way that none of the other movements do. It is the movement that emphasises liberation through Christ in communion with others. This is the movement of which Mgsr Luigi Giussani, the subject of this book of essays, is the founder and leader. If the movements are as important a phenomenon as the Pope thinks and given that Communion and Liberation is one of the three largest of the movements, Giussani should be seen as one of the most significant figures in the contemporary Church.

In terms of the new evangelization that the Pope has called for, it is notable that the movement grew out of Giussani's own experience in leaving a prestigious academic chair for the school classroom in order to see how Christianity could be made real to an increasingly secularised youth. He is above all an educator, and Communion and Liberation is the movement most concerned with intellectual and cultural evangelization.

But *Christianity* is the wrong word, for it is an abstraction, whereas at the heart of Giussani's thought is the insistence that to be a Christian is to encounter a historical person, Jesus Christ. To put it in another way, Christianity is not an ism or a doctrine or even a message: it is nothing other than the Christian *fact*. And the response to this fact, which we call faith, has to come out of our own experience of our human nature and how Christ gives meaning fulfilment to human life. It is this concrete, pragmatic, and experiential approach that makes him seem so Anglo-Saxon. Indeed, he has been deeply influenced by such as English writers as Newman, Chesterton, T.S. Eliot, and C.S. Lewis.

In the English-speaking world, where the movements are relatively weak compared to their strength in the Latin countries, Giussani is still not a well-known name even in Catholic circles. This will change, but in the meantime a book of essays devoted to an examination of his work and achievement is much to be welcomed.

Ian Ker

NOTES

1 *Lumen Gentium*, no. 12
2 *Movements in the Church: Proceedings of the World Congress of the Ecclesial Movements Rome, 27–29 May 1998* (Vatican City: Pontificium Consilium pro Laicis 1999), 221, 16, 222–3.
3 *Movements*, 222.

# Introduction

ELISA BUZZI

Luigi Giussani's work, which is clearly evident in the ecclesial, cultural, and social dimensions of Comunione e Liberazione (Communion and Liberation), the Catholic lay movement he founded in the 1960s, needs no introduction. Communion and Liberation (CL) is now present in more than seventy countries worldwide. In addition, several of Giussani's principal texts have been translated into English, and they now circulate widely even in the Anglo-American world. In any case, an extensive general presentation of Giussani's work is well beyond the scope of this book, which will have achieved its purpose if it awakens in readers a desire to know more for themselves. The approach of all the essays in this collection, a reflection on Giussani's thought as it emerges in his writings, will be seen to be far more specific, yet really fundamental, if we are willing to grasp all the depth and richness of the word "thought" and if we do not yield to intellectualistic reductionisms of any sort.

One of Giussani's deepest and most passionate convictions, a conviction that has constantly enlivened his pastoral and educational action, is that "no tradition or, indeed, no human experience, can challenge history and stand against the flow of time, except insofar as it comes to express and communicate itself in ways that possess cultural dignity."[1] This judgment can be usefully juxtaposed with another remark that is every bit as significant: for Giussani, theologising, or simply thinking, and being committed to a missionary or educational work are not at all separate activities. Indeed, he says he cannot understand "how it is possible to theologise unless theology is a systematic and critical self-awareness of an experience of faith in action and thus a commitment to the mystery of Christ and of the Church; a passion for the salvation of the world, therefore."[2] From these brief, intense brush-strokes emerge the fundamental outlines of a style of thought that Angelo Scola analyses with deep critical insight in chapter 1 of this volume. "Generative thought," another expression from the same chapter, defines further the very nature of Giussani's style of thought and has been chosen as the title of this collection.

As we shall see, this term identifies Giussani's originality as "his capacity for describing in an articulate way man's elementary experience ... in the mainstream of the *traditio catholica*." We may interpret this suggestion in a way that provides this collection with its proper context and justification: Giussani's thought is also generative in the sense that, getting directly to the origin, that is, to the fundamental questions of meaning in human experience and the Christian Event, with a deep awareness of their wide-ranging existential, theoretical, and cultural implications, it "generates" thought in a constant, passionate dialogue with the most varied of interlocutors. This dialogic impetus, the capacity to reach the very core of his interlocutors' beliefs and concerns and thereby to provoke their free and rational responses at a level in which theoretical seriousness, the search for truth, is not dispersed in an idly academic battle of ideas, is one of the most striking and fascinating characteristics of Giussani's style and method, a feature that has shaped his work as an educator, "an extraordinary educator" – to quote from another contributor to this volume, Mark Ouellet – in a decisive way. A dialogue of this kind can reach the level of "an experience of the communal genesis of understanding [that is] a unity of conception, directed both in its organization and in its every particular," as is attested to in the article by Javier Prades.

In addition, even for those who do not belong to the movement founded by Msgr Giussani, who come from different, even very different, backgrounds and experiences and can therefore only give it a look that is "both affectionate and distant," the engagement is nonetheless deep and fruitful, to the point of producing living examples of genuine ecumenical and intercultural dialogue. The main aim of this book, therefore, is to offer a preliminary introduction to Giussani's writings, showing the lively dialogue that the encounter with such generative thought solicits in thinkers with different backgrounds, temperaments, intellectual motivations, and concerns. For this reason, rather than imposing a uniform style on the contributions, I thought it best to let the very distinguished contributors speak for themselves, respecting, as far as possible, the original structure of the individual texts – which for the most part were public lectures or discussions of Giussani's books – in order to preserve the varying perspectives and styles of thought. The essayists mostly focus on a single work by Giussani, but they are clearly well aware of his oeuvre as a whole. Moreover, in spite of their varying perspectives, some common features or interpretative paths are evident in all the contributions, and this has made it possible to group them into four sections.

The first section, "Passion for Human Destiny," is intended as a general and systematic overview of the main themes of Giussani's thought, covering its key concepts from the perspective of its cultural and historical context (Scola), its deep philosophical implications (Brague), and the self-awareness of the Church as living experience of a present Event – the mystery of Christ's Incarnation – (Albacete). The second section, "Faith Reasonably Communicated," brings into focus Giussani's understanding of the religious sense as it is described and probed in the first volume of his trilogy. (The three volumes are titled *The Religious Sense, At the Origin of the Christian Claim,* and *Why the Church?* and are published by McGill-Queen's University Press). All the essays in this second section converge in pointing out the density of Giussani's idea of experience as a radical faithfulness to reality according to the original human evidences and needs, that is, according to the deepest longings the Bible identifies with human "heart." Each essay takes note of Giussani's integral notion of reason as related to the heart and to affectivity and as openness to reality in all its aspects (Waldstein, Stafford, Bergoglio). Among other things, the essays in this section also make clear the far-reaching consequences of these conceptions when they are applied to an educational method (Ouellet, but also Feliciani in the closing essay) and their diagnostic power in the context of contemporary secularism and, in particular, with respect to the dualistic stance of American religious positivism (Schindler).

In the third section these dominant themes are reconsidered from the perspective of the Christian Event and of the changes its original nature and claim bring in the context of natural religiosity and the life of human subject. The authors (O'Connor, Prades, Del Colle, Howsare, and Caffarra) articulate here Giussani's idea of the "overturning of religious method" brought about by Christ's Incarnation. They explore its implications from the vantage point of their personal, pastoral, and theological knowledge and experience and show thereby the significance of this position for the generation of a really new cultural presence of the Church and of Christians in contemporary world.

The final section, "At Home with Truth," concerns the ecumenical, or, more generally, inter-religious dimension, of Giussani's thought and its reception outside the Christian context, showing the beginning of a dialogue with the Jewish religion, Buddhism, and Islam. As some of the essayists note (Lobkowicz, but also Scola, Prades, and Caffarra) and as Giussani himself never tires of reminding us, ecumenical openness is not an extrinsic appendage, a sort of "fashionable new theology," as Jonathan Edwards would say, devised in order to address a recent, though important, cultural trend. In fact, from the start his ecumenism represented one of the most original and discriminating traits of Giussani's thought. It is rooted in his total commitment to the person of Christ as "the truth of all that is contained in history." This truth neither excludes nor diminishes anything of human value; indeed, so convinced is Giussani of this point that, in his view, ecumenism represents, as he often says, the only adequate way to express the true, nonideological meaning of culture.

These last points bring me back to my initial observations on the essentially dialogical character of the present collection and to a further remark along the same lines that in no way means to detract from the richness of the individual contributions. Viewed as an ensemble, the overall impression conveyed by them is of the extraordinary relevance of Giussani's thought both on a personal, existential level and for the wider context of contemporary culture. Giussani, a profound and learned scholar of North American Protestant theology, very often likes to quote the words of one of his favourite authors, Reinhold Niebuhr: "Nothing is so incredible as an answer to an unasked question." This quotation reminds me of an indictment Niebuhr used to make against the "liberal" theologians of his day: they were so absorbed in attempting to prove the Gospel "credible" for modern culture and science – Niebuhr observes quite ironically – that they did not realize that it was becoming altogether irrelevant for modern men and women. Together these remarks provide a clue to understanding a salient trait in all Giussani's work: his capacity to propose the Christian Event as the answer to the deepest and most pressing questions of contemporary people and their culture. With a clear and vigorous awareness of the cultural, philosophical, and theological issues that are central to the contemporary debate and of their concrete, often dramatic, experiential implications, Giussani succeeds in translating the truth of the Catholic tradition into "an anthropology that would render it existentially reasonable" (Lobkowicz) and is thereby able to overcome the impasse imposed by the nihilism and prejudicial dualisms of our age. In this sense Giussani's work fully reveals its original and unitary "generative" character as the thinking of a man of our time who lives in the utmost wonder and thoughtful recognition of a novelty, an Event that entered into the world and continues to live on in history. As one the Fathers of the early Church would say, Quid est veritas? Vir qui adest. (What is truth? A Man who's here, present.)

NOTES

1 See L. Giussani, *Il Movimento di Comunione e Liberazione* (Milan: Jaca Book 1987) 13. Translated by Patrick Stevenson.
2 Ibid., 178.

# PART ONE

# Passion for Human Destiny

# 1 A Style of Thought

ANGELO SCOLA

## A CHOICE AGAINST THE STREAM:
## A SUBJECT ASSERTS ITSELF

"It greatly concerns us to use our utmost endeavors clearly to discern, and have it well settled and established, wherein true religiosity consists."[1] This affirmation of Jonathan Edwards, whom Luigi Giussani, a scholar versed in North American Protestant theology,[2] defines as "the greatest philosopher-theologian of American Puritanism,"[3] gives a good description of Giussani's intentions in *Religious Awareness in Modern Man*.[4] Concern for the true nature of the religious fact pervades the whole of Giussani's work and constitutes – as his imposing bibliography shows[5] – one of the main lines of the articulated web of his thought.[6]

Giussani himself offers us another surprising analogy with Edwards when he answers a question about the connection between expression and reflection, between art (creativity) and critique (with particular reference to the relationship between pastor and theologian). He affirms that "Theologising and being committed to an immediate activity of apostolate do not seem to me at all separate or incompatible. I would say rather that I cannot understand how it is possible to theologise unless theology is a systematic and critical self-awareness of an experience of faith in action and thus a commitment to the mystery of Christ and of the Church, a passion for the salvation of the world therefore ... Jonathan Edwards was able to write a colossal work like *Freedom of the Will* (1754), with pages of extraordinary value on freedom, on religious affections and so on, while he was living with his family amidst grave poverty, committed to the mission amongst the Indians of the village of Stockbridge in the remote woods of Western Massachusetts in the first half of the eighteenth century."[7] While in the experience of the famous American thinker, who was involved in the religious phenomenon of the Great Awakening, the *forced choice* of the mission among native Americans was of major relevance,[8] in Giussani's life a key aspect was a *free choice* that went completely against the current, in the panorama of Italian culture, both lay and Catholic, in the postwar years. We can say at once that this choice explains his conception of culture (including the relationship between theology and the pastoral approach), because it shows that the subject of knowledge is inseparable from the object. But let us allow this biographical fact – which is important for the scientific development of Giussani's thought – to emerge from his own direct witness:

At the time, I was a lecturer in Venegono seminary, teaching Dogmatic Theology in the seminary courses and Oriental Theology in the faculty courses, and I never imagined the abrupt change of direction that was to come about. It all started from a small episode that was nevertheless destined to change my life. I was on my way to the Adriatic coast for a holiday. In the course of the train journey I happened to talk with some students and found them fearfully ignorant of the Church. Honesty compelled me to ascribe their disgust and indifference towards the Church to this ignorance. I thought of dedicating myself to the rebuilding of a Christian presence in the student environment. So I asked, and was allowed by my superiors, to leave Venegono and to come to Milan. I was sent there to teach religion in a high school, Liceo Berchet. From the first days at Berchet, the original intuition aroused by that meeting on the train sadly was fully confirmed. I would stop the few students wearing the badge of Catholic Action or of the Scouts, whom I used to meet during the breaks, in the corridors or on the stairs, and would ask them explicitly, "Do you really believe in Christ?" They would look at me dumbfounded and I don't remember if even one of them answered "Yes" with the spontaneity of someone who has a true root of faith inside him. Another question I would put to everyone at first was, "In your view, are Christianity and the Church present in school, are they relevant to school life?" The answer was almost always amazement and a smile.[9]

At that time such a decision went completely against the stream, not only in the Catholic milieu or in the lay-liberal milieu – identified, by way of example, with people linked with the Partito d'Azione – but also among the followers of Marxism, which in 1954 was close to achieving hegemony in Italy. If we stay within the Catholic world, even people like Milani and Mazzolari – whom Giussani always followed attentively, despite the differences in judgment, which were at times considerable[10] – "learned" this intrinsic link between subject, thought, and addressee, because they were in some way forced to do so, albeit in virtue of, as it were, extreme choices. That Giussani's choice, though a free one, was no less radical than theirs we can conclude from the substantial distance at which he was kept, for a long time, by the established authority.[11]

In the inverting of the intellectualistic concept of culture (knowing) and therefore of science that is implied in the free and personal choice of starting off from experience[12] – here not understood individualistically but as the people's experience of faith[13] – we can grasp not a few distinctive traits of Giussani's personality. Here it will serve to recall two of these. He appears, first of all, as a great educator,[14] gifted, in the second place, with an acute sense of lived experience in its ideal dimension, lived experience that is constantly compared with the historical (cultural and social) datum.[15] In Giussani's thought there is a category that exhaustively synthesises this vision of reality and that is at once constructive and critically aware: the category of method. The Christian method has two pivots, the first of a theoretical nature. The contents of faith need to be embraced reasonably; in other words they have to be "presented as potentially capable of improving, enlightening and enhancing authentic human values." We can express the second pivot by saying that such a presentation must be verified in action; in other words, the rational evidence can be enlightened to the point of conviction "only from within" the experience "of a human need" acknowledged from within a participation in the Christian fact, and such participation is "an involvement that would treat Christianity as a social, communal event."[16]

I have introduced these brief biographical references with the aim of situating Giussani's meaning when he speaks of religiosity (religious sense) and, therefore, of setting his meaning in the context of the whole of *Religious Awareness in Modern Man*. It is superfluous to point out that this text, the objective limits of which the author himself points out,[17] is in the nature of a synthetic reading, in a certain sense dynastic (I will explain this term in a moment) and not historiographic. Giussani does not overlook the complexity of the phenomenon of modernity and of its humanistic origin, but his interest does not lie in researching its genesis and its development and going along with its interpretations and assessing how they conflict.[18] His concern, rather, is to grasp the main stages that mark the evolution of modernity's religious consciousness, so as to be better able to throw light on that critically aware Christian experience that constitutes, today more than ever, the precious resource for human beings and the community. The fact that the subject should not try to hide itself behind the (in fact, nonexistent) scientific neutrality of research but should instead propose itself as personally involved in the experience of the *humanum*, assuming it critically in a thought (culture) in order to make it communicable (and by this very fact demanding a thoroughgoing critical comparison), is sufficient to explain the peculiar nature of Giussani's approach to modernity.[19] I have spoken of a dynastic reading, because it is aimed at pointing out the dynasties of thoughts (the leading philosophical, theological, and cultural currents) that give a general outline of the development of religious consciousness concerning the Christian proposal. Before expounding synthetically Giussani's reading of modernity, it may be useful to ask ourselves where Giussani got the energy for a choice, so against the current, like that of leaving a chair of theology of great prestige (and not only in the enormous Diocese of Milan) for obscure work among students, work that had still to be invented and, moreover, that he undertook within an organisation like the Italian Catholic Action, which was still at the peak of its development and so strongly structured hierarchically that it was not too open to adventures?[20]

The answer can only be very partial, for it cannot take into account the unfathomable mystery of grace-freedom that guided the step that Giussani took in 1954, one that was vocationally so decisive for him personally and for thousands of others. One aspect deserves to be considered in detail here: the singular formation that took place in that great foundry of life and study that was then the Major Seminary of Milan, the seat of the Theological Faculty. I cannot describe all the important elements (but I will point out that in the 1940s more than two thousand people were living a quasi-monastic life at Venegono).[21] Nor can I consider the contents and teaching methods in themselves and in relationship to the pastoral life of the great Ambrosian diocese. Suffice it to say that during the years in which his thought was formed (1933–54), Giussani was placed in a position to receive a vision of knowledge so broad and critical that it allowed him to integrate poetry, art, literature, philosophy, and theology and to do so with particular reference to American Protestant theology and Orthodox theology. As he himself says, "The theological school of Venegono was essentially open."[22] His teachers – among whom the most famous was Bishop Carlo Colombo, one of the experts most consulted by Paul VI[23] – were able to combine a fidelity to Rome that was not merely passive with vigilant attention to the principal German, French and English theological schools.[24] There was no lack of tools of the highest levels of learning, like the library, complete with newspapers and periodicals, a philosophical and theological review – *La Scuola Cattolica* – and scientific journals.[25] In the Milan Theological Faculty in those years an urgent need was felt for an accurate study of the Bible, of the Fathers, and of the history of dogmas. At the same time, in balanced synthesis between the historical and speculative method, two principles were held to that guaranteed a global openness: Christianity as Event of grace, and the Church as the sign (sacrament) of the Christian Event that extends itself in time.[26] Theological opinion – which was connected with the exegetic polemics over *desiderium videndi Deum*, the uniqueness of the supernatural end[27] – was at the centre of the studies at Venegono, and little by little was to direct the whole of the faculty towards paying particular attention to the question of theological method.[28] It would not be a mistake to say that the turning point in Giussani's personal life permitted his thought to become a meaningful variant of his methodological research, which does not avoid, as Cardinal Biffi likes to say, getting to the *res* (Biffi was first Giussani's student at Venegono and then his colleague).

In any case, I had better conclude this observation by noting how, from the 1930s (if I limit my scope to theological studies) Giussani was able to tackle organically the works of thinkers like Neibhur and Tillich and, later on, of all American Protestantism, at the same time as he was assimilating important authors of Orthodox thought.[29] Could we understand the import in Giussani's thought of the category of experience, with the methodological implications we have already hinted at, or that of *communio* – not to speak of his accurate use of poetical and literary sources – without understanding these formative roots?[30] Moreover, without understanding them, how could we take into account the extraordinary pedagogical efficacy, which was intent on giving back substance to faith in order to renew the body of the Church, that marked the "cure" for whole generations and that now, through the movement of Communion and Liberation, touches men and women in dozens of countries in the world?[31] To be sure, the story of the singular formation of Luigi Giussani's thought is not unrelated to the prophetic choice he made in 1954.

## THE CHRISTIAN FACT AND MODERNITY

"I am convinced that as regards the religious fact in general, and Christianity in particular, we all believe we know already. But if we tackle it again, it is not impossible to discover some aspects of new knowledge."[32] Giussani made this judgment as a premise to the conversation that was to become *Religious Awareness in Modern Man*. The wholly positive intention of the author in these "short notes" – this is how he describes them – is to demonstrate the *cum-venientia* (appropriateness) of the Christian fact in a moment, like the present one, in which "people are far more open to the religious sense that coincides with the search for destiny."[33] In order to reformulate the Christian proposal to show the pertinence of its "objective claim," he examines the factors that, in the modern social and cultural situation, have tended to hamper it.[34] In this way the experience of a personal and communitarian (ecclesial) subject, well identified in its ideal traits but inserted in history, is proposed to human beings, simply and without complexity, on the strength of its intrinsic reasons.[35] And consequently, it is not afraid of an all-round confrontation. So in Giussani the same dynamism sustains the emergence and the development of experience and of the thought that confirms the fact that experience, when it is authentic, contains its own *logos* (it does not receive it from outside) and, in its turn, thought, when it is integral, cannot fail to "recount" reality as such. The two basic components of Giussani's reflection are in this way assured.

In his impassioned teaching and in his writings, the Milanese priest never fails to keep his attention fixed on the historical-cultural context, in order to communicate a dramatically situated experience/thought of freedom to his listener. Reality (and therefore history and culture) and knowledge (and therefore reason and faith) make human experience open to truth and keen to communicate it. For truth is not truly known until it is communicated.[36] Nor should it escape us from this point of view how Giussani's work neatly disposes of every dichotomy and all that is extrinsic in considering the relationship between reason and faith (and, therefore, between nature and the supernatural, human and Christian), without for this reason forsaking distinction in the unity.[37] It will return to this point, but for the time being this observation about method allows me to take up again the theme of religious consciousness in modern times. *Religious Awareness in Modern Man* articulates this theme synthetically, but the whole of Giussani's œuvre continually returns to it and elaborates on it, always respecting the methodological choice that I have defined as dynastic and not historiographic and responding to Giussani's predominant intention.

Msgr Giussani's assessment of the situation of Christianity in Italy in the 1950s is particularly enlightening about his judgment of modernity: It was "A situation that saw Christians politely eliminate themselves from public life, from culture, from popular reality, amidst the encouraging applause and the heartfelt consensus of the political and cultural forces that were planning to replace them on the national stage."[38] Even though the Catholic world still seemed to be in control of society in an imposing way by means of an elaborate network of parishes and official associations, Giussani perceived with lucidity the wave of secularisation that was about to sweep over Catholic Italy, whose effects were to be visible on a grand scale from 1968 on. In a situation quite different from that of other European countries such as France (where at the end of the nineteenth century, before the famous pastoral initiatives of Cardinal Suhard, one could already speak of a mission country), where could such a prophetic judgment come from? It came from the perception that such a massive presence was nothing but the inertial heritage of the past: "At the time it appeared clear to me that no tradition or, indeed, no human experience can challenge history and stand against the flow of time, except insofar as it comes to express and communicate itself in ways that possess cultural dignity."[39] Already for some time Christianity had had a minimal presence in the schools and universities, not to mention the workplace,[40] partly because of the dualistic conception of the relationship between Church and world, which was in its turn connected – as I have noted above – with the dualisms human/Christian, nature/the supernatural, faith/reason, and freedom/grace. Not for nothing are these the contents of the debate, sometimes bitter, but always respectful, that found Giussani and his first followers in dialectic with the Catholic intelligentsia of the Diocese of Milan.[41] These recollections can make it easier to grasp, as I have said, the framework of Giussani's consideration of modernity.

Giussani's analysis in *Religious Awareness in Modern Man* takes its cue from T.S. Eliot, because in a few powerful and intense lines the poet describes the human religious journey up to the present disturbing situation.[42] Though Eliot limits himself to recording the fact of the journey, leaving aside the questions concerning when, how, and why the present situation could have developed, Giussani sets aside the poet's caution and proposes instead to give an answer, though a summary one, to these questions. In his analysis, the break-up of that powerful unitary conception of humanity, of the cosmos and of history that had characterised the Medieval synthesis, began with humanism.[43] In fact, it was the humanists who started the process, but without the intention of abandoning Christianity. Humanism became progressively tied up with a vision that more and more made the value of human beings coincide with their "success," a vision that placed absolute trust in nature and in reason as the instrument of dominion over reality, to the point of bending nature itself in order to bring about human happiness.[44] However, more than in the process itself, Giussani is interested in grasping the outcome, which he describes with effect using the lapidary formula of the Italian philosopher Cornelio Fabro: "If God does exist, he doesn't matter."[45] The formula is further illuminated as follows: "The Protestant theologian, Tillich, rightly said, 'Atheism, in the etymological sense, is impossible.' Atheism is, in fact, existentially possible: there can be a god who no longer matters in one's life, a god to whom one pays lip service, one who is even perhaps honored with dogmas, but who is thought to have nothing anymore to do with existence."[46]

Let us ask ourselves, then, how does such a process affect the constitutive categories of human experience: reason, freedom, consciousness, and culture? Even without studying the passages in various publications where Giussani illustrates the reduction of these key terms, we can record a synthetic judgment.[47] However positive the inheritance it has left us, modernity can be reduced to a parabola whose apex coincides with what is defined as an "optimism syndrome" but whose downward slope represents the features of an "anthropology of dissolution." In his recent reflections, Giussani describes the end result of the modern parabola as follows: "There is an irreligiosity in our world that starts off with a separation that is made between God as the origin and meaning of life and God as a fact of thought ... This is reduced to *a separation of the meaning of life from experience* that in its turn implies a separation of morality from man's action."[48] The passage in T.S. Eliot that inspired *Religious Awareness in Modern Man* culminates in the agonized question, "Has the Church failed mankind, or has mankind failed the Church?"[49] In the second part of *Religious Awareness in Modern Man* Giussani does not back away from this question but has the courage to lay bare the responsibility of Christians and of ecclesiastics for the break-up of the Medieval synthesis (this too is a theme that returns insistently in the whole of his work).[50] In order to describe the effects of this process Giussani brings into play a radical category, that of "the protestantizing of Christianity." The first effect of the protestantizing of Christianity is "a subjectivism in [the face] of destiny, both in theory and in practice. The second is the stress on a moralism in the face of values exalted by the dominant culture. Finally, we have mentioned the weakening of the living unity of the people of God with [their] tradition."[51]

I should point out that the use of this category in no way casts aspersions on the Protestant confessions. Not only has Giussani been an attentive scholar of Protestantism (especially American Protestantism) – whose best intuitions he has borne in mind in his method of Christian life – but from his younger days he has been a convinced supporter of ecumenism,[52] a theme to which he has kept returning in recent years.[53] Even when he speaks of protestantizing, Giussani's intention, however crude it may appear, is that of describing realistically a precise situation or tendency. The value of this category, therefore, is, again, dynastic not historiographic. In any case, Giussani's diagnosis ends with a cry of alarm. The symptoms that reveal that Christianity today is paying a debt to what has by now become the dominant mentality are the three grave "reductions," or failures: "subjectivism, moralism and the weakening of the organic unity of the Christian fact," of which it is the victim. Giussani's recent book *Generare tracce nella storia del mondo* describes the situation we have come to in this way: "the incomprehension and the hostility of the modern mentality towards the word 'event' are reflected in a reduction made concerning the way of conceiving 'faith.' In refusing prejudicially to consider the method chosen by God to answer man's need for total meaning – a fact in time and space – the modern mentality confuses 'religious sense' with 'faith' ... The whole of modern consciousness is frantic in wrenching from man the hypothesis of Christian faith and in sending him back to the dynamics of the religious sense and to the concept of religiosity, and this confusion is unfortunately penetrating the mentality of the Christian people ... faith is recognizing an exceptional presence that corresponds wholly to one's own destiny, and adhering to this presence."[54] Another text reformulates this diagnosis effectively in the following terms: "in the modern era, by losing the true nature of reason, rationalism makes *confusion between religious sense and faith* quite habitual ... this empties faith, too, of its very nature, because the true nature of faith is that of a judgement that involves freedom: affectivity complements the content of this judgement. All this is born from experience."[55] In this context Giussani points out a whole series of reductions as the salient features of contemporary man's religious consciousness: God without Christ, Christ without the Church, the Church without the world, the world without the "I," the "I" without God.[56]

Before taking up again the central content of Giussani's judgment – the confusion of religious sense with faith (more than ever manifesting itself in the present phase of secularisation as the explosion of *sacré-sauvage*)[57] – we need to observe how Giussani's synthetic analysis both of modernity and of the transition to postmodernity is in no way reducible to the category of antimodernism.[58] For, as we shall see below, one cannot understand Giussani without key concepts that are part of the modern sensibility, like those of experience, of freedom[59] – whose existential primacy is constantly affirmed – of truth as event,[60] of knowledge as structurally connected with affection,[61] of being as gift, of subject as implied in the very gift of being,[62] of real sign as the locus of the revelation of natural being and, through grace, of the very face of the Triune (the foundation).[63] In this sense it would be a serious mistake to read Giussani's thought as a mere return to classic realism. His realism, through which the existence and the knowability of the veritable foundation of the real is objectively affirmed – since, according to Giussani, it is from this ontological affirmation of "things as they are" and only from this that human beings can understand ethics[64] – is built upon the basis of what von Balthasar has called a dramatic anthropology.[65] In fact, the wholly modern richness with which Giussani develops this theme in one of his most highly esteemed books, *Alla ricerca del volto umano*,[66] would be incomprehensible without acknowledging the import of the most central categories of current philosophical/theological debate. Apart from the concepts already mentioned, I should add those of the other, difference, affection, and friendship.[67] Nothing, therefore, could be more mistaken than to place Giussani (and the imposing international ecclesial reality he gave life to) within an out-dated scheme of dialectic between conservatives and progressives that was in vogue up to at least a few years ago. Giussani's passion for "orthodoxy", has to do, if anything, with his intense familiarity with English-speaking authors like Chesterton, Newman, Eliot, and Lewis. This reveals another root of this thought.

## A THOUGHT FROM EXPERIENCE: REALITY, REASON, AND FAITH

These last notes lead us to a further step, by the very logic of the Milanese priest's thought. I have already said that in Giussani the subject-witness cannot be separated from the proposal and therefore from the judgment concerning the historical-cultural period in which it is situated, since the concept of experience particular to this author[68] is the unifying element of these three aspects.[69] For the communication of a personal and communitarian experience to be convincing to its audience, revealing to the interlocutor's free will the reasons for its suitability, the historical-cultural situation must be critically examined.[70] We have seen that this critique is carried out in the first section of *Religious Awareness in Modern Man*. Thus we can understand why the last two chapters of this book are centred on the proposal of the Christian fact.[71] First its objective lines are shown, as opposed to the subjectivistic reduction (protestantization) and moralism, and then two peculiar characteristics are described: the Christian Fact as a totalising event and faith that becomes culture, ending up, through the category of sign, with its nature as present event.[72] It is therefore necessary to look at the Christian Fact, considered in its unity and its entirety, as it expresses itself in the experience of ecclesial life that takes place in the here and now of history.[73]

The simplest and most objective answer to the question, What is the Christian fact? comes to us, then, through the description of the early steps of the Christian community as described in Holy Scripture.[74]

They tell us that the Christian fact is the event of Jesus Christ dead and risen, that it is the Incarnate Son of the Father, who, by the working of the Holy Spirit, makes himself present – in the Church and through the Church – in the today of history, communicating himself in a gratuitous and surprising way to human beings who are situated with their unforeseeable freedom and their inevitable belonging to peoples, cultures, and traditions. From this point of view, which sees the infinite freedom of God mercifully bending over the finite freedom of man, every abstraction is removed from the reality of the Church. She imposes herself first of all as a Fact that happens to me, that comes my way (ad-venio). The Christian Fact, which is identifiable in history, lives therefore in the event of the Church.[75] With Giussani, the Christian Fact – always considered in keeping with the traditio catholica, starting from the Bible – objectively demands that religious sense and faith be kept in dual unity (without confusion and without separation).[76] For a faith that would empty the religious sense does not respect human freedom but confines it to a state of mere external passivity,[77] while a religious sense that is not surprised, thanks to faith, by the event of Christ runs the risk of extenuating man's religious consciousness in a tormented problematicism.[78] Yet from the point of view of the Christian Fact, the same reality is manifested to human knowledge in a dual unity.[79] The thing in itself (reality), considered in its essential completeness, indeed reveals that being maintains, on the one hand, its natural consistency, that it is opened wide to the religious sense as the apex of reason capable of Mystery,[80] yet it reveals, on the other hand, through faith in the ecclesial event of Jesus Christ, the merciful face of the Triune.[81] Thus *"faith is the feast of reason."*[82]

Here a unitary and articulated conception of reality is at play – wonderfully described in *The Religious Sense*, one of Giussani's key works – a conception that is central in Giussani's thought.[83] To this is related a precise notion of reason,[84] of faith,[85] and of their relationship[86] that is ultimately determined by a vision of cognition[87] – a vision that, with exquisite contemporary sensitivity, presents an accurate analysis of human factual freedom.[88]

Here I can give only some hint of this original structure of Giussani's thought – inevitably running the risk of impoverishing it – to which he comes back again and again with the acute methodological sensitivity that I have already described.

To outline synthetically Giussani's conception of reality I shall say a word about the two poles that constitute it, paying special attention to the unitary factor within which this duality is always kept.

Reality ("the thing," being in its broad sense) is *presence to the "I."*[89] In this sense, being is an event that happens to my freedom and engages it.[90] Event, among other things, indicates that being comes my way from beyond (*e-venio*).[91] In the experience of presence, being reveals itself, though remaining veiled, so that properly speaking things (reality) are the sign of it.[92] In this synthetic proposition of the first pole of reality we can easily recognize the weight of the classical theme of *real distinction*, newly taken up in the contemporary one of *ontological difference*.[93] The essentialist nature of Giussani's thought is thus brought to perceive that the difference between being and *ens* penetrates the "thing" and its transcendental properties (one, true, good, beautiful) without breaking its unity.[94] In conceiving of reality, Giussani's thought, while remaining faithful to the tradition of Christian realism, forcefully penetrates contemporary sensitivity.

When by grace the Mystery reveals itself, it is to communicate the full face of being, dissolving the very enigma of freedom right at the moment in which it exalts its drama. "Christ everything in everybody," so that *"God may be all in all"*: here is the second pole of reality![95] If the Mystery gives itself, it is in order to show itself as the very depth of things and not as a mere veneer applied on the outside. It tells us that things lie in the merciful light of the Triune God, locus of the originary friendship.[96] Jesus Christ, in his precise historical identity and in his universal singularity is thus revealed as "the Sign of all signs."[97] Every dualism is eliminated at the root, since the difference between being and *ens* is not kept in an indefinite oscillation (Heidegger) but becomes the principle for discovering the face of the Mystery in the gift of Covenant that begins in creation[107] (theological difference).[98] Not only does the category of event (the event of Jesus Christ developed by Giussani in all its various implications: Trinitarian, Christological, ecclesiological, sacramental, anthropological, and ethical) throw light on the nature of this second pole of reality, just as it enabled us to understand the first, but, more properly, it takes on the task of showing the unity of the real in which alone the two poles live and engage each other[99]. In the horizon of the Christian fact we can "see" the totality of the real.[100] Thus, necessity and history, metaphysics and revelation, appear as two constitutive, inseparable, and unmistakable dimensions of this totality.

The truth is an event in which the real – in both its natural and supernatural dimensions – and the freedom of the "I" meet: "The totality of the presence of the Mystery and its claim on our lives ('God all in all') ... explains [why] to God we must say 'You,' and 'You, O Christ,' we must say to the man, Jesus of Nazareth. Both the Mystery and His physical presence in our life, all of this is the source of the relationship we have with the truth and with the whole of reality."[101] According to the most genuine classical tradition, analogy is at work in Giussani's thought, learnedly revisited in an anthropological key.[102] For, as a meaningful fruit of the primacy of experience and against any intellectualistic temptation (even modern), analogy is understood by Giussani as *analogia libertatis* (analogy of freedom) rather than *analogia entis* (analogy of being).[103]

Now I can easily touch on the concept of reason to which Giussani has dedicated an impressive number of reflections, both critical and poetic.[104] It would be impossible to grasp his thought without giving proper place to the esteem for reason that flows from all his writings. Reason is "the capacity to become aware of reality according to the totality of its factors."[105] It is not the measure of all things but a window wide open onto the whole of reality.[106] This implies a conception of the phenomenon of human knowledge that reveals the intrinsic reasonableness of intellect, reason, will, and faith.[107] The categories – all of them simultaneously involved in the act by which the consciousness of the "I" addresses the real – are laden with analogy and present therefore an important aspect of homogeneity.

From the critical point of view Giussani is committed to proving the theoretical and practical irrelevance of both the rationalistic and fideistic reductions, to which, since the dawn of the modern era, thought, especially Western thought, has subjected reason.[108] Thus the critical and poetic analysis of the category of reason naturally comes to the very topical theme – unfortunately constantly disregarded – of the morality of cognition: "Applying this to the field of knowledge, this is the moral rule: *Love the truth of an object more than your attachment to the opinions you have already formed about it.* More concisely, one could say, 'love the truth more than yourself.'"[109]

Once the integral meaning of reason has been opened up to embrace the whole arc of the possible,[110] the category of faith, too, can be seen according to its authentic nature. Giussani makes it visible in two ways: first by affirming forcefully the cognitive capacity of faith,[111] and then by stressing – even in the case of Christian faith, which originates only from grace – its homogeneity (always analogical) with reason itself. Against any mutual exclusivity between faith and reason, which is responsible for so many isms that *Fides et Ratio* critically stigmatised,[112] faith and reason are proposed by Giussani as two dimensions of the one cognitive energy with which the "I" addresses reality![113] If we keep in mind that reason and will, and therefore affection, live intertwined with each other and if we think adequately of the gratuitous genesis of faith in this way – that is, that it originates not in a manner juxtaposed and superadded – the most genuine Catholic doctrine of the *fides quae* and the *fides qua* finds a dynamic interpretation.[114] This conception of faith, in itself and in its relationship with reason, necessarily places the category of freedom in the forefront.[115]

We must look at this category for a moment if we wish to complete the attempt at reconstructing the mosaic of the theoretic nucleus of Giussani's thought, the main segments of which I have identified. If the truth is the event where reality and the "I" meet, and if this event is given always and only in sign, we can understand that ultimately there is no possibility of knowing the real (the truth) without a decision.[116] That is not all: for Giussani the very act with which consciousness addresses reality, inexorably reveals the decision of the self-awareness of the "I" as regards existence and its foundation.[117] The fact that for Giussani freedom holds such an originary position explains why all his works dedicate an acute analysis to this theme. In particular his analysis of the factual freedom of human beings, which starts off by pointing out the weight carried, in its originary nucleus, by natural human inclinations, passes through the interpretation of freewill to culminate in the explication of freedom as adherence/obedience to the attraction of the Infinite.[118] Thus, freedom is linked with fulfilment and satisfaction. Yet the most original aspect in the restatement of this scheme, which after all is the classical one, is seen in Giussani's capacity to retain the best results of transcendental thought about freedom. I am referring to the conviction – proposed several times with sharper and sharper nuances – that the factual freedom of the "I" is called to transcend itself, yet it is incapable (in the ontological sense of the Mediaeval *capax*) of doing so by itself.[119] Each single act of freedom is factual, therefore always historically determined, and therefore irreducible. (Here too human beings discover again the weight of difference and of alterity!) In this sense freedom has to be freed. It needs an event that will make it possible: the Christian fact, in the free surrender (*sponte*) of the Crucified to the Father through the Spirit, brings about that perfect correspondence between the Foundation (infinite freedom, Trinity) and created freedom that makes this possible for every act of human freedom. Not because Christ can decide in my place but, on the contrary, because Christ makes it possible for me in every action to decide, in Him, for the Foundation (Trinity). In other words, Jesus Christ effectively liberates my freedom. Now we are equipped to understand better why for Giussani religious sense and faith must be kept in a deep dual unity.

A final note regarding method, perhaps the most acute expression of the genius of Giussani's thought. The method that takes pride of place in the encounter between reality in its totality and the "I" in its freedom is the *sacramental method*.[120] For Christ happens today to my freedom in the sign represented by every circumstance and every relationship; but the complete form of this sign is the sacrament.[121] The sacramental method, however, requires the simplicity of a child:

The method the Mystery has used to give Himself, to reveal Himself to His creature is the sacramental method: a sign that in this sense contains the Mystery of which it is the sign. The community of the Church is the aspect of this sign, it is the aspect of that face, it is the visible aspect of that face. It is the clothing of that Presence, like Jesus' garments were for the little children who came near Him. The tiny children, 4–5 years old, who milled around Jesus, grabbing hold of his legs, sticking their noses into His clothes, didn't see his face, they didn't remember his face, perhaps they didn't even look at it. But they were there with Him. So that the clothes, the seamless tunic in which Jesus was clad, were more fixed in their eyes than His face. In the same way Jesus makes himself perceivable to us in the ecclesial community, as if it were the clothing with which our smallness enters into relationship with His real presence.[122]

## A GENERATIVE THOUGHT

This presentation of *Religious Awareness in Modern Man* has brought me to risk an interpretation of some of the major aspects of Giussani's thought. Obviously it is just an attempt, and its limits are objectively evident, first of all, in the wholly rhapsodic character of the enterprise and, secondly, in the inevitable choice implied in every interpretation. In this case I have submitted Giussani's experience and reflections to my sensitivity to its theoretical nucleus without being able to exhaust its fascinating polyhedricity. I hope that this objective impoverishment – owing among other things to the quantitative breadth of Giussani's writings – will challenge my readers to study Giussani's works for themselves.

To conclude I would like to make a note about what seems to me the salient nature of Giussani's thought. I introduce it with three points, not without first recalling the unitary method proper to the process of Giussani's experience and thought. In the movement of the communication of a convincing personal and communitarian experience, the historical-cultural situation is critically sifted in such a way that the reasons for the suitability of that very experience that the subject proposes are more accessible to the freedom of the counterpart.

First, one cannot deny the fact that Giussani's proposal, by its very nature, mobilized and continues to mobilize tens of thousands of persons of the most diverse social groupings in all continents to a direct personal and communitarian involvement. This happens, among other things, through a systematic study of his writings. In the second place it is worth pointing out the surprising openness of the horizon of a thought that has led to impassioned contestation, dialogue, and – and why should it not have done so – dialectic in the most diverse lay and religious milieus, from the Jewish world to the speculative, learned forms of Buddhism, from the confrontation with both Orthodox and Protestant personalities to the point of dialogue with significant exponents of lay, philosophical-scientific, and artistic thought. In addition, Giussani's affinities and friendships with great figures of the Catholic world, starting with the Holy Father himself and von Balthasar, are particularly significant. Nor can the desire of many university teachers to meet for the study of Giussani's work be passed over in silence. Suffice it to recall the recent convention held in Washington in September 1998, the presentation of his book at the UN headquarters in New York in December 1997 and in May 1999, and the fact that this chapter was originally presented as a UNESCO lecture in Paris in January 1999.[123]

Finally, as I have already shown, the central themes of Giussani's work and their development are consonant with what is most actively debated in contemporary philosophical circles that are sensitive to the veritative basis and theological literature, especially in the "fundamental" field. Keeping these things in mind, it seems to me that Giussani's thought can be defined as a *generative thought*. With this adjective I mean to point out his capacity for describing in an articulate way elementary human experience as it is perceived by him in the mainstream of the *traditio catholica*. It is probably the genius of the educator that expresses itself through a noteworthy deepening of the philosophical-theological discourse. In this sense Giussani's thought presents two peculiar characteristics. Seeing it from the outset, one cannot consider it to be simply the result of many influences; rather, it is precisely *generative*. So it is to be looked at at its origin and in itself. Even the thinkers and the currents that contributed to its formation, when analysed in themselves and in the articulated confluence do not explain the form (gestalt) of Giussani's thought. In this sense I therefore propose reading Giussani's work from the point of view of what von Balthasar has called a "style" of thought.[124]

The second characteristic of Giussani's thought that testifies to its original nature is given by the fact that without passing directly through the vast ocean of modern and contemporary philosophical literature – simply because the *scholar* of far-away 1954 has had to come to terms with his role as the pastor who is hemmed in on all sides – his itinerary manages not only to tackle the more important theoretical contents of the contemporary debate but to do so without sacrificing anything to critique, revealing an impassioned desire to get to the matter at hand.

A generative thought and therefore a style of thought! An authentically Christian thought and one that is therefore dramatically open –

like that of the great Catholic tradition – to human freedom and its multifaceted and variously situated cultural expressions! All the more because a generative thought, like a prime number, cannot be broken down: it cannot be imprisoned in the filter of interpretation I have had to use. In order to understand Giussani you have to meet Giussani in person!

NOTES

Translated by Patrick Stevenson.

1 J. Edwards, *A Treatise concerning Religious Affections* (1746; New Haven, CT: Yale University Press 1953), 89.

2 See L. Giussani, "Atteggiamenti protestanti e ortodossi davanti al dogma dell'Assunta," *La Scuola Cattolica* 79 (1951): 106–13; "L'Eucaristia nella Chiesa anglicana," *Ambrosius* 29 (1953): 164–74; "Da Amsterdam ad Evaston (Cronaca ecumenica)," *La Scuola Cattolica* 82 (1954): 133–50; "Il problema dell' 'Intercomunione' nel protestantesimo attuale," *Ambrosius* 30 (1954): 258–63; "Il ricupero dei valori religiosi nel personalismo americano e la filosofia di Edgar Sheffield Brightman," *Filosofia e vita* 8 (1967): 71–85; "Aspetti della concezione della storia in Reinhold Niebuhr," *Rivista di Filosofia neo-scolastica* 60 (1968): 167–90; *Teologia protestante americana* (Vengono: La Scuola cattolica 1969); *Reinhold Niebuhr* (Milan: Jaca Book 1969); "La teologia protestante americana," in AA.VV., *Problemi e orientamenti di teologia dogmatica* (Milan: Marzorati 1979), 691–728; *Grandi linee della teologia protestante americana* (Milan: Jaca Book 1989).

3 Giussani, *Il Movimento di Comunione e Liberazione* (Milan: Jaca Book 1987), 178.

4 Giussani, *La coscienza religiosa nell'uomo moderno* (Milan: Jaca Book 1985), now in Giussani, *Il senso di Dio e l'uomo moderno* (Milan: Rizzoli 1994), 77–139. In its original core was a lecture delivered by Msgr Giussani in several Italian and foreign universities. English translation: "Religious Awareness in Modern Man," *Communio* 25 (spring 1998): 104–40, from which I quote. Among many others, I should mention the French translation, *La coscience religieuse de l'homme moderne* (Paris: Le Cerf 1999), to which this essay originally refers.

5 A comprehensive bibliography of Luigi Giussani that includes his writings from 1951 to 1997 (essays and articles in periodicals, in newspapers, interviews and unpublished texts and translations) can be found in Giussani, *Porta la speranza* (Genoa: Marietti 1997), 205–60.

6 Giussani's reflections on the religious sense, first set out in written form in 1957, were reworked in 1966 and reached their definitive form (up to now) in 1997: *Il senso religioso*, vol. 1 of *PerCorso* (Milan: Rizzoli 1997); English translation, *The Religious Sense* (Montreal: McGill-Queen's University Press 1997). It is undoubtedly one of the most important works on the subject (the volume, whose speculative density makes it very demanding, has been translated into seventeen languages and has sold hundreds of thousands of copies).

7 Giussani, *Il Movimento*, 178.

8 See E.H. Davidson, *Jonathan Edwards: The Narrative of a Puritan Mind* (Cambridge: Harvard University Press 1968); A.O. Aldridge, *Jonathan Edwards* (New York: Washington Square Press 1964).

9 Giussani, *Il Movimento*, 12–13.

10 See ibid., 29–30.

11 See ibid., 14, 44–8, 59–61.

12 See Giussani, *The Religious Sense*, 4–6; "Tracce d'esperienza cristiana," in Giussani, *Il cammino al vero è un'esperienza* (Turin: SEI, 1995), 47–8; "Appunti di metodo cristiano," in Giussani, *Il cammino al vero*, 97–8.

13 See Giussani, *Tracce*, 65: "The 'we' becomes fulness of the 'I,' law of the fulfilment of the 'I.'"

14 Education is one of the problems Giussani tackles expressly, as can be seen by the titles of some of his early writings. See Giussani, "Risposte cristiane ai problemi dei giovani," *Realtà e giovinezza: La sfida*, (Turin: SEI 1995), 125–47; "Come educare al senso della Chiesa," *L'Azione Giovanile* 52 (1960), 14–16; "Valore educativo della scuola libera," *Vita e Pensiero* 43 (1960): 401–8. For an articulate presentation of the educational problem see Giussani, "Il rischio educativo," *Il rischio educativo: Come creazione di personalità e storia* (Turin: SEI 1995), 3–56. English edition: *The Risk of Education*, trans. Rosanna M. Giammanco Frongia (New York: Crossroad 2001), 31–102.

15 This is the judgment with which Giussani describes the origins of the experience of Communion and Liberation: "Our attempt was born as an answer to this situation of crisis and the absence of Christians from the more vivacious and concrete environments in which the vast majority of people, including Christians, spent their lives." Giussani, *Il movimento*, 19.

16 Giussani, *The Risk of Education*, 32–3.

17 "In the following conversation I shall first try to identify our cultural and social situation insofar as it is an impediment to an authentic religious awareness; secondly, I shall point out the attitude of Christianity in the face of this situation." Giussani, *Religious Awareness*, 104.

18 See R.L. Guidi, *Aspetti religiosi nella letteratura del Quattrocento* (Rome: LIEF 1973) H. de Lubac, *Pic de la Mirandole* (Paris: Aubier-Montaigne 1974).

19 From the start Giussani considered culture as one of the dimensions of the Christian call. See Giussani, *Appunti*, 123–31; *Il Movimento*, 36–7.

20 See *Il Movimento*, 17–20, 59–61.

21 Venegono is a village to the north of Milan where the Major Seminary of the Archdiocese of Milan was built, rather like a huge monastery, on the fringe of the surrounding woods. On the school of Venegono see *Annuario Teologico 1984* (Milano: Istra-Edit 1985), 9–88. Of particular interest are the conversations published in the same volume with Gaetano Corti (115–20), Carlo Colombo (121–26), Giacomo Biffi (127–30), and Luigi Giussani himself (131–5).

22 L. Giussani, "Conversazione con Luigi Giussani (6 gennaio 1984)," in *Annuario Teologico*, 131. He continues: "what made it so open, in my opinion, was the firmness of two attitudes: 1 Christianity as event of grace that challenges the world; 2 an ecclesiology that was clear in its enunciation."

23 See J. Grootaers, *I protagonisti del Concilio Vaticano II* (Cinisello Balsamo: San Paolo 1994); M. Leonardi, *Carlo Colombo*, (unpublished dissertation, Pontificia Università Lateranense, 1993).

24 See F. Bertoldi, "L'atto di fede e il metodo teologico in Carlo Colombo," in *Annuario Teologico*, 30–2.

25 See T. Citrini, "La Scuola Cattolica. Anno 125," in *La Scuola Cattolica* 125 (1997): 3–27.

26 See *Annuario Teologico*, 131: "The Christian event, despite a rather abstract idea of grace, recovered its function of sign by means of ecclesiology. Thus the event was rethought in its patristic sense: the Church as Christian event that prolongs itself in time is precisely a patristic idea."

27 In this sense Giacomo Biffi affirms that "The first idea was that of the supernatural, which in the Milanese environment, even before it came from the theological schools, came from the pastoral work of Msgr Francesco Olgiati." *Annuario Teologico*, 129–30.

28 Even today it is one of the basic concerns. See the volume of G. Colombo, *La ragione teologica* (Milan: Glossa 1995).

29 Apart from the writings on Protestantism already quoted, as regards Orthodoxy I would mention Giussani, "L'Eucaristia presso gli orientali," *Ambrosius* 29 (1953): 49–54; "Maria nell'Oriente cristiano," in *Ambrosius* 30 (1954): 57–64.

30 One of Giussani's teachers, Giovanni Colombo, was a great expert in literature. See M. Fraschini, "Letteratura e catechesi in Giovanni Colombo," *Annuario Teologico*, 61–88.

31 See *Communion and Liberation: A Movement in the Church*, ed.
   D. Rondoni, trans. Patrick Stevenson and Susan Scott (Montreal:
   McGill Queen's University Press 2000).

32 See Giussani, *Religious Awareness*, 104. Acutely the author starts off
   from an affirmation of Barbara Ward: "Men do not learn when they
   believe they already know." See B. Ward, *Faith and Freedom* (New
   York: W.W. Norton 1954), 4.

33 Giussani, *Religious Awareness*, 105.

34 Significantly, the second volume of Giussani's trilogy is entitled *At the
   Origin of the Christian Claim* (trans. Vivian Hewitt, Montreal: McGill-
   Queen's University Press 1998).

35 "What characterizes experience is our *understanding* something, discovering its meaning. To have an experience means to comprehend the
   meaning of something." Giussani, *The Risk of Education*, 98–9.

36 St Thomas, in reference to the *quaestio* regarding the fact that those
   called to a contemplative life should also teach, replies significantly
   that it is better to communicate what one contemplates than simply to
   contemplate it, pointing out the need for what is known to reach the
   public dimension: "Sicut enim maius est illuminare quam lucere solum,
   ita maius est contemplata tradere quam solum contemplari," St Thomas,
   *Summa Theologiae* IIa IIae, q.188, a.6.

37 "The experience of their encounter with that Man, of their life with
   that Man – impassioned, anxious, uncertain – all at once forged
   into another experience, absolutely unforeseen, disconcerting – the
   experience of the divine reality, the encounter with , life together with
   God, brilliant, certain, strong. Christ so present, so concrete to us,
   one of us, is at the same time that "beyond" which solves the enigma
   of existence. Christ is the meaning of history and the Lord of the
   Universe. Christ is the point of view that explains everything." Giussani,
   *Tracce*, 63.

38 Giussani, *Il Movimento*, 19.

39 Ibid., 13.

40 In this sense perhaps we can see a vague analogy from the point of
   view of the vocational choice in itself – but not so much as regards the
   contents and methods of pastoral action – between Giussani's decision
   to leave the theological faculty for a mission among the students and
   that of the first French "worker priests." In fact, Giussani was very
   interested in that phenomenon.

41 See Giussani, *Il Movimento*, 17–20.

42 "The words of the poet [Eliot] clarify the context in which the religious sense finds itself today: overwhelmed by a steady attempt to
   prevent it from acting as an existentially vital factor at work in the
   dynamics of education and social relationships – as if to make it rigid,

something obsolete. But because the religious sense is the culmination of reason – the future Paul VI, in his first letter as Cardinal of Milan, defined it as 'the synthesis of the spirit' – it cannot, as such, be uprooted; it cannot be ignored for long. Thus in an epoch such as ours, God's absence is filled by the presence of something else ... Men can certainly eliminate the names of all the gods, but they will in any case find some god for themselves without even knowing it and bow to it in unnatural slavery. Eliot identifies these as 'Usury, Lust and Power,' and they can be reduced to one thing: mutual instrumentalization, a compensating projection of ultimate subjection, deceptively conceived." Giussani, *Religious Awareness*, 108.

43 Giussani's analysis finds an impressive confirmation in that of John Paul II in *Fides et ratio* 45: "From the late Medieval period onwards, however, the legitimate distinction between the two forms of learning became more and more a fateful separation. As a result of the exaggerated rationalism of certain thinkers, positions grew more radical and there emerged eventually a philosophy which was separate from and absolutely independent of the contents of faith. Another of the many consequences of this separation was an ever deeper mistrust with regard to reason itself."

44 See Giussani, *Religious Awareness*, 108–13. Remo Guidi, in his impressive work on a great number of inscriptions and manuscripts, shows in the dialectic between humanists and mendicants the substantial pertinence of Giussani's judgment on humanism. See R.L. Guidi, *Il dibattito sull'uomo nel Quattrocento* (Roma: Tiellemedia 1989).

45 See Giussani, *Religious Awareness*, 114: "Cornelio Fabro summed it up well: 'If God does exist, he doesn't matter.' God has nothing concrete to do with man. God is now extrinsic to human cares and human problems. Within this sphere, man is his own measure, his own master, the source both of the formulation of his plans and of the energy needed to bring them about, the origin even of the ethical intention implicit in all he does. Thus, even if God does exist, within the sphere of human problems it is as if he did not. In this way, a division between the sacred and the profane comes into being, as though there could exist something outside the 'temple' of God that is the entire cosmos. So it is that rationalism has embraced this division as its own, gradually at first, and, after the French Revolution, through political force. This division has in turn come to be the common ground of the learned; it has determined the cultural air we breathe; it has now become the dominant culture. And the novel substance of this culture has, after several centuries, and by means of public education, infected the hearts and minds of all people, so as to become a social mind-set."

46 Ibid., 129.

47 In particular, see L. Giussani, *Why the Church?* (trans. Viviane Hewitt, Montreal: McGill-Queen's University Press 2001), 27–61.

48 L. Giussani, *The Miracle of Change. Exercises of the Fraternity* (Milan: Coop. Nuovo Mondo 1998), 14–20: "In order to defend God in His truth and in order to defend the need for man to conceive his life as His and to tend in everything to please this supreme creator and manager of all that is, we need to recover the word 'reason' from our heart. It is the word that is most confused in modern day parlance. If the word reason is used wrongly then all man's knowledge as a building on reality, of reality, is put in jeopardy … If reason is used wrongly, then there are three possible grave reductions that affect all our behaviour [Ideology in place of an Event; the reduction of sign to appearance; the reduction of the heart to feelings]."

49 See T.S. Eliot, *Choruses from "The Rock,"* in *Collected Poems, 1909–1962* (New York: Harcourt, Brace & World 1963), 177.

50 *Religious Awareness in Modern Man* is divided into two parts, and their titles correspond to the two parts of Eliot's question, "Has Mankind Failed the Church?" "Or Has the Church Failed Mankind?" (see 105ff., 129ff.).

51 Ibid., 133.

52 His support can be seen from the following affirmation as regards the ecumenical movement: "It is an enterprise a Catholic cannot ignore. It is remarkable that the Protestant churches have started to find in some way a common expression, a common visible manifestation of that invisible unity of the Church of Christ in which they believe. The fact that they have managed to organise themselves in a single movement, to establish a vast reciprocal contact, to perceive the significance of a common interest, to express before the religious, social and political world one single voice, all this is so serious a fact as to merit accurate attention. And great comprehension." L. Giussani, "Da Amsterdam ad Evaston (Cronaca ecumenica), in *Porta la speranza*, 132–3.

53 See L. Giussani, S. Alberto, and J. Prades, *Generare tracce nella storia del mondo* (Milan: Rizzoli 1998), 156–61.

54 Ibid., 20–2.

55 See Giussani, *The Miracle of Change,* 31.

56 See ibid., 32–8.

57 See A. Scola, *Questioni di Antropologia Teologica* (Rome: Pontificia Università Lateranense-Mursia 1972), 175ff.

58 I am stealing Maritain's great title: J. Maritain, *Antimoderne* (Paris: Editions de la revue des jeunes, 1922).

59 See Giussani, *The Religious Sense,* 4–10; *At the Origin of the Christian Claim,* 96–7.

60 See Giussani, *Si può (veramente?!) vivere così?* (Milan: Rizzoli 1996), 92: "If the Mystery is the truth of man and as Mystery the truth cannot be known, if the Mystery coincides with that man, then the truth is that man. *Quid est veritas? Est vir qui adest.* What is truth (which is a theoretical question, truth should be a theoretical concept)? It is this man here present."

61 See Giussani, *The Religious Sense*, 23–33.

62 In fact, Giussani, on the one hand, speaks of the "profound gratuitousness of our being, of our very existence" (*Tracce*, 64) and, on the other hand, conceives of life as a gift of oneself (See *At the Origin of the Christian Claim*, 92–5).

63 See Giussani, *The Religious Sense*, 110–18.

64 In this regard see L. Giussani, "Moralità: Memoria e desiderio," in *Alla ricerca del volto umano* (Milan: Rizzoli 1995), 127–235; English edition, *Morality, Memory and Desire*, trans. K. D. Whitehead (San Francisco: Ignatius Press 1986). Giussani, Alberto, and Prades, *Generare tracce*, 78–93.

65 See H.U. von Balthasar, *Teodrammatica*, vol. 2 (Milan: Jaca Book 1982), 317. English edition: *Theo-drama: Theological Dramatic Theory* trans. Graham Harrison (San Francisco: Ignatius Press 1988).

66 See Giussani, *Alla ricerca del volto umano*, 19–92.

67 See Giussani, *The Religious Sense*, 115–16; *"Tu" (o dell'amicizia)* (Milan: Rizzoli 1997), 15–86, 208–9; *Alla ricerca del volto umano*, 83–92.

68 Giussani himself acknowledges this: "I think the category of experience is totally original, because in those days no one spoke of experience, so much so that I had taken Mouroux' book because it spoke of experience, but I had read only a few pages." *Annuario teologico*, 134.

69 On the category of experience in Giussani see *Tracce*, 47–8; *The Religious Sense*, 4–10; *The Risk of Education*, 98–102; *Why the Church?* 203–9; "Decisione per l'esistenza," in *Alla ricerca del volto umano*, 109–14; *Si può (veramente?!) vivere così?* 80–4; *"Tu" (o dell'amicizia)*, 84–5; *Vivendo nella carne* (Milan: Rizzoli 1998), 20–2.

70 This is a critique, however, that implies the person in a continuous comparison with concrete reality. The insistence on the need for a continuous comparison is one of the characteristics of Giussani's educative method: "If the person of Christ gives meaning to every person and every thing, then there is nothing in the world or in our life that can live by itself, or that can avoid being invincibly linked to Him. Therefore the true Christian cultural dimension is brought into play by the

comparison between the truth of your person and our life in all its
implications." Giussani, "Gioventù Studentesca: Riflessioni sopra
un'esperienza," in *Il cammino al vero*, 13.

71 Giussani insists on the methodological relevance of the nature of Chris-
tianity precisely as a *fact*. "A fact is a criterion that everyone can grasp.
We can encounter a fact, come face to face with it." Giussani, *At the
Origin of the Christian Claim*, 40.

72 See Giussani, *Religious Awareness*, 134–9: "The presence of the
Christian Fact lies in the unity of believers ... This is the miracle,
the sign" (139).

73 See Giussani, *Why the Church?*, 20–6.

74 See ibid., 8–9; 66–71; 72–4.

75 A. Scola, "La realtà dei movimenti nella Chiesa universale e nella
Chiesa locale," in *I movimenti nella Chiesa: Atti del Congresso mondi-
ale dei movimenti ecclesiali: Rome, 27–29 May 1998* (Vatican City:
Pontificium Consilium pro Laicis, 1999). Giussani explicitly affirms that
"Primarily, the Church presents itself in history as a relationship with
the living Christ ... In the eyes of those men, the only teaching that
could not be doubted was the presence of their Master, Jesus alive. And
this is exactly what they transmitted: the testimony of a Man, present
and alive. The birth of the Church is none other than this company
of disciples, this small group of friends who stayed together even after
Christ's death. And why did they stay together? Because the risen
Christ made himself present in their midst." Giussani, *Why the Church?*
66–7. Also see Giussani, *Religious Awareness*, 138–40.

76 "Insistence on religiosity is the first and absolute duty of the educator,
that is to say, the friend, he who loves and seeks to help humanity
along the pathway towards its destiny ... Jesus' understanding of
humanity induces him to drive men forcefully back towards their origins, towards what will give meaning and zest to life, towards religiosity." Giussani, *At the Origin of the Christian Claim*, 87.

77 "It would be impossible to become fully aware of what Jesus Christ
means if one did not first become fully aware of the nature of that
dynamism which makes man human. Christ proposes Himself as the
answer to what 'I' am and only an attentive, tender, and impassioned
awareness of my own self can make me open and lead me to acknowledge, admire, thank, and live Christ. Without this awareness, even Jesus
Christ becomes just a name." Ibid., 6.

78 "In this sense faith in Christ surpasses and clarifies the world's religious sense ... Faith surpasses and clarifies man's religious sense. It
reveals the object of man's religious sense, the object that reason could
not reach." Giussani, *The Miracle of Change: Exercises of the Fraternity*, 29. See also Giussani, *Si può (veramente?!) vivere così?* 542–3.

79 The category *dual unity* can be easily traced in Giussani's writings.
I quote some examples where a unity of a dual character is affirmed.
In the anthropological reflection: "A unity composed of two irreducible factors, where the emergence of the second is conditioned by
a certain development of the first, is perfectly within our grasp, and
thus rationally plausible. Thus the human body has to evolve to
a certain point in order to be suitably tuned for the genial expression
of the human spirit. This conclusion values the irreducible two-fold
make-up of man's nature as it manifests itself in the experience of the
present, without censuring or reducing anything." Giussani, *The
Religious Sense*, 44. In the gnoseological reflection: "The sign is a
reality whose meaning is another reality, something I am able to
experience, which acquires its meaning by leading to another reality."
Ibid., 111. In the christological reflection: "That Jesus is a man-God
does not mean that God has been 'transformed into a man.' Rather, it
means that the divine Person of the Word possesses not only the divine
nature, but also the concrete, human nature of Jesus the Man."
Giussani, *At the Origin of the Christian Claim*, 103. In the ontological and Trinitarian reflection: "The nature of Being is relationship,
like the 'I-you' relationship ... the dogma of the Trinity explains again
– it's not that it says everything: it says something definitive about the
nature of the 'I' and about the things that the human mind would not
have had the faintest perception and knowledge – that Being is communion." Giussani, *"Tu" (o dell'amicizia)*, 69–70. In another text,
though, Giussani offers a critique of the category of duality: "The
We is not 'I and You,' in order to be able to say 'I and you' one must
have discovered the event of the we. For one cannot discover the
mystery of Being without discovering a we, because it is Trinity, not
duality. Religions, the most alive of them, reach duality at best." Ibid.,
264. I believe that in this passage our author is criticising not so much
the category of dual unity but rather a dualistic scheme for understanding reality, all the more so since, precisely at the anthropological level,
the dual unity of man-woman, because of its objective openness to a
child, is an analogue with the Trinitarian we. For this see A. Scola,
*Il mistero nuziale, 1: Uomo-donna* (Rome: Pontificia Università Lateranense 1998).
80 See Giussani, *The Religious Sense*, 139–40: "The world is a sign. Reality calls us on to another reality. Reason, in order to be faithful to its
nature and to the nature of such a calling, is forced to admit the existence of something else underpinning, explaining everything ... Reality is
a sign, and it awakens our religious sense."
81 See Giussani, *Why the Church?* 166–9.
82 Giussani, *"Tu" (o dell'amicizia)*, 43.

83 Giussani, *The Religious Sense*, 100–9; ibid., 143: "Reality is a sign, and, when human consciousness interprets this sign, it understands the existence of mystery. In this sense, then the world by its very structure is the revelation of God."

84 Ibid., 12: "The distinctive characteristic of that level of nature that we call man, that is, the capacity to become aware of reality according to the totality of its factors."

85 Acknowledging that "Jesus Christ is our salvation, both in history and in reality." Giussani, *Morality: memory and desire*, 10.

86 Giussani, *Si può (veramente?!) vivere così?* 177: "The faith-reason problem involves love for the truth." In this same sense Cardinal Ratzinger in his presentation of the encyclical *Fides et ratio,* affirmed, "The central problem of the Encyclical *Fides et ratio* is in fact the question of truth, which is not just one of the many problems that man must tackle, but the fundamental one, that cannot be eliminated, that passes through all times and seasons of the life and history of mankind." In *L'Osservatore Romano,* 16 October 1998, 25.

87 See Giussani, *The Religious Sense*, 8: "Knowledge is the encounter between human energy and a presence. It is an event where the energy of human knowledge is assimilated to the object. How do you produce such an assimilation? This is a fascinating question that we can only partially answer." The three premises with which *The Religious Sense* begins describe in synthesis this vision of the phenomenon of knowledge typical of Giussani: see ibid., 3–33.

88 "To arrive at a definition of freedom," Giussani reminds us, "we must observe our own experience." Giussani, *At the Origin of the Christian Claim*, 96. Also see L. Giussani, *Un avvenimento di vita cioè una storia,* ed. Carmine Di Martino (Rome: EDIT-Il Sabato 1993), 224–7, in particular: "This absolute relationship (I' – mystery) is the foundation of human freedom whose dynamism we have hinted at (cognitive and affective perception of reality that is born from within, that as work develops into judgement and that is translated into creative praxis). Without this absolute relationship, without a direct relationship with the infinite, the word freedom is just ... 'hot air' because man would be totally determinable by the reality in which he is immersed, a product of the given causes and of whoever has the luck or the chance to hold power at that moment." Ibid., 227. See also Giussani, *The Religious Sense*, 23–33, 120–3, 125ff.

89 Ibid., 100–1: "First of all, to make myself understood, I will stir your imagination. Picture yourself being born, coming out of your mother's womb at the age you are now at this very moment in terms of your development and consciousness. What would be the first, absolutely your initial reaction? If I were to open my eyes for the first time in this

instant, emerging from my mother's womb, I would be overpowered
by the wonder and awe of things as a 'presence.' I would be bowled
over and amazed by the stupefying repercussion of a presence which
is expressed in current language by the word 'thing.' Things! That's
'something'! 'Thing,' which is a concrete and, if you please, banal
version of the word 'being.'"

90 Speaking of the dynamics of freedom, Giussani explains how freedom
emerges precisely through the relationship with reality: "it is the capacity to reach destiny; freedom is the link, the relationship with final destiny, the capacity to reach God as final destiny." Giussani, *Si può vivere
così?* (Milan: Rizzoli 1994), 69ff. Freedom's involvement with the event
becomes the rule for life, so it cannot be surpassed, "Since you have
been struck, surprised and grasped, at a given time and in a given
place, by a given kind of event, the fundamental rule is to be wholly
faithful to that event and to the rules that the event implies." Giussani,
*Si può (veramente?!) vivere così?* 583.

91 "Another great word which must intervene to clarify further the meaning of 'given' is 'other, otherness.' Let us take up again our image: if I
were to be born with the consciousness that I now have, and my eyes
were, for the first time, to fly open, then reality would disclose itself as
the presence of something 'other' than myself." Giussani, *The Religious Sense*, 102.

92 See, on the category of sign, Giussani, *Il senso di Dio*, 25–30; *The Religious Sense*, 110ff.

93 Thomas is not concerned expressly with the problem of the *distinctio
realis*, but as a result of long discussions today it is not doubted that he
sustains the real distinction between essence and being. The expression
*distinctio realis*, as such, is not found in his writings, but he sometimes
used the term *compositio realis* (*De Ver.*, q.27 a.1 ad8). Thomas and
Heidegger both affirm the difference between *esse* and *ens*, but their
interpretations of the difference disagree from the start. For Thomas it
is the expression of contingence, while Heidegger absolutises it, closing
it in on itself. See E. Pérez De Haro, *El Misterio del ser*, (Barcelona:
Santandreu Editor 1994), 152–62. Not a few authors have compared
Thomas and Heidegger on the problem of metaphysics and, in particular, on the conception of being: C. Fabro, *Tomismo e pensiero moderno*
(Rome: Pontificia Università Lateranense 1969), 21–45.

94 "The prime original intuition then, is the awe in front of this given
and of the 'I' as part of it. First you are struck, and then comes the
recognition that you have been struck." Giussani, *The Religious Sense*,
103.

95 See the significant exegesis of Col 3:11 compared with that of 1Cor
15:28, in L. Giussani, *You or about Friendship: Exercises of Fraternity*

(Milan: Coop. Nuovo Mondo 1997), 23–4; Giussani, *The Miracle of Change: Exercises of the Fraternity*, 28.

96 See Giussani, *You or about Friendship*, 17–18: "For the Mystery has wanted to be acknowledged by our freedom, has wanted to generate the acknowledgement of Itself. But in God Himself the acknowledgement is given by the Son, by Him who was spoken to us as Word, Son. For Jesus Christ God is Father, and for the Father Jesus Christ is Son, therefore participant in the Word, as the theology of the Most Blessed Trinity says. Thus in His person, in His behaviour towards God, the Mystery is revealed as Trinity. Now, let's proceed, to accept love creates reciprocity, generates reciprocity. This, in the Mystery, is nature. The nature of Being revealed itself in Jesus of Nazareth as love in friendship, that is as love acknowledged. Thus the mirror of the Father is the Son, the infinite Word, and in the infinite mysterious perfection of this acknowledgement – in which vibrates for us the infinite mysterious beauty of the Origin of Being, of the Father (*Splendor Patris*) – proceeds the mysterious creative power of the Holy Spirit. Now, the 'I', the human 'I', made in the image and likeness of God, reflects originally the Mystery of the one and triune Being, proper to the dynamism of freedom, whose law will therefore be love, and the dynamism in which this love is lived can be nothing else but friendship. There remains yet a point that is mystery for my reason: why has God desired this, why does Being desire the participated being, why does the Creator desire the creature, in such a way that the participated being may not confine, may not tie Being within its boundary, may not rob anything from Being . This – how the participated being does not rob anything from Being (with a capital *B*) – this is the heart of the mystery, this is the Mystery."

97 See Giussani, *The Miracle of Change*, 29; *At the Origin of the Christian Claim*, 31–5.

98 See Giussani, *Decisione per l'esistenza*, 95–6: "The foundation is He who, as the mother of the Maccabees said, calls 'to existence the things that don't yet exist' (2 Mac 7: 28). He is the object, at least unconsciously sought, of that acknowledgement of our own consistency which begins to exist, to happen."

99 See Giussani, *Un avvenimento*, 477–8; *Alla ricerca del volto umano*, 13–18; Giussani, *You or about Friendship. Exercises*, 12–18; Giussani, *At the Origin of the Christian Claim*, 43ff.; *Why the Church?* 8–9, 183–9; *Morality*, 31–6; *Vivendo nella carne*, 116; *Decisione per l'esistenza*, 108: "The choice of life most adequate to a Christian man is therefore that of applying the method with which the fact that resolves his humanity came to be clear. This event is Christ, the God made man,

who can become today a present existential encounter in which can be verified His proposal to give a meaning to our life: following Him"; *The Miracle of Change,* 16: "Christianity is an event and is therefore present, it is present now, and its characteristic is that it is present as a memory, and Christian memory is not the same as a remembrance, or better, it is not a remembrance, but the re-happening of the Presence itself, of the same Presence." See also Giussani, Alberto, and Prades, *Generare tracce,* 36–9.

100  "'Reality' is Being, so here it's a question of identifying Jesus of Nazareth with the Mystery, with the origin of reality itself." Giussani, *The Miracle of Change,* 33.

101  Giussani, *You or about Friendship,* 55–6.

102  Giussani, *The Religious Sense,* 109: "This is the value of *analogy*: the structure of the 'impact' of the human being with reality awakens within the individual a voice which draws him towards a meaning which is further on, further up – *ana*. Analogy: this word sums up the dynamic structure of the human being's 'impact' with reality." At this point inevitably arises the question about the 'I' in as much as it is originally involved in the veritative event; and along with this that of freedom which is the emblem of the 'I,' and also of the knowledge (reason and faith) that he can have of this veritative foundation.

103  In this case the syntony with von Balthasar is considerable, confirming the fecundity of the "great friendship" that bound the two from 1971 onwards. Balthasar asserts that the "analogy of the truth of being is far from getting lost in abstractions, to the point of placing itself before the most vital questions of faith and Christian life ... In what way, ontologically thinking, can God become man, or in other words: in what way, when this fundamental mystery has made itself radiant, is it possible within the world and its logic to think of something like an imitation of Christ on the part of beings that cannot repeat the mystery of the incarnation? How can a reality like the 'Church' (as *Body* and as *Spouse*) be ontologically conceivable since it is the determining premise for such an imitation?" Hans Urs von Balthasar, *Theo-Drama: Theological Dramatic Theory: I Prolegomena,* trans. Graham Harrison (San Francisco: Ignatius Press 1988), xxx. He then elaborates an *analogia libertatis,* understood as perfect correspondence (*Entsprechung*) between God's historic self-manifestation in Jesus Christ and a human freedom that is in effect free. A synthetic look at the Christological *analogia entis* is to be found in von Balthasar, *Theo-Drama: Theological Dramatic Theory: 3* (San Francisco: Ignatius Press 1988).

104  Giussani speaks of reason in innumerable passages. The pages dedicated to faith in *Si può vivere così?* are a paradigmatic example. Here

one can sense how reason is always implied in the act of faith and how it is not independent of human freedom. See Giussani, *Si può vivere così?* 19–109.

105 Giussani, *The Religious Sense*, 12.

106 See Giussani, *Religious Awareness*, 115–17.

107 "How is faith born reasonably? Faith is a human act, so it must be born in a human way, it would not be human if it were born without reason; it would be unreasonable, that is to say not human. The way in which it is born reasonably – in other words carrying within it for man, for any man, the evidence of its consistence, the evidence of its reason – is an encounter, is the event of an encounter: of an encounter between man's awareness – intelligence, sensitivity and affectivity – and an exceptional human Presence." Giussani, *Si può vivere così?* 60–1.

108 See Giussani, *Religious Awareness*, 108–19; *Why the Church?* 32–59.

109 Giussani, *The Religious Sense*, 31.

110 See ibid., 51: "philosophy must possess the profound humility to be a wide open attempt, earnestly seeking adjustment, completion, and correction; it must be dominated by the category of possibility." Giussani, *Si può (veramente?!) vivere così?* 89: "The final position of reason, the very last, is called, from the cognitive point of view, the *category of possibility* and from the existential point of view, *begging*."

111 See Giussani, *The Religious Sense*, 21–2; *Si può (veramente?!) vivere così?* 97–9.

112 See the criticism of fideism and rationalism expressed in *Fides et ratio* (FR 55), as well as that of eclecticism (FR 86), historicism (FR 87), scientism (FR 88), pragmatism (FR 89), and nihilism (FR 90).

113 "Faith first of all is not only applicable to religious subjects, but is naturally born of indirect knowledge: of knowledge though! ... Reason is something living that, therefore, for every object has its method, its own way; it develops its characteristic dynamics; it also has a dynamics for knowing things that it does not and cannot see directly; it can know them through the testimony of others: indirect knowledge by mediation." Giussani, *Si può vivere così?* 23.

114 Ibid., 33: "Faith is a method of knowledge. Who is it that knows? My reason; we call 'reason' that energy proper to man by which man knows. So faith is a method – a way – of reason, one of reason's ways of knowing or, more briefly, a method of knowledge. What method of knowledge? It is a method of indirect knowledge. Why indirect? Because it filters; it is mediated by the fact that reason depends upon a witness; it does not see the object directly, immediately itself, but comes to know about the object by means of a witness. We have said that this method is the most important of all the methods of reason ... Other methods of reason use only one piece of man, whereas this method, the

method of faith, uses the whole man. Why? Because in order to trust a person in a just and reasonable way one has to apply the acumen of observation, one has to imply a certain dialectic, one needs a sincerity of heart, one's love for the truth must be stronger than one's dislike, for example." The question of Christian faith therefore becomes, "How can one get to know Christ? Evidently, of the methods we have mentioned, used by reason, that which will be applied here will be faith," Ibid., 36–7.

115 See ibid., 62–4.

116 Giussani, *At the Origin of the Christian Claim*, 33–4.

117 Giussani, *Decisione per l'esistenza*, 95–100.

118 Giussani, *At the Origin of the Christian Claim*, 97–8.

119 Giussani, *The Religious Sense*, 49–51, 57–8.

120 Giussani, *Why the Church?* 184–5: "The sacrament is the first aspect of this self-communication of the divine within human experience. In this sense, the Church describes itself as sacrament, a place where the presence of the divine strength, of the person of Christ who conquers the world, is and will always be seen." Giussani, *Decisione per l'esistenza*, 114: "we have to commit our own freedom in order to grasp the connection between Christian reality and our humanity. This connection is indicated by the word sign. This is a disturbing word because through the sign the presence of the transcendent touches the flesh."

121 See Giussani, *Why the Church?* 190: "The sacrament really is the divine act of the Risen Christ who knocks on the door of our personality. He presses on it." Giussani, *You or about Friendship*, 32–3; *The Miracle of Change*, 28–9.

122 Giussani, *"Tu" (o dell'amicizia)*, 31.

123 The Religious Sense Symposium: Person, Meaning, and Culture in America, 10–12 September 1998, Georgetown University Conference Center, Washington, DC (sponsored by McGill-Queen's University Press; Communio Communiom and Liberation; and Centre for Faith and Culture, Oxford University); Presentations of *The Religious Sense* and of *At the Origin of the Christian Claim* on the occasion of the publication of the English editions, Auditorium of the Dag Hammarskjöld Library, New York, 11 December 1997 and 26 May 1999.

124 See H.U. von Balthasar, *Gloria*, vol. 2 (Milan: Jaca Book 1978), 11–78. English edition: *The Glory of the Lord: Theological Aesthetics* vol. 2 of *Studies in Theological Styles Clerical Styles* (San Francisco: Ignatius Press 1984).

# 2 Christianity: A Fact in History

REMI BRAGUE

I discovered Luigi Giussani's *Religious Awareness in Modern Man* only very recently, and I will treat it in a way that is both affectionate and distant, as a friend and as one who does not belong to the movement founded by Msgr Giussani. Thus I will try to appropriate its content for myself and to transmit what I have absorbed. I have heard a voice speak to me, and I can do nothing other than return the favour. The booklet collects the texts of a few conferences, edited very simply and directly, and is divided according to a similarly simple plan: it is a sort of a diptych that contains in its first panel a kind of critical history, a genealogy, or, as is said these days, a deconstruction of contemporary religious consciousness. This is followed by an attempt by Giussani to reformulate Christian faith, after he has described some reductions that, according to him, it has undergone and that make it somewhat too well known, that make it, in fact, like an old story that one would rather forget.

One of the original aspects of *Religious Awareness* is that this genealogy, this history that attempts to explain why we have come to the point at which we find ourselves, is not done only or mostly through a reading of philosophers; being a philosopher myself, at first I felt a bit offended. But I soon changed my mind when I realized that Msgr Giussani proceeds by reading various poets of all the traditions of European poetry and, in particular, uses a poem by T.S. Eliot as the leitmotif for his discussion. It seems to me that precisely because rigour is not extraneous to poetry – on the contrary, in our times poets perhaps speak with greater rigour than philosophers – this leitmotif is extraordinarily fruitful. Since I am only a philosopher – and the most prosaic man in the world – I will propose a simple, entirely personal, and perhaps subjective reading of *Religious Awareness* that concentrates, not on a poem, which I would be entirely incapable of composing, but simply on four cornerstones, four fundamental ideas.

The first of these ideas, constantly asserted in Giussani's text, is that Christianity is not something verbal, something that belongs to the sphere of words. Neither is it a doctrine or, as is said too often, I think, a message. It presents itself not as something verbal but as a fact. I do not want to say that it is a reality. I am not yet dealing with Christianity's claim to offer itself as the truth; I am saying only that it presents itself as something that happened, as much more than a verbal message that was written down and that would count as a doctrine, even a system. This is something so true that one can even ask whether the word Christianity has become inadequate. It originally indicated a way of behaving, just as Hellenism indicated not a doctrine but a manner of behaving that was Greek and just as Judaism indicated not a theory, or even Judaic thought, but a practice, the daily practice of the Law. If that is what Christianity means, I have no objection. The problem is that language has evolved and words ending with "ity" or "ism" lead us to think, or at least suggest, that we are faced with a system, a group of doctrines.

Given these reservations and the current use of the word Christianity, I greatly appreciate the fact that Msgr Giussani does not speak of Christianity but of what he calls the Christian fact. This expression does not really work well in French, but it seems to me that it very effectively underlines the idea that what we are dealing with in Christianity is not a doctrine, not even a message, but a person who must be taken as such and for whom one must make space in one's life. To convey this idea Giussani uses a splendid metaphor describing how the birth of a child forces the entire universe of a family to reorganize: "When a child is born into a family, it is clear to the parents, to the grandparents, to the whole family and to friends that this is a fact. There is nothing to dispute: a new bed is needed, perhaps another bedroom; we have to give thought to how to take care of the new arrival; we are concerned about feeding, clothing and protecting him or her; we get up at night if he or she needs us. The shape of daily life is transformed by virtue of this fact ... Christianity is a 'fact' in the same way. It entered history just as a child enters the house of a husband and wife. Christianity is an irreducible event, an objective presence that desires to reach man; until the very end, it means to be a provocation to him, and to offer a judgment of him."[1] This is a marvelous image for me personally and as the father of a family; it should really be recognized as an image of the dimension of event, of fact, proper to Christianity: it evokes something that happens and that, like the baby, does not speak in the beginning. It is present before speaking. Thus Christianity is also a fact that we have not yet finished explaining for ourselves, that we have not yet finished letting speak.

The second fundamental idea of *Religious Awareness* is an attack that I liked very much, because it showed that Msgr Giussani and I have the same adversaries. While discussing the reductions of Christianity to something verbal, to something that deforms it, Giussani writes two very dense pages on what he calls moralism. The essence of moralism is to subject life to an exterior criterion, to judge it; but judging life means killing it. Nietzsche said as much (perhaps he was not a good Christian, but he was a thinker). In this case, morality reduces life to a few values by which it is judged and evaluated and always found lacking. Values, explains Giussani, are the instruments of the dominant culture, of real power, of a power that establishes certain values, quoting them as one quotes in the stock market, deciding what is good and what is not. This real power that Giussani speaks about can be, naturally, economic or military power, which one thinks of right away, but it is above all the power of the dominant ideology, which provides objectives for the economy and the military: the ideological power decides what is worth accepting and defending.

Now, the fundamental problem for the Christian is never the sphere of morality; that is, it is never about knowing which morality to propose; it is not a question of a so-called Christian morality. It is never about knowing what to do. One never needs a revelation, in theory, in order to know what to do. Instead, one needs to reflect on how to put into practice in concrete cases of infinite complexity and variety the moral rules that we already know – I was about to say, "that we know all too well." Some foolish people say, believing that they have made a great discovery, that there is no need for religion to establish morality. I will let them be content with this banal observation. If they want to crash through open doors, let them go ahead. But in reality this banal observation does not face the problem. What is the problem that Christianity tries to answer? It is that we know very well what we should do, but we do not do it – you perhaps, but certainly not me. Saint Paul said, "I do not do what I want, but I do the very thing that I hate" (Rom 7:15). Giussani prefers to cite the poet Ovid to demonstrate that we are dealing with a general human condition. Christianity did not appear on earth to add to the burden of laws that we know all too well. The presence of these laws, which we do not follow, which we cannot follow, is in Saint Paul, but it is also in Seneca, Ovid, and Epittetus, who all know very well that our problem is not our knowledge of good and evil – our problem is doing what is good or not doing it. Thus, moralism consists in knowing our inadequacy to do what we should and stopping there; to cite Giussani, it always "accuses man." Moralism can only accuse us of being what we are, but it can not help us.

What must be done to get out of this impasse? I turn now to the third fundamental idea that I shall focus on by citing the new formula of Msgr Giussani: "It is absolutely necessary that the meaning of life should once again befriend life."[2] *Religious Awareness* is not very long, and at first glance it gives the impression of being rather quick and superficial, but a formula like this truly deserves to be looked at in depth. What life is involved in this case? In T.S. Eliot's poem *The Rock* (1934), which Giussani uses as touchstone, life is one of the idols that the poet enumerates as substitutes for God; it is life with which one seeks to replace God. Eliot's "life" certainly refers to the idea of the life force, which was dear to Bernard Shaw and which was still in vogue at the beginning of the 1930s; similarly, it clearly alludes soon after to race (we are in 1934), evidently reffering to Nazism and to dialectic, with reference to Marxism. But the life of which Giussani speaks is not biological: it is not that blind life force that would be powerful enough even to judge both those who distance themselves from it and those who conform to it, so much so that to subordinate oneself to evolution would be the supreme good (as if we could do otherwise). Instead, the life of which Giussani speaks is the life with which Christ identifies himself when he says, "I am the Life."[3] Thus, perhaps, following Giussani's new formula, we must learn anew how important it is (to cite Nietzsche once again) not to allow morality to condem life, a life that is not biological but the life that is Christ. My point is this: for a very long time, perhaps millennia, the love of life has been in evidence. Now – and this could give rise to one of the tasks that await us in the next century – the love of life is becoming, or becoming again, praiseworthy, a virtue.

Giussani assumes that meaning and life have been separated and that without the other each one degenerates. Meaning degenerates thus into a moralism that claims to dominate reality and can only condemn it without helping it to become more profoundly itself; for its part, life degenerates into a kind of excitement, a frenzy. The love of life that I want to defend here is normally taken for granted. When one speaks of love of life, when one says that someone loves life, one means above all that he loves his life, that he wants to enjoy it, no matter whether in a bestial, vulgar manner or in an extremely refined manner. *Love of Life* is the title of a film about the pianist Arthur Rubinstein, who was certainly not vulgar. "Love of life" is ambiguous, like the love of truth that Augustine speaks about in the tenth book of the *Confessions*. In most cases what we call love of the truth is our enjoyment of truth, a truth that illuminates what we want to know and that enables us to enjoy our capacity for domination. This domination is first theoretical and then practical in relation to the objects that truth has introduced us to. But we begin to love truth a bit less when it turns against us and speaks frankly to us, revealing what we really are, which is much less than what we would like to be. To love life, we do not need to consume it, burn it in a frenzy, in a sort of Brownian movement, but we need to transmit it, live it profoundly, nourish it. It is necessary for us to let live, and life cannot come from nothing. This attitude to life must manifest itself in behaviour that, according to the formula used by Giussani, flows from the intrinsic dynamism of the event to which one belongs, not from a set of principles, not even from values.

The fourth and last point is this: how can we correspond adequately to this event, this fact? This is a general question that, given that we know reality, suggests, case by case, a correct manner in which to correspond – I use this verb deliberately, because it is vague – to whatever presents itself to us, a manner that varies according to the circumstances. One corresponds to music by listening or dancing to it. One corresponds to the laws of the state by behaving in a manner that conforms to them. One corresponds to the profound reality of nature by observing it through scientific knowledge. For each manifestation of reality there is thus a way to correspond to it, to allow it the possibility of expressing itself, to present itself for what it is.

In the light of this very simple point one can understand the importance of a sentence that is apparently also very simple but nevertheless provocative, one that appears twice in *Religious Awareness*: "The religious sense is the culmination of reason ... The religious sense is the culmination of reality ... Faith is the incandescence of reason."[4] At first sight, this affirmation seems quite strange, since we learned in elementary school and it was continually repeated in middle school that faith and reason are two separate things, oppposites. Well, if to every phenomenon there corresponds a certain attitude, if there is a correct way to embrace every phenomenon according to how it reveals itself, then for Christians phenomena exist that reveal themselves in faith. And faith is the right attitude in relationship to, in front of, in the presence of, a certain number of phenomena, an attitude that is essentially free, since, ideally, it can be dictated only by the object itself from the way in which it reveals itself. One cannot oblige belief, just as one cannot force listening, looking at a picture, for example, or dancing to a certain rhythm. I would almost like to go beyond this formula, or in any case beyond its first meaning. I would like to say that the religious attitude is the essence of rationality, because it is above all precisely the way to accept the given just as it is, without imposing on it any external criterion. It is in this sense, it seems to me, that Giussani speaks of reason as an "open gaze," a gaze that does not blink, does not shift, but looks, takes into consideration all that manifests itself. Reason is precisely the capacity to accept the given for what it is, to respect it, to receive it without deforming it. It is interesting to note that in fact this is the meaning of the Greek word that we have translated as "reason," that is, the word *logos*, which everyone knows because it has passed intact into all languages. *Logos*, then, or reason, is "a gathering, a grasping, an understanding" of reality, a gathering in which one lays out the fruit with delicacy, in good order, as one lays out raspberries on a bed of leaves, placing them with careful attention, taking care of reality. There is one way of taking care of reality, having concern for reality, when it presents itself through scientific laws. There is another way when reality is a person. There is a third way to embrace reality when it presents itself in a work of art. One could list all the various ways of such welcoming. In the case of the Christian fact, of what one is given in the faith, this welcoming, this way of "gathering," this form of reason, is faith itself. It is therefore clear how taking a position against the reduction of the Christian fact to something purely verbal does not at all lead to an obscure irrationalism, nor does it lead to a disavowal of reason in favour of more or less hazy experiences – but exactly the contrary. And it is at this point, for that matter, that Msgr Giussani understands perfectly the meaning of the last Encyclical *Fides et Ratio*, in which it is demonstrated how faith has currently taken on the task of defending reason against its own attempts at self-reduction. The book is therefore a wager: the object itself that is presented by faith, or better, the object that faith gathers, presses towards an assent that, if one can say so, needs no other arguments than the object itself as it presents itself in the faith. I would dare to say so with empty hands and pockets, with no trickery. It seems to me that a similar assent is able to bring along reason itself, and that is why as a philosopher I can be at ease with this perspective.

NOTES

1 L. Giussani, "Religious Awareness in Modern Man," *Communio* 25 (spring 1998): 134.
2 Ibid., 129.
3 See 11:25, 14:6.
4 See Giussani, "Religious Awareness," 108, 116.

## 3 The Spirituality of Luigi Giussani

LORENZO ALBACETE

In terms typical of Giussani's thought, "spirituality" can be defined as a relation with a Mystery that is perceived by the religious sense as totally transcendent and yet at the origin and as fulfillment of those defining human experiences that he calls the "original" desires of the heart.[1] Giussani also uses the expression "original experiences of the heart,"[2] which is similar to Pope John Paul II's concept of "primordial experiences" in the "Wednesday Catechesis on Human Love," where he uses this concept to construct what he calls an "adequate anthropology." The point of departure for both, therefore, is the experience of being human, of being a person, of being someone unique and unrepeatable. The word "heart" is a metaphor for the subject, the acting agent, the "I," or self, that engages with reality. In this engagement with a reality that is not created by the self, the subject experiences its own originality. This experience is the point of departure for "spirituality."

It is important to note, therefore, that for Giussani spirituality is a response to a presence: spirituality is the response of the self to the encounter with reality as other.[3] It is the response to an event, to the experience of an event. Its defining characteristic is "wonder" (*stupore*) at Being.[4] It is a going out of the self before it is a going within. The capacity for this experience is what Giussani calls the religious sense.[5] It is what defines the human being as such. This is why the real point of departure for Giussani's vision is not the religious sense as a human capacity but the event that awakens it.[6] Applied to Christian spirituality, this vision means that the starting point is the encounter with

Jesus Christ, the Incarnation of the Transcendent Mystery perceived by the religious sense.[7]

The point of departure of Christian spirituality is thus the historical event of Christ proclaimed in the New Testament and celebrated as a continuing reality in the life of the Church. Giussani constantly repeats the idea that there is nothing in the religious sense, or opening, that necessarily "requires" its fulfillment in the encounter with Christ. In real life the encounter comes first. The dominant category in his thought is thus not the religious experience but the event of encounter with a historical Presence.[8] Therefore, in one of his latest books, *L'autocoscienza del cosmo,* (The Self-Consciousness of the Universe), in spite of the title Giussani makes it clear at the very beginning that:

The religious sense is in all men and women. Each one, each human type, develops the consciousness of this religious sentiment according to his or her temperament, according to his or her personal history, to his or her character, to certain experiences to which he or she is subject. Still, some have introduced a grave fallacy, namely the identification of the God made flesh with the religious sense, within all human beings and with all its expressions ... My point of departure is not the religious sense, because if I departed from the religious sense, I would have to say that all the different constructions made over the religious sense are all good, all true ... If this religious sense is Christ, then whatever expression anyone gives to the religious sense is Christian. And this would be the true and total elimination of Christ as a historical fact, unrepeatable and unequaled, as a fact without precedent, without anything similar happening before (Christ is not the consequence of what happened before). Instead, we construct our education exactly saying this: saying that the religious sense would be fragile – one can hardly see anything; it's all dark, foggy, a *gran pasticcio*, leading to a *bailamme* of constructions, expressed in a storm of dust – if God, the Mystery, had not become man, and in that great *piazza* of the world he had not cried out: 'I am the Way to destiny because I am the Destiny,' if this man had not come and not dared identify himself – this man who ate, drank, slept, watched and was in fact killed and rose from the dead – if he had not identified himself with Divinity, with the destiny of man, with the true object of the religious sense.[9]

A crucial part of Giussani's thought is the exploration of the cultural impediments to an authentic Christian faith and spirituality, even if the external trappings remain. The Christian claim is dissolved when faith is reduced to an abstraction, to an inspiration for moralism. Christian action on behalf of a better world thus becomes voluntarism. In this case, Jesus Christ is not a factual presence that becomes the decisive factor for the organization of all of life, and as a result, spirituality becomes an escapist spiritualism or degenerates into idolatry or, in its secularized form, ideology. The proposed antidote to this malady is a method of education based on the event, the experience of encounter with Christ.[10] Indeed, Giussani does not present himself as an academic theologian; his theology and philosophy are at the service of an educational method that gives birth to a "movement" in the Church.[11] The movement is not designed a priori; it is born and sustained from the educative experience of the "school of community."[12] Giussani is, above all, a teacher.

This method is developed as a trilogy that goes from the religious sense as the anthropological openness to the encounter with Christ, to the original historical encounter as such, to its continuing presence in the Church. Still, Christ is not incarnate in a vacuum. The result of His Incarnation and work of redemption is not to "add" to the human being a dimension of life that is totally independent of what was there before. Human life is that point where the universe becomes capable of receiving divine life, as a grace, thus reaching the fulfillment – the destiny – for which it was created.[13] Already in the 1950s Giussani embraces the theology personified by de Lubac and his teaching on nature and grace, especially on the "natural desire" for Divine (specifically, Trinitarian) life.[14] Indeed, the human is the very structure of this capacity, a capacity that in absolutely no way allows us to predict the form of its fulfillment, since it is all-surpassing. On the human side, this capacity is governed by what Giussani calls reason.[15] For him reason is the human opening to reality in all its dimensions.[16] When applied to the ultimate questions about meaning, reason guides the religious sense. Much of Giussani's educative method is dedicated to rescuing reason from rationalism and fideism, from the cultural forces that diminish reason's scope, weakening or eliminating our capacity for transcendence.

Freedom, another important concept, is the possibility of exercising this capacity.[17] It is the power to act according to our link with Infinity, with the Ultimate Mystery. The suppression of the religious sense, therefore, is an attack against freedom. There is thus no freedom without "spirituality." To say that in Giussani spirituality is a "passion for the human" is to say that he has in mind the defense of human freedom and all its expressions.[18] Spirituality is the history of freedom's attempts to reach the Infinite, to which we are linked. An authentically human spirituality is one that will not stop along the way, will not replace the Mystery with a human creation, synthesis, or project, and will not abandon or deform the point of departure in order to reach the destiny (spiritualism).

*Et Incarnatus est.* The Incarnation is the event upon which Giussani's proposal is grounded. The Incarnation is understood totally in a

Catholic, Chalcedonian way, that is, affirming the uniqueness, historical and material concreteness and unicity of Christ. (*Dominus Jesus*,
the recent decree of the Congregation for the Doctrine of Faith on the
unicity of Jesus Christ corresponds perfectly to Giussani's fundamental
concern.) This is indeed what awakened his vocation as a teacher, leading to the creation of Communion and Liberation, namely, the "dis-
Incarnation" of Christ that he perceived among those who thought of
themselves as Christians. Making this dis-Incarnation possible – indeed,
likely – is modern culture itself, which is a culture of abstraction in
which the unique and the particular disappears from consciousness.
Indeed, for Giussani it is only the Incarnation that allows us to grasp
the real in all its dimensions, since it is the Presence of the Ultimate
within creation itself.[19] The Incarnation unveils the "ultimate truth" of
what exists. Without acceptance of the Incarnation, our grasp of the
real is dissolved, sooner or later, into abstraction. (This is one of the
consequences of seeing creation as the "predestination of Christ" and
of "reality in Christ," what has been called "objective Christocentrism.") The Incarnation is, of course, the definitive basis of that "passion for the human" that Paul VI said was the key to the Church's
mission after Vatican II.

Taking the Incarnation seriously also means that Christian spirituality has a very definite, incarnate, tangible and sensible expression, or
form, outside of which it simply does not exist. For Giussani, spirituality cannot be separated from this concrete, historical shape, since the
Christian's relation with the Ultimate Mystery always passes through
the historical, structured form of the Christ-event.[20] Spirituality, therefore, is a way of experiencing and living life in this world, the world
where the Incarnation took place. The after-life is not seen as something added to this one, but as the very truth behind life in this
world.[164] This truth certainly goes beyond what life in this world can
achieve by its own power or dynamism, but spirituality does not seek
to escape this world; on the contrary, it seeks to make the life of this
world all it was created to be. Spirituality is life according to the event
of the Incarnation, and since the Incarnation is the "purpose" of creation, spirituality is simply human life itself faithful to the way it was
created. "Spirituality" is thus an expression of the "passion for the
human" provoked by the Incarnation.

The Incarnation determines the fundamental form, shape, or dynamic
law of spirituality; therefore, it will be characterized by the following
dimensions. It will be the result of an event. An event is something
that happens to us, something that "comes to us from outside of us"
(e-vent).[22] An event is an encounter with a reality that does not orig-
inate in us. Christian spirituality, therefore, is not created by the religious sense. Rather, it guides it and sustains it, keeping it tied to the

event of the encounter with Christ. If the spirituality generated by the religious sense is the effort to discover God as "All in all," Christian spirituality is the recognition of Jesus Christ as "Christ in all."[23] The encounter with Christ gives birth to a new way of looking at the world, at reality: it brings about a conversion, a change of mentality. Christian spirituality will express this new way; in fact, it is this new way. This is the way of child-like wonder and amazement, of child-like surrender and trust so wonderfully exemplified by the figure of St Therese of Lisieux.[24]

The newness discovered in the Incarnation is, of course, the work of the Holy Spirit. Christian spirituality, therefore, is the experience of the work of the Holy Spirit, as Louis Bouyer insisted. Experienced in the encounter with the Incarnate Son sent by the Father, brought about by the power of the Holy Spirit, Christian spirituality is always Trinitarian. As such, Christian spirituality experiences human life as inherently communal. It brings together liberty and belonging, communion and liberation. Christ is encountered through this communion called the Church.[25] Christian spirituality is thus ecclesial. The *communio* that is the Church is created and sustained by the Eucharistic Presence of the Risen Christ. Christian spirituality, therefore, is Eucharistic. Christian spirituality is Eucharistic life in this world.

The Holy Spirit always creates the Body of Christ. We, therefore, do not create the Church; the communion is not the creation of our religious needs. The "dynamic law" that reveals the work of the Spirit is the law of election for mission. The "elect" is the one sent. Such is, of course, the shape of the Christ-event. Jesus Christ, the Incarnate Son, is the chosen or predestined one (the predestination of Christ "before all ages"), and as such He is the One sent by the Father.[26] Creation itself is an expression of the election of Christ. According to Giussani, the history of the election of Israel and of the individual elections within the life of Israel is the great teacher of what will happen to all of humankind through the Incarnation.[27] The Incarnation occurs within the body of Mary, chosen, elected, created, and shaped for this event from the first moment of her existence. With Mary begins the election of the Church as the place of the diffusion of the Risen Body of Christ throughout history, the creation within the world – for the world – the "House" (a key word in Giussani's thought) where Jesus Christ is Lord of the universe.[28] Christian spirituality is always lived with reference to this House; it is the life of this House in the world. Christian spirituality is thus inseparable from Mary, the Church, and the houses where the Church becomes a reality (parishes, families, monasteries, and convents and the houses established by the ecclesial movements and communities).[29] Christian spirituality aims to turn the entire world into a house where men and women are at home with Christ, to restore to creation itself its truth as the "house of Christ."[30] Through baptism, each Christian is chosen and sent into the world for this purpose, to embrace the circumstances of his or her life in such a way as to make Jesus Christ present as Lord of the Universe.[31] Christian spirituality, therefore, is oriented to work, to recreation, to the struggle for justice and peace in the world. For this reason, it will embrace the challenges that characterize today's world mentioned by Louis Bouyer: family and work, the dignity and mission of women, technology and the humanization of the environment, and so on.

The Incarnation, of course, cannot be separated from the Paschal Mystery. The Eternal Son of God became incarnate in the "flesh of sin."[32] The "newness" brought about by the Holy Spirit through the Incarnation can be described as the forgiveness of sins; the Incarnate Son is the Redeemer of Man, and the Invisible Father revealed through the Incarnate Son is the "Father of mercies." Human insufficiency before the vocation to divine life (the religious sense) is further augmented by the poison of sin that has taken residence in the human heart. For Giussani, the human posture before the Mystery is thus that of the "blind beggar" before Christ.[33] Spirituality is the cry for mercy. The gesture or act through which Christ restores reality to its original truth is "sacrifice," understood as a participation in the Cross.[34] As a result of truth, fidelity to the truth about reality and the openness to Divine Trinitarian Life engraved in it always involve sacrifice. That is why there cannot be spirituality without asceticism, as Louis Bouyer insisted. This asceticism is thus not a denial of the goodness of creation and the world but the affirmation that the distortions brought about by sin are not the ultimate truth of the world. So powerful is the redeeming sacrifice of Christ that Giussani can say that what sin has brought about "doesn't exist," that the only reality is Christ, who is, through sacrifice, all in all.[35] Awareness of this reality allowed Peter to declare his love for Jesus in spite of having betrayed him. This yes of Peter is paradigmatic for Christian spirituality in the thought of Giussani.[36] Indeed, the sacrifice that makes it possible ensures that the "passion for humanity" that is characteristic of the Christian is not obscured or destroyed by sin. As such, this kind of asceticism is the greatest contribution the Christian can make for the good of the world. It is the highest form of charity. Christian spirituality thus understood is a sacrificial love for the world, seeing and living our life in Christ as the Original and Ultimate Truth of all that exists, by the power of the Spirit, to the glory of the Father.[37]

NOTES

1 See L. Giussani, *The Religious Sense*, trans. John Zucchi (Montreal: McGill-Queen's University Press 1997), 7–9.
2 Ibid., 9.
3 Giussani, *The Religious Sense*, 100.
4 Ibid., 100.
5 Ibid., 45.
6 Ibid., 108.
7 L. Giussani, S. Alberto, and J. Prades, *Generare tracce nella storia del mondo* (Milan: Rizzoli 1998), 5.
8 Ibid., 24.
9 L. Giussani, *L'autocoscienza del cosmo* (Milan: Rizzoli 2000), 14, 16–17.
10 Giussani, Alberto, and Prades, *Generare tracce*, 40.
11 See L. Giussani, "How a Movement is Born," in *Communion and Liberation: A Movement in the Church*, ed. Davide Rondoni, trans. P. Stevenson and S. Scott (Montreal: McGill-Queen's University Press 2000), 105ff.
12 The "school of community" provides the usual occasion for catechism and for meeting together, for high school and university students and for adults.
13 See, e.g., Giussani, *L'autocoscienza del cosmo*, 137–46.
14 See H. de Lubac, *Il mistero del soprannaturale* (Milan: Jaca Book 1978). Original edition: *Le mystère du surnaturel* (Paris: Aubier 1965).
15 Giussani, *The Religious Sense*, 12ff.
16 Ibid., 12.
17 Ibid., 87.
18 See L. Giussani, "Più società meno Stato," in *L'io, il potere, le opere. Contributi da un'esperienza* (Genova: Marietti 2000), 44.
19 L. Giussani, *L'uomo e il suo destino* (Genoa: Marietti 1999), 127.
20 Giussani, Alberto, and Prades, *Generare tracce*, 43.
21 L. Giussani, *Vivendo nella carne*, (Milan: Rizzoli 1998), 185.
22 See Giussani, Alberto, and Prades, *Generare tracce*, 11.
23 See Giussani, *L'uomo e il suo destino*, 11, 25.
24 See Therese of Lisieux, *The Story of a Soul* (Wheathampstead, England: Anthony Clarke Books 1973).
25 L. Giussani, *Why the Church?* trans. Vivian Hewitt (Montreal: McGill-Queen's University Press 2001), 119ff.
26 See Giussani, Alberto, and Prades, *Generare tracce*, 53–6; L. Giussani, *Il tempo e il tempio* (Milan: Rizzoli 1995), 14.
27 Giussani, Alberto, and Prades, *Generare tracce*, 52.
28 Ibid., 98; see Giussani, *Il tempo e il tempio*, 11ff.

29 Ibid., 15ff.

30 Ibid., 15.

31 Giussani, Alberto, and Prades, *Generare tracce*, 67.

32 See Rom 8:3.

33 Giussani, Alberto, and Prades, *Generare tracce*, 29–30.

34 L. Giussani, *At the Origin of the Christian Claim*, trans. Viviane Hewitt (Montreal: McGill-Queen's University Press 1998), 92ff.

35 L. Giussani, *Si può (veramente?!) vivere così?* (Milan: Rizzoli 1996), 21.

36 L. Giussani, *You Can Live Like This: Exercises of the Fraternity*, trans. Damian Bacich (Milan: Coop. Nuovo Mondo 1995), 36–44.

37 L. Giussani, *At the Origin of the Christian Claim*, 92ff.

PART TWO

# Faith Reasonably Communicated

# 4 Living the Real Intensely

MICHAEL WALDSTEIN

*Astonished and at Home*

In the first chapter of his book *Orthodoxy*, G.K. Chesterton tells the story of "an English yachtsman who slightly miscalculated his course and discovered England under the impression that it was a new island in the South Seas." One might think the man felt rather stupid, Chesterton notes, but he points out that "His mistake was really the most enviable mistake ... What could be more delightful than to have in the same few minutes all the fascinating terrors of going abroad combined with all the humane security of coming home again ... What could be more glorious than to brace one's self up to discover New South Wales and then realize, with a gush of happy tears, that it was really old South Wales?" Chesterton goes on to draw a rather far-reaching conclusion from this paradoxical story. "This ... seems to me the main problem for philosophers ... How can we contrive to be at once astonished at the world and yet at home in it?"[182]

This coincidence of opposites was my experience with the writings of Msgr Giussani when I studied them in the weekly School of Community with my friends in the movement Communion and Liberation: first during my four years as a doctoral student in New Testament at Harvard and then during my eight years as a professor of New Testament at the University of Notre Dame. It is still my experience in the School of Community we have in Gaming, Austria.

### Thought and Experience

This is the first thing to be said about the great three-volume *PerCorso*, Giussani's main work, which is now being introduced to the English-speaking public. Great as the *PerCorso* may be when one measures it by the academic criteria of sustained and penetrating theological thought – and I think it is great indeed – one sees its true greatness only when one realizes how it is saturated by an experience that is its immediate origin and target. The *PerCorso*'s thought flows from reflection on the experience of faith in the web of friendships which is Communion and Liberation, and it is directed back into this experience as a pedagogic stimulus for the steps to be taken in an actual life of faith. Here lies the reason for the Chestertonian coincidence of opposites experienced by those who study the *PerCorso*. In St Irenaeus's words, "Christ brought all newness by bringing himself."[2]

### Ecumenical and Catholic

Consider a characteristic page, perhaps the most characteristic and important page of the *PerCorso*'s first volume, *The Religious Sense*.

What is the formula for the journey to the ultimate meaning of reality? Living the real. There is an experience, hidden yet implied, of that arcane, mysterious presence [that is] to be found within the opening of the eye, within the attraction reawakened by things, within the beauty of things, within an amazement, full of gratitude, comfort, and hope ... Now the question is this: How can this complex, yet simple, this enormously rich experience of the human heart ... become vivid, how can it come alive? How can it become powerful? In the *"impact" with the real*. The only condition for being truly and faithfully religious, the formula for the journey to the meaning of reality, is to live always the real intensely, without preclusion, without negating or forgetting anything.[3]

One thing is immediately evident in this text: a position of openness that embraces everything. A glimpse of this openness was the main reason I was attracted to Communion and Liberation when I first encountered it fifteen years ago while studying at the Biblicum here in Rome. It is one of the main reasons I have remained with this movement since. The Christian Event concerns the entire inhabited world, or in Greek, the entire *oikoumene*. It is radically ecumenical. Another way of saying the same thing is to say that the Christian Event is completely universal, or again in Greek, *katholikos*. Ecumenical and Catholic: both for the same reason and both as forming the heart of the Christian. That is the heart of the matter.

## THE THREE PARTS OF THE *PerCorso*

### The Religious Sense

The *PerCorso* unfolds this heart in three dimensions. The first volume, *The Religious Sense*, focuses on the question of the human heart, on the longing that finds fulfillment only in God. Giussani explains the importance of this first step in the words of Reinhold Niebuhr: "Nothing is so incredible as an answer to an unasked question."[4] He argues that the most serious obstacle to the acknowledgement of Christ consists in the lack of awareness of one's own human need, of the question that constitutes our humanity. He diagnoses a certain spiritual anorexia in our culture, a deadly lack of desire for the fullness of life, that brings with it a loss of the self, a loss that exposes those who suffer it to manipulation by the powers of this world.

The Religious Sense formulates its central point also in terms of reason. According to Aristotle, the human soul is in a certain way all things. It is open to being in its entirety. Nothing that is, is foreign to it. Reason is therefore the power that allows us to consider reality in *all* its aspects. In our culture this open reason is often replaced by an instrumental-practical reason that serves particular interests and therefore precludes particular aspects of reality. But the true openness of reason is required if we are to recognize the gracious event of God's incarnation among us.

### At the Origin of the Christian Claim

The second volume of the *PerCorso*, *At the Origin of the Christian Claim*, focuses on the event in which God answers the longing that He himself has placed in the human heart. The category of event is decisive here. *At the Origin of the Christian Claim* resists a reduction of the Christian event to moral discourse. This reduction is the great temptation for Catholics today. It is welcomed by the power of this world in politics and culture because it allows the power of this world to harness the energies of Catholics to its interests.

In this context Giussani often quotes Solov'ev's short story *The Anti-Christ*, because it powerfully expresses the central point. In that story the Anti-Christ, who has become emperor of the whole world, offers Christians his support. To the Pope and Catholic leaders in general he offers world-wide moral authority for the common good of peace and justice, to Protestants he offers a splendidly endowed world institute of free inquiry into the Scriptures, and to the Orthodox he offers a world museum of Christian archeology and the reinstituting of sacred customs.

Many Christians accept the offer, but Pope Peter II, the Protestant professor Pauli, and the Orthodox elder John refuse, together with a small number of followers. Then the Anti-Christ says to them, in a tone of sadness, "What more can I do for you? Strange men! What do you want of me? I do not know. Tell me yourselves, you Christians forsaken by most of your brothers and leaders and condemned by popular feeling: What is dearest to you in Christianity?" Elder John rises up like a white candle and answers gently, "Great emperor! Dearest to us in Christianity is Christ himself – He himself. Everything rests on him, for we know that in him all the fullness of Godhead dwells bodily."[5] At this point the Anti-Christ flies into a rage and betrays himself.

### Why the Church?

The third volume of the *PerCorso*, *Why the Church?* continues the argument of the second volume by bringing it into the present time. How is Christ present *now*, so that he transforms his followers *now* in the late twentieth century? This is our question as people who do not live at the time of Christ. The Church as the body of Christ – this is the central thesis of *Why the Church?* – prolongs Christ's humanity in history to reach us here and now as an efficacious sign of God's presence. In the Church as a living institution that can be seen and touched the power of God is sacramentally at work.

The third volume of the *PerCorso* speaks of the Church with a particular emphasis and temperament that is characteristic of Msgr Giussani. Again of fundamental importance is the category of event. The Christian Event, made present here and now by the Church, is like the birth of a baby for young parents (Remi Brague discusses this point in chapter 2 of this book). A birth has a privileged role in educating the parents precisely as an event that endures in the baby's presence. In anticipation the parents prepare their house. In the joy of the baby's living presence their lives are changed. *Why the Church?* shows that Christ changes us in a similar manner, not by substituting something else, as one would replace a defective part in a machine, but by transfiguring us. He eliminates nothing but enlivens our relationship with ourselves, with other people, with the world of things, with everything. It is the same humanity that becomes different, the same humanity in relation to everything. It is our way of loving, our way of looking at nature, our way of experiencing and facing suffering that become different. *Memores Domini* – the Church, and in particular the piece of the Church in which we live, effectively recalls the presence of Christ.

## THE WAY OF *THE RELIGIOUS SENSE*

To give a more concrete view of the *PerCorso*, let me return from this bird's-eye view to the passage from *The Religious Sense* quoted above: "The only condition for being truly and faithfully religious, the formula for the journey to the meaning of reality is to live always the real intensely, without preclusion, without negating or forgetting anything."[6] This passage stands at the conclusion of a chapter that describes the dynamic of human reason in its impact with reality in five interlocking steps.

Let me introduce these steps with a fragment from one of Aristotle's lost dialogues:

Suppose there were men who had always lived underground, in good and well-lighted dwellings, adorned with statues and pictures, and furnished with everything in which those who are thought happy abound. Suppose, however, that they had never gone above ground, but had learned by report and hearsay there was a divine spirit and power. Suppose that then, at some time, the jaws of the earth opened and they were able to escape and make their way from those hidden dwellings into these regions which we inhabit. When they suddenly saw earth and seas and skies, when they learned the grandeur of clouds and the power of wind, when they saw the sun and realized not only its grandeur and beauty, but also its power, by which it fills the sky with light and makes the day; when again night darkened the lands and they saw the whole sky picked out and adorned with stars, and the varying light of the moon ... Most certainly when they saw these things would they have judged both that there are gods and that these great works are the works of gods.[7]

I find it hard to escape the impression that the *PerCorso* sees our impact with reality with eyes that have much of this Aristotelian amazement at the world in which we are at home. They satisfy with great precision Chesterton's demand that philosophy should allow us "to be at once astonished at the world and yet at home in it."

### Awe of the "Presence"

As I open my eyes – this is the first step described by Giussani – I am drawn into awe before the presence of beings I did not make, an awe that contains a strong attraction. "It is, indeed, truly superficial to repeat that religion is born of fear. Fear is not a human being's first sentiment – it is attraction ... Attachment to being, to life, awe in front of the evidence comes first ... Religiosity is, first of all, the affirmation and development of the attraction."[8]

### The Cosmos

Within and among the beings whose presence imposes itself on me there is an order that is not merely functional or mechanical but beautiful. Giussani calls to mind how a look at the starry sky almost made Kant doubt his *Critique of Practical Reason*, which denies precisely the possibility of contact with a true presence of being.

### "Providential" Reality

The ordered cosmos is not only beautiful in its grandeur. Its order in some way aims at me, allowing me to live. Giussani quotes Paul's statement in the *Acts of the Apostles*: "Yet in bestowing his benefits, he has not hidden himself completely, without a clue. From the heavens he sends down rain and rich harvests; your spirits he fills with food and delight."[9]

### The Dependent "I"

Encountering the real in awe as an ordered reality that allows me to live, I discover myself *as* dependent precisely as myself. I stand vis-à-vis the mystery of my source. "It is that which is more than I, more 'I' than I myself. It is that by means of which I am."[10] In every instance I am begotten and stand thus as son before God as Father, before God, not as one among other beings, but as all. As the source of being, God is all. Here lie the foundations of peace. "All human actions, therefore, inasmuch as they aim towards peace and joy, seek God, the exhaustive substance of our lives."[11]

### The Law of the Heart

The movement of gift in which I receive myself as a creature of God is completed in the writing of God's law on my heart. By understanding this law, I am most fully given into my own hands, I am truly self-moving, self-impelled. Yet, at the same time, this law written on the heart sets me on a journey into God. God as my origin thereby draws me to himself as my goal.

### CONCLUSION

Let me conclude by returning to the passage from *The Religious Sense* that I quoted above. It will resonate more fully at the end of my remarks, I hope, than at the beginning. "What is the formula for the journey to the ultimate meaning of reality? Living the real. There is an experience, hidden yet implied, of that arcane, mysterious presence [that is] to be found within the opening of the eye, within the attraction reawakened by things, within the beauty of things, within an amazement, full of gratitude, comfort, and hope ... Now the question is this: How can this complex, yet simple, this enormously rich experience of the human heart ... become vivid, how can it come alive? How can it become powerful? In the *'impact' with the real*. The only condition for being truly and faithfully religious, the formula for the journey to the meaning of reality, is to live always the real intensely, without preclusion, without negating or forgetting anything."[12]

NOTES

1 G.K. Chesterton, *Orthodoxy* (New York: Image Books 1959), introduction, §2.

2 "Quid igitur novi Dominus attulit veniens? Cognoscite quoniam omnem novitatem attulit semetipsum afferens." St Irenaeus, *Adversus Haereses*, 4.34.1.

3 L. Giussani, *The Religiouse Sense*, trans. John Zucchi (Montreal: McGill-Queen's University Press 1997), 108.

4 R. Niebuhr, *The Nature and Destiny of Man*, vol. 2, *Human Destiny* (London and New York: Nisbet 1943), 6.

5 See V. Solov'ev, *War, Progress, and the End of History, Including a Short Story of the Anti-Christ: Three Discussions.* Trans. from the Russian by Alexander Bakshy (London: University of London Press 1915).

6 Giussani, *The Religious Sense*, 108.

7 Aristotle, fragment 12, Ross.

8 Giussani, *The Religious Sense*, 101–2.

9 Acts 14,17.

10 Giussani, *The Religious Sense*, 106.

11 Ibid., 107.

12 Ibid., 108.

# 5 The Religious Sense

## J. FRANCIS STAFFORD

In the fourteenth chapter of *The Religious Sense* Msgr Luigi Giussani recalls the change of Jacob's name to Israel at Penuel.[1] His reflections on the patriarch's story point up the incommensurability between infinite human desires and finite human capabilities. Its usefulness in understanding Giussani's *apologia* for the religious experience will become apparent.

Giussani highlights the need for engaging every bit of human strength in the search for God. Here is his account:

Returning home from exile: that is to say, from the dispersion or a foreign reality, [Jacob] reaches the river at twilight, and darkness is rapidly descending. Already the herds, servants, children, and women have passed by. By the time it is his turn to wade the ford, it is completely dark, but Jacob wants to continue on. But before he sets foot in the water, he senses an obstacle in front of him. A person confronts him and tries to prevent him from crossing. Jacob cannot see this person's face but, with all of his strength, he starts to wrestle with him in a match that will last the entire night. Finally at the first rays of dawn, the strange person manages to inflict such a blow on Jacob's hip that from then on, for the rest of his life, Jacob will be lame. But at the same moment, the strange individual says to Jacob, "You are indeed great. You shall no longer be spoken of as Jacob, but as Israel, which means, 'I have wrestled with God.'"[2]

Giussani continues, "This is the stature of the human being in Judeo-Christian revelation. Life, the human being, is a struggle, that is to say a tension, a relation 'in darkness' with the beyond; a struggle without seeing the face of the other. He who realizes this about himself goes among others as lame, singled out. He is no longer like the others. He is marked."[3]

Jacob was the ambitious trickster, the one who could not be trusted. He was fearful of his brother, Esau, whom he had wronged, yet he hoped to heal their disrupted relationship through gifts of appeasement. The drama included the crucial scene of the all-night wrestling with the mysterious, unnamed person. The contest took place while Jacob was still an exile. It required the total engagement of Jacob's energy – physical, emotional, intellectual, spiritual. A dramatic tension arose between an unpredictable fraternal reconciliation and an all-encompassing personal struggle that preceded it. The stranger even seemed to assume the distant features of Esau. Jacob found the dawn and a new name. But he now had a limp for all the world to see and for himself to bear. Paradoxically, he was now also more confident that he could move from the condition of exile to being reconciled with his brother. We have here Israel's most sophisticated theology. On the one hand, Jacob/Israel challenged the divine visitor for a blessing and the revelation of his name. On the other hand, Jacob became a cripple with a unique blessing. "Israel must ponder how it was that blessings were given and at what cost."[4]

Weakness in power and power in weakness move this text toward the New Testament and the threshold on which Giussani's book ends, the gospel of the cross. The same elliptical existence stands behind Jesus's encounter with his disciples. They want thrones, which is equivalent to demanding to know the name of God. Jesus counters by asking them about cups and baptisms and crosses. Like Jacob, they are invited to be persons of energy who prevail, but they walk into their future with a limp. Jacob's energetic struggle anticipates the crucified one. Giussani's description of the all-encompassing human search for and encounter with God is profoundly moving. This story, with its emphasis on Jacob's total engagement is important for grasping Giussani's point.

I will now summarize the purpose and argument of *The Religious Sense*, which was the first volume of his Italian trilogy, the *PerCorso*, to be translated. Its central chapters are the fifth, "The Religious Sense: Its Nature"; the tenth, "How the Ultimate Questions Arise: The Way of the Religious Sense"; and the fifteenth, "The Hypothesis of Revelation: Conditions for Its Acceptability." Keeping these chapters in mind, after some introductory remarks I will discuss five general themes: the religious sense and St Thomas's *Quodammodo omnia*; the three premises of the author's method, realism, reasonableness, and the impact of morality on the dynamic of knowing; six obstacles before the ultimate question; the ultimate question and childlike wonder and awe; and the hypothesis of revelation. While highlighting his central themes, I will more or less follow the logic of the argument of Giussani himself.

## INTRODUCTORY REMARKS

Luigi Giussani's *Religious Sense* grew out of his experience of priestly work after World War II as an instructor of young people and adults in Italian Superior Schools and the Sacred Heart University in Milan. His vision was conceived and born within a century not dissimilar to the time several centuries earlier when Italy's civilization was so desolate that Alessandro Manzoni compared it to a cultivated vineyard gone wild. Comunione e Liberazione, (Communion and Liberation) which Giussani initiated after the war, has become one of the most significant lay movements in the Catholic Church. The method and content of his teaching have made a profound impact upon the lives of people of all ages in dozens of countries.

Giussani contextualizes his work. He knows that the peril of modernity is the loss of the sense of human being. The Enlightenment's rejection of the *quodammodo omnia* of Aristotle, and St Thomas Aquinas and the even more radical skepticism of the deconstructionists – those of the afterword, of the epilogue – have led to the deeply felt emptiness of modern people. Since people today accept no real norm beyond human autonomy, *homo democraticus* has become acutely conscious of the dangers of totalitarianism. Consequently, politics are characterized by mistrust and conflict. In a world after liberalism, thinkers perpetually question the dignity of human existence.

Another effect of democratic modernity, Giussani maintains, is "the uncertainty in relationships," and he adds an even more sobering endnote: "It is difficult to become certain about relationships, even within the family."[5] Pervasive mistrust, beginning with spouses and children, is like "the passing of a scythe which lays low grass and flowers together," to quote Manzoni's description of the bubonic plague and its effects on Milanese families. I recall reading in a very different forum about this modern explosion of mistrust. In an essay in the *New York Times Magazine* (21 January 1996) Meghan Daum, a New York-based writer, reveals her disillusionment with the 1990s. Her upbringing and education had held out for her generation the pursuit of a sex life in which "women should feel free to ask men on dates and wear jeans and have orgasms." She describes her discontent. "Two decades after *The Joy of Sex* made sexual pleasure permissible for both sexes and three decades after the pill put a government-approved stamp on premarital sex, we're still told not to trust each other. We've entered a period where mistrust equals responsibility, where fear signifies health." For Ms. Daum the sexual revolution has led to the dead end of a universal mistrust of others. She writes acutely that "trusting anyone is an irresponsible act, so that having faith in an intimate partner, particularly women in relation to men, is a symptom of such naivete that we're obviously not mature enough to be having sex anyway." And so distractions cover their fears and mistrusts: sports, body-building, work, acquisition of goods, consumerism, violence, drugs, war, and sexual activity.

Giussani says that the great challenge to the Church is to keep the spirit of trust and hope alive. His book reveals a fundamental Christian optimism in the human capacity to overcome the dehumanizing characteristics of modern society. His hope is sustained by the capacity of individuals to reassert their dignity.

Of the fifteen chapters in his book, the first fourteen describe, argue for, and insist upon the existence of a religious *sense* in man analogous to the five traditional senses, although Giussani does not explicitly draw that parallel. In human beings there has always existed and continues to exist a universal transcendence to God. The religious sense is part and parcel of being human in every epoch. The fifteenth chapter concludes his metaphysical reflections with the dawn of the particularity of the biblical event.

## THE RELIGIOUS SENSE AND ST THOMAS'S *QUODAMMODO OMNIA*

Human dignity is founded on the capacity to be open to the infinite and on the possession of reason. This is fundamental for Giussani's project; he underlines it with a sharp contrast. "As I see it, only two types of men capture entirely the grandeur of the human being: the anarchist and the authentically religious man. By nature, man is relation to the infinite: on the one hand the anarchist affirms himself to an infinite degree, while, on the other, the authentically religious man accepts the infinite as his meaning."[6]

In other words, the truly courageous man, today's Jacob, has only two real choices: to be an anarchist or to believe, to lead a tragic life or to embrace the Christian experience. Reinhold Schneider observed the world of the anarchist and of the Christian believer and remarked: "Tragedy is indignant revolt; Christianity means the total penetration of the world in the spirit of unwearying love. Christ handed himself over publicly to the world in order to transform it ... He himself lived this task unconditionally." The religious sense is to know a fact, namely, the religious experience. It does not mean just to think about it but to know it oneself and not through the opinions of experts. Giussani speaks of the dignity of man in terms of his being challenged by reality: "The intriguing problem for man is how to adhere to reality, to become aware of reality. This is a matter of being compelled by reality, not one of logical consistency."[7] His method does not present the reader with a theological or philosophical treatise in the technical sense, something born from elaborated theory. Since his preoccupation is with the education and formation of students by communicating the reasonableness of the Christian fact, he focuses on the experience of their individual humanity. Rather than defining the nature of the category *religious sense* he urges the reader to draw upon experience, elementary experience, he calls it. It is the total "original impetus with which the human being reaches out to reality, seeking to become one with it. He does this by fulfilling a project that dictates to reality itself the ideal image that stimulates him from within."[8] He identifies this elementary experience with the "heart." It is here that one again sees a parallel with the all-consuming struggle of Jacob.

But Giussani's work is not without conscious philosophical presuppositions. His method is an affirmation of the primacy of existence over essence. The unfolding of the vocation of humanity is the affirmation of *esse*, the act of being: existence is reality. With Etienne Gilson, Giussani knows that outside of what is most perfect and most profound in the real, there is nothing. Giussani asserts many times that judgment alone can penetrate existence. To form a judgment is to signify that a certain external form, therefore a certain act, exists actually in the subject. As Gilson insists, existence is not the predication of the composition of essence and existence but rather the predication of a composition of the form with the subject which it determines. This will become clearer in the next section.

Giussani's starting point for and description of the nature of the religious sense is from the premise of the "real" in the affirmation of Aristotle and St Thomas Aquinas: Anima est quodammodo omnia (The soul is in a sense all things). It means that the dignity and transcendent nature of human beings is established by "the openness of human reason to all reality." This openness precedes the experience of faith. As Pope John Paul II points out in his encyclical letter *Centesimus annus*, it is also transcultural.

*Quodammodo omnia* is an illuminating and radically simple phrase meaning that the soul is open to all realities in its own particular measure; or in other words, spiritual nature is open to the universality of being that it both wills to know and must will to know before all individual acts of free choice. Giussani understands that the adverb *quodammodo* is the charged Latin word; it translates into the English phrase "in a certain measure," or "in man's own finite way." With this personal desire for the infinite, universally present in all people, there arises the conclusion that the "I" of every individual is a "promise".[9] Within the created spiritual nature (the human "I") there is a *capacitas*, an *aptitudo passiva*, a natural desire or striving, a powerful needful energy, for the perfect good that can never be satisfied by human effort. There is a natural longing in human beings for complete, exhaustive self-possession, which even in its coincidence with the possession of being as such would not be satisfied. Again we see the parallel with the all-encompassing struggle of the patriarchal story at Penuel.

The paradox can be further elaborated: human beings strive to fulfill themselves in an Absolute. With Gilson, Giussani would assert that a human being is *causa sui*; i.e., through human reason alone we are capable of judging our own judgment and thus capable of being cause of our own selves in autonomous motion. Yet we are incapable of achieving the Absolute by our own power or by attaining any finite thing or good. Human judgment alone cannot satisfy the infinite desire of human beings. This constitutes the paradox of human dignity and misery.

Another point of reference may be helpful in casting light on the religious sense. It is one with what St Thomas Aquinas called the *desiderium naturale visionis*. This natural desire for the vision of God was the focus of the studies of Henri de Lubac in his *Surnaturel* (1942) and *Le Mystère du surnaturel* (1965). All human beings are interiorly conformable to the fulfilling order of grace, without in the least possessing this grace in anticipation, that is, without in any way being able to make a claim upon grace as a right. Nature awaits the finishing touches of grace. Giussani's description of the structural disproportion or distance between the end of the investigation and the depth of the question echoes the work of de Lubac and of von Balthasar.[10] It assumes the capacity of natural reason to search for ultimate meaning in our lives.[11] It is a universal capacity shared by all human beings.

I must also mention the principle of the analogy of being. Introducing this fundamental principle of Catholic philosophy and theology more formally in the tenth chapter of *The Religious Sense*,[12] Giussani insists on its central role and cites a biblical passage to support this: "For from the greatness and the beauty of created things their original author, by analogy, is seen."[13] In his rejection of making gods out of created, understandable things, Giussani still insists that it is equally important that created reality be seen as a sign by which our religious sense is awakened.[14] The fundamental Catholic principle of the analogy of being is asserted here. Reason's highest intuition is that a mystery exists that is hinted at in all the multifarious forms of the created world. And reason understands that this mystery exceeds the measure of reason itself.[15] *Deus semper maior est.*

### THREE PREMISES OF GIUSSANI'S METHOD: REALISM, REASONABLENESS, AND THE IMPACT OF MORALITY ON THE DYNAMIC OF KNOWING

What premises are involved in claiming the existence of the religious sense? Giussani insists on the *passion* for reasonableness: "We are made for truth, and truth is the correspondence between reality and consciousness."[16] He expands this statement into three premises needed to substantiate his method. They coincide with the titles of the first three chapters of *The Religious Sense*: realism, reasonableness, and the impact of morality on the dynamic of knowing in confronting the universally human religious sense. The importance of human judgment, mentioned above, becomes more apparent here. I will look at each of these premises.

### Realism

In the opening chapter Giussani introduces the universal question asked by human beings: "What is the meaning of everything?" It is a question known to all people. The universal question points to the primacy of the object outside of the self. Realism is meant to recognize and affirm this primacy. Emphasizing the personal courage necessary to acknowledge this universal question and to embrace the response one eventually gives to it, Giussani is confident that his method will lead to a successful, i.e., fully human, response. Jacob's unnamed stranger confronts everyone.

The criterion for judging the truth of the religious sense "must emerge from within the inherent structure of the human being, the structure at the origin of the person."[17] The criterion becomes apparent only within the universal needs and "evidences" arising from the face-to-face meeting with what exists. "This 'self' is nothing more than the clamorous, indestructible, and substantial exigency to affirm the meaning of everything. And it is exactly in this way the religious sense defines the self: it is the level of nature where the meaning of everything is affirmed."[18]

Finality is imprinted in human reason. The Absolute is the horizon of the world's origin and goal. Central to this realism is Giussani's frequent insistence on the need for human beings to come to the formation of a judgment. He says, "Let us begin to judge. This is the beginning of liberation."[19] Only a proposition – a judgment – is able to penetrate to the *ipsum esse* of created reality. Giussani perceives St Thomas's philosophy and his own as fully and consciously existential, as based on the indispensable formation of judgment in the discovery of truth. Giussani affirms that judgment goes to the very heart of the act-of-being. It alone is liberating. Intellection of the idea reaches only the essence that the definition formulates. The judgment, the composition, reaches the very act of being. "Prima operatio respicit quidditatem rei, secunda respicit ipsius esse." (The first operation regards the essence of a thing, the second, its being.) *Esse*, which is at the heart of every judgment, designates an act, like every verb. It is not skill in argumentation as much as judgment that is the key to attaining certitude concerning the truth of nonlogical subjects. Newman called this intellectual judgment the "illative sense." Giussani makes the nineteenth-century cardinal's insight his own by acknowledging and accepting the exigency of the religious sense.

Giussani elaborates further on the criterion for determining the truth of the judgment. The elementary experience is rooted in the complex of needs and evidences, already mentioned above, that accompany our coming face-to-face with all that exists. The growing awareness of the "I" in the infant's relation to his or her mother is central to Giussani's understanding of truth, freedom, and God. The I-Thou relationship of mother-child is at the centre of his epistemology and metaphysics. The distinctive part of Giussani's thought inserts itself at this point. Like Hans Urs von Balthasar, Giussani's meta-physics, his reflection on what is beyond the physical sciences, could more accurately be described as a meta-anthropology, because of his radical emphasis, not on cosmology, but on the relational, rational, and transcendental nature of man.

Giussani's realism is relentless. He holds tenaciously to the inherent power of human reason to be open to reality. Evidence of this power begins with the infant's relationship with the mother: the "other" is necessary for the emergence of the "I" of the child. "True self-consciousness is well portrayed by the baby in the arms of his mother and father – supported like this, he can enter any situation whatsoever, profoundly tranquil, with a promise of peace and joy. No curative system can claim this, without mutilating the person."[20]

Unlike John Locke and other English empiricists, Giussani does not consult his own ideal of how the mind should work. Rather, he interrogates human nature as an existing thing, as it is found in the world: "Modern mentality reduces reason to a group of categories in which reality is forced to find a place, and whatever does not fall into these categories is defined as irrational. But reason is like an eye staring at reality, greedily taking it in, recording its connections and implications, penetrating reality, moving from one thing to another yet conserving all of them in memory, trying to embrace everything."[21] One notes his passion in describing the cyclopaedic *eros* of man.

## Reasonableness

The second premise for grasping the religious sense highlights the acting subject. Reasonableness requires more than the element of common sense. And that "more" is the truly comprehensive action of our reasoning powers. It leads to the moral certitude, or existential certainty, arising as "the consequence of a complex of indications whose only adequate meaning – whose only adequate motive and whose only reasonable reading – is that certainty itself."[22] Only this comprehensive embrace of the examined phenomenon by the acting subject can overcome the charge of "the vicious circularity of the argument."

How do human beings know themselves to have been grasped by the truth? It is in part through the faculty of reason by which human beings, having come to the threshold of religious faith, arrive at and cross over to certainty. Human reason is not a narrowly logical faculty, as it was for those in the Age of Reason, but rather it is open-ended in its capacity for grasping the truth. Reason is the distinctively human characteristic that participates in infinitude, that is, in complete existence, in the *actu essendi illimitato* (unlimited act of being). This is the epistemological realism Giussani affirms.

Freedom and reasonableness are closely connected. Reasonableness highlights "concern and love for rationality" in the reasoning subject.[23] In one of his lectures on Giussani's *Religious Sense*, Msgr Lorenzo Albacete has observed that reasonableness is an indispensable condition for true liberty – the liberty to allow reality to be what it is, including the willingness to allow one's own self to be itself.[24] Consequently, reasonableness is necessary for liberty. Giussani scornfully rejects any attempt to "play it cool" before the ultimate question. Yet the culture insists on the prevailing convention of avoiding the ultimate question. Individuals today are weakened in their capacity, either intellectual or expressive, to overcome metaphysical bankruptcy. George Steiner has described our deconstructionist culture as not being up to "the act of *poiesis*, the act of making," thereby signifying the human inability to give form to any meaning.

## The Love of the Truth

The third premise of Giussani's method, the impact of morality on the dynamic of knowing, brings us to the love of the truth, a love that overcomes one's attachment to opinions one has already formed about the truth.[25] Here Giussani speaks of the relationship of virtue to the pursuit of truth.

It might be useful to cite the explicit convergence of Giussani's thought on the relation between truth and virtue with the teaching of Pope John Paul in his encyclical letter, *Veritatis Splendor*. Pope John Paul writes, "Indeed, at the heart of the issue of culture we find the moral sense, which in turn is rooted and fulfilled in the religious sense."[26] He then gives a reference to his earlier encyclical letter, *Centesimus Annus* no. 24, where the religious sense is described at greater length: "At the heart of every culture lies the attitude man takes to the greatest mystery: the mystery of God." In Giussani's understanding, the love of the truth requires a childlike "sincerity in front of the real ... Children have their eyes wide open."[27] I will be highlighting this aspect of his thought in a later section.

### THE SIX OBSTACLES TO THE ULTIMATE QUESTION

Yet the making of judgment is contrary to the natural tendency of reason. George Bernanos has cited "the refusal to judge ... people suffering from a paralysis of their conscience" as pervasive today.[28] It is this paralysis of conscience that Giussani insists must be overcome in recovering the religious sense.

Giussani describes six illegitimate reductions of the religious sense to the merely finite. They bear a striking resemblance to the chimeras of Dostoevsky's *Underground*. Each represents a different way of responding to the ultimate question. Giussani calls them "temptations" or "actual attitudes all of us live" in response to the ultimate question, "What is the meaning of everything?"[29] The six illegitimate responses are as follows.

1 Some simply declare the ultimate question to be theoretically "senseless." Charles Taylor describes this response as a turning against "depth," the freighting of things with meanings, with a kind of euphoric liberation. In a passage in *Aaron's Rod*, D.H. Lawrence likens the lifting of the weight of discovering obligatory meaning in experience to the escape from "a horrible enchanted castle, with wet walls of emotions and ponderous chains of feelings and ghastly atmosphere."[30] Giussani calls this a theoretical denial of the ultimate question.

2 Others empty the question of meaning by reducing it simply to "self-affirmation," the will to act, the will as the only "voluntaristic force" or energy. Theirs is a Schopenhauerian world where, according to Charles Taylor, the human will "is nothing but wild, blind,

uncontrolled striving, never satisfied, incapable of satisfaction, driving them on, against all principles, law, morality, all standards of dignity, to an insatiable search for the unattainable."[31] Many of our contemporaries who assume this position after having broken with Christianity seek liberation through an explicit espousal of Buddhism. Like Schopenhauer, they seek meaning in an escape from the self and the world and God altogether.

3  Others empty the question of any meaning by a practical denial of its content. This response is the contemporary expression of the early Puritan ideal, "God loveth adverbs; and careth not how good, but how well." It is the absolute and exclusive affirmation of ordinary life.

4  Others, reducing the ultimate question by aesthetic or sentimental evasion, reflect the characteristics of Romanticism. "In this position, although the person accepts the questions, measures and calibrates them with feeling, he does so without self-involvement, without committing his own freedom. Rather, the individual finds enjoyment in expressing the emotions stimulated by the questions. The search for life's meaning, the urgency, the need for life to have a meaning becomes a spectacle of beauty: it assumes an aesthetic form."[32]

5  Modern rationalists see a response to the ultimate question as impossible and ultimately insoluble. Theodor Adorno, a representative of the pessimism of the Frankfurt school, believes that the religious sense, i.e., hope for salvation, is "an obsession." Giussani comments, "Rationalism [of this type] destroys the very possibility of reason, of reason as a category of possibility."[33]

6  Finally, there are those who, in the name of progress, isolate and marginalize the "I"; it has no personal meaning or significance other than its contribution to some collective fulfillment in the unknown future. Giussani's critique here is typical of his critiques of the other responses: only by emphasizing the priority of judgment in discovering the religious sense is one enabled to overcome every idol, whether economic, academic, political, or utopian. He cites Dostoevsky to prove "the most evident truth": "The bee knows the secret of its beehive, the ant knows the secret of its anthill, but man does not know his own secret – the structure of a human being is a free relationship with the infinite, and therefore, it has no limits. It bursts through the walls of any place within which one would want to restrain it."[34] By refusing to make a judgment about their relation with the infinite, individuals as well as whole cultures, experience the breakdown of communication and face the isolation and disintegration characteristic of post-religious man.

Here Giussani's argument coincides with themes of the *Pensées* of Blaise Pascal. In a special way *Pensée* no. 416 echoes Giussani's description of the terrible paradox of human wretchedness and greatness. Pascal says, "In a word, man knows that he is wretched, because he is so; but he is really great because he knows it."

## THE ULTIMATE QUESTION BEGINS
## WITH CHILDLIKE WONDER AND AWE

Giussani identifies the religious sense both with religious experience or sentiments and with religious awareness – each is interchangeable, one with the other.[35] The religious sense arises and is inseparable from both the response to the ultimate question (What is the meaning of everything?) and the question itself. All religious inquiry becomes straightforward and simple before that question, which can be stated in even more radical terms: Why is there anything at all, and not simply nothing? The inquiry can only begin with wonder and awe. Before the unfolding miracle of being and love, human beings taste the sweetness of childlike wisdom.[36] "The Lord gave an example, a paradigm of this attitude of love for the truth: 'I assure you, unless you change and become like little children, you will not enter the kingdom of God.'" The religious sense "coincides with the radical engagement of the self with life, an involvement which exemplifies itself in these questions."[37]

In reading about the Christian experience in others and reflecting on my own, I have been struck by how radically childlike it is. In *The Path to Rome* Hilaire Belloc narrates the effects of early memories on his mature years. Recalling his tears at being "taken up and transfigured by the collective act" of all the men and women of the village of Undervelier attending vespers in their parish church one Sunday evening during his pilgrimage in 1901, he probes deeper into the origins of his own Christian experience. The return to belief, he writes, "is [caused by] the problem of living; for every day, every experience of evil demands a solution. That solution is provided by the memory of the great scheme which at last we remember. Our childhood pierces through again ... But I will not attempt to explain it."[38] He is rediscovering the wonder and awe of his childhood in adult life.

I am convinced that Jesus' teaching on childlikeness is revolutionary. The biggest surprise of my nearly seventy years' journey as a Christian has been the unfolding of the meaning of the teaching of Jesus about the discipleship of spiritual childhood. Giussani also gives it prominence. He writes, "You [must] face reality wide open, loyally, with the bright eyes of a child, calling a spade a spade, embracing its entire presence, even its meaning."[39] We all owe much to the newest doctor of the Church, St Thérèse of Lisieux. She taught that childhood is the last resource of the world, its last chance (a point that Lorenzo Albacete also touches on, above). She urged us to pursue it "with energy," which she identified as one of the chief virtues. Jesus entrusted to his disciples in every century the task of keeping the soul of childhood alive in the world. Giussani knows that it is the challenge of the new millennium.

## THE HYPOTHESIS OF REVELATION

Only in the fifteenth and final chapter of *The Religious Sense* does Giussani address the hypothesis of revelation and the conditions for its acceptability. He calls for an openness to the hypothesis and illustrates this openness by describing a prophetic passage from Plato's *Phaedo*: "At the extremity of life's experience, at the edge of this passionate and hard-won consciousness of existence, in spite of himself, this cry of the truest humanity breaks out as an entreaty, a begging. And then emerges the great hypothesis: 'unless someone take this passage on a more solid craft, that is to say, with the revealed word of God.'"[40]

Ending this first part of his trilogy, Giussani also quotes a similarly reinforcing thought of Franz Kafka (in a footnote) from Gustav Janouch's *Conversations with Kafka*: "Perhaps this quiet yet unquiet waiting is the harbinger of grace or perhaps it is grace itself. I do not know. But that does not disturb me."[41]

## CONCLUSION

Since the death of St Thérèse of Lisieux in 1897 we have been experiencing the continued, gradual loosening of the social order. This has been a theme of many Church leaders. It received a pastoral expression in the letters of Cardinal Suhard of Paris after the Second World War. The French author and editor of the intellectual journal *Le Débat*, Marcel Gauchet, argues that "modern man is torn, perpetually dissatisfied, and ironic ... Conflict characterizes his politics and must characterize them lest we succumb to the totalitarian temptation. Our societies explode with individualist demands, so (*pace* libertarians) the more we loosen our morals, the more the state expands."

The same mindset informs believers. Ecclesial communities abound with conflict, suspicion, instrumentalism, irony, with each person demanding to give themselves their own moral law. It is a disenchanted world in which humans are the measure of all things. Deaf to their spiritual ancestors, people now organize their political, cultural, economic, and, in part, their religious institutions solely with the future in view. With reality totally desacralized it is difficult today to repeat with Pascal that all things hide a mystery; all things are veils hiding God. But Giussani revives what is being lost, namely, the capacity to make the metaphysical act. He reawakens the openness to the infinite in us, the sense of the sacred among us. Over the decades since the war, he has heard in his Milanese community the same melodies that St Ambrose of Milan heard and that the Church still uses for morning prayer, *Splendor paternae gloriae* (Radiance of the Father's splendour).

How has Giussani moved beyond the skepticism and irony and conflicts of this age? How has he become attuned again to the silent music? How has he enabled young people of the past generation to recognize and overcome those modern characteristics that not only inhibit the community of the Holy Spirit but tend to kill it? He has said that true human happiness rests on our willingness to ask the fundamental questions that haunt reason and to struggle mightily for the answers. He concludes his work with the reference to the biblical patriarch with which I began this chapter: "The realization of the existence of this supreme unknown, upon which all history and the world depends, is reason's pinnacle and its vertigo. This means that, ideally, a human being who fulfils his true capacity, his by nature – with all of his will for life, his affection for the real – ought to be at the mercy of, hanging on moment by moment to this unreachable, indecipherable, ineffable, absolute Unknown ... "One needs great courage. Like Jacob, of whom we have spoken, who spent the entire night, the time of existence, struggling with this unseizable, indecipherable, faceless Presence. Here man feels his head spin."[42] As the years go by and I enter the midpoint of my seventh decade, I have discovered how difficult it is to grow old today. It is as difficult as it is to become a saint, i.e., to remain open to infinite love. To grow old is to discover that the two, holiness and spiritual childhood, are related. To become a saint is to become a child before God.

My pastoral ministry confirms Giussani's insight. The 1993 World Youth Day at Butterfly Hill in Cherry Creek Park, Denver, was a kind of metamorphosis for the Church of Denver and for many local churches throughout the world. It taught us again that the language of saints is written in the language of wonder and awe, the language of spiritual childhood. World Youth Days convey a mighty message: that the world loves childlikeness, the impulse of youthfulness. That should not be a surprise. We understand this because every adult was once young and has known the challenge of the young Jacob at Penuel in his or her own life. And so does Msgr Giussani.

NOTES

1 L. Giussani, *The Religious Sense*, trans. John Zucchi (Montreal: McGill-Queen's University Press 1997).

2 Ibid., 134.

3 Ibid.

4 W. Brueggemann, *Genesis: A Bible Commentary for Teaching and Preaching* (Atlanta, GA: John Knox Press 1982), 271.

5 Giussani, *The Religious Sense* 19.

6 Ibid., 9.

7 Ibid., 14.

8 Ibid., 9.

9 Ibid., 54.

10 See ibid., 49–50.

11 See ibid., 34.

12 See ibid., 104.

13 Wis 13:1–5.

14 See Giussani, *The Religious Sense*, 140.

15 See ibid., 132.

16 Ibid., 34.

17 Ibid., 7.

18 Ibid., 47.

19 Ibid., 11.

20 Ibid., 106–7.

21 Preface, ibid., xv.

22 Ibid., 20.

23 See Ibid., 22.

24 See L. Albacete, "The Challenge of Liberty," in *The Religious Sense and Modern Man* (Milan: Coop. Edit. Nuovo Mondo 1998), 13–17.

25 See Ibid., 31.

26 John Paul II, *Veritatis Splendor*, 98.

27 Giussani, *The Religious Sense*, 32.

28 Hans Urs von Balthasar, *Bernanos: An Ecclesial Existence* (San Francisco: Ignatius Press 1996), 91.

29 Giussani, *The Religious Sense*, 59.

30 Quoted in C. Taylor, *Sources of the Self: The Making of Modern Identity* (Cambridge: Cambridge University Press 1989), 466.

31 Ibid., 442.

32 Giussani, *The Religious Sense*, 70.

33 Ibid., 72.

34 Ibid., 79.

35 See ibid., 4.

36 See ibid., 32–3.

37 Ibid., 45.

38 H. Belloc, *The Path to Rome* (London: Thomas Nelson, n.d.), 159.

39 Giussani, *The Religious Sense*, 122.

40 Ibid., 143.

41 Ibid., 154.

42 Ibid., 141–2.

# 6 An Extraordinary Educator

MARC OUELLET

Let me start with a quotation from Dostoevsky. "The bee knows the secret of its beehive, the ant knows the secret of its anthill, but man does not know his own secret – the structure of a human being is a free relationship with the infinite, and therefore, it has no limits. It bursts through the walls of any place within which one would want to restrain it."[1] This quotation (which is also discussed by Cardinal Stafford in chapter 5 of this collection) is cited by Giussani in *The Religious Sense*. That book bears witness to the paradoxical nature of human beings, who are open to the infinite but too often do not know their own secret. Giussani asserts with persuasive strength that the way to the religious sense is the thirst for meaning that is distinctive of the human person. This thirst is an elementary experience that does not require the mastery of a particular knowledge but emerges naturally within an open mind that raises and carries to the end the question of the meaning of life. Reason and reasonableness in Giussani's opinion must not illude, reduce, or uproot this question from its metaphysical depth. It must address positively the secret of human openness to God, including the supreme possibility of divine revelation. In these few remarks I want to highlight his methodology, his critique of modern rationalism, and his retrieval of the metaphysical question of human freedom thirsting for God. But let me begin with a preliminary remark on the nature of this book.

*The Religious Sense* is not the theory of an isolated philosopher, it is in my opinion the result of an encounter between an extraordinary educator and a community fascinated by his testimony to Christ and by his articulation of the meaning of life in rational terms. The book proceeds from this whole, personal, and communital experience and engages in a rational dialogue concerning the ultimate meaning of life. The scope of the book is not to provoke conversions but rather to form converts to a deeper understanding of and witnessing to the truth. In this regard it provides a path of reflection that can be very fruitful for the dialogue between the believer and the secularized culture.

As for the methodology, *The Religious Sense* appears to me as a provocation at both the theoretical and practical levels of searching for the truth. It is not so much a provocation in the style of Diogenus of Sinal, who used to walk through Athens by daylight with a lantern in his hand searching for an honest man. It is rather a provocation in the pedagogical style of Socrates. It is an exercise in giving birth to the soul, in raising awareness of the self by challenging the "I" to stand up and engage in positive relationship with the infinite. What Socrates did, Giussani does, asking again and again, What is reason? What is faith? What is freedom? He thus invites his readers to consider all the factors involved in the question and helps them to persevere on the way to assessing the reasonableness of the hypothesis of God. What is faith? What is reason?

The way these questions are raised and dealt with in this book reveals a new consciousness of the narrowing of human reason in modern times. The author is fully aware of the slide of modern autonomous reason into functional and oppressive ideologies. He denounces the fall of human reason into the trap of its own abstract dialectic and its loss of rootedness in the soil of affectivity, community, and tradition. By becoming entirely autonomous and self-constructed, the enlightened modern man ended up being Promethean and therefore inhuman. Giussani's essay is an attempt to rehabilitate a dimension of rationality that was ruled out by the Cartesian model of mathematical certainty applied to philosophical methodology. His concept of reason originates from a clear and conscious epistemological realism. Thus, it does not operate in the void of a cold, objective, neutral application of the human mind to religious questions. Moreover, his use of reason stems from the awareness of the complexity of reality, which is never reducible to one single analysis. His basic conviction is that the adequate method of knowledge of the truth must be dictated by the object and not established a priori. For example, methodologically mathematical deduction does not fit the religious question, for it does not involve human freedom in its realm of knowledge. One of the most deleterious consequences of modern rationalism is the reduction of the human factor, the factor of freedom and communion. The age of critical reason has ruled out the original awe before the mystery of being.

Reason has reduced itself to mastering the world, instead of keeping the mind open to listening to and becoming enriched by reality in all its dimensions.

Giussani provides a glimpse into the reasons for trusting the real more than oneself in the search for truth and for engaging one's freedom in reading the signs of a presence. His whole book is a concrete dismantling of the fundamental dogma of the enlightenment, the impossibility of revelation: "The hypothesis of Revelation cannot be destroyed by any preconception or option. It raises a factual issue to which the nature of the human heart is originally open."[2] The liberation of human freedom from sin and from human limitation is ultimately guaranteed only by affirming this ultimate possibility.

*The Religious Sense* addresses the challenge of overcoming the prejudice concerning the irrationality of the religious question. The essay has no pretension to be a theoretical demonstration that would meet the standards of modern rationality. It is, rather, a thorough questioning of the modern separation between reason and faith. It is an effort to bridge the gap between both realms of knowledge. Giussani engages himself forcefully in digging out the depth of human striving for the ultimate meaning of things. He does not fear to be decisively counter-cultural and to advocate the rational legitimacy of the metaphysical question. "To be conscious of oneself right to the core is to perceive, at the depths of the self, an Other. This is prayer: to be conscious of oneself to the very centre, to the point of meeting an Other. Thus prayer is the only human gesture which totally realizes the human being's stature."[3] Prayer brings human freedom face to face with divine freedom. Therefore the pursuit of the ultimate meaning of life is inseparable from engaging one's freedom in the prayerful interpretation of the signs. The One who made me in freedom, does not expect less than a free response.

*The Religious Sense* is an apology for freedom as the only human way to meet the Other. The thrust of Giussani's argument is thus not to prove God's existence in a rational and objective way that would be compelling for any unprejudiced human being. His main concern is rather to reaffirm the reasonableness of the "I", striving for a full affirmation of reality. According to him the consideration of all factors involved in the "I in action" is the only way to discover and fulfill one's own humanity. His original methodology does not lead to the discovery of a new theory about the ultimate meaning of reality. Actually, the market of ideology and religious experience already provides too many new products of knowledge of the unknown. But while people are marketing the right, and maybe the orthodox, answer, Giussani raises the question afresh. The religious problem of our time is not the lack of answers but the superficiality of the question. The social and cultural context in which we live does not allow our human person to attain the depth of our own heart when the living experience of reality refers to something else, namely, to God. Actually, the religious question is often dealt with from the perspective of psychological well-being or from the point of view of social adaptation or as a way to find access to cultural and artistic treasures or maybe, in the best case, from the perspective of a coherent worldview. But very seldom is the religious sense rooted in the metaphysical need for truth, justice, love, and happiness.

Giussani addresses the forgotten truth of creatureliness, the fact that the "I" is dependent, which implies the awareness of the self as ontological gift and thus the call to respond to the gift. Hence the methodology of attention, awe, and acceptance as a fundamental way of affirming and discovering one's relationship with the mystery. No doubt the challenge of liberating oneself from prejudice entails an experience of solitude in breaking away from social patterns of thought, but it implies, as well, a deep sense of companionship, because I am given to myself and therefore I can rely on the goodness of the Giver, which shines forth in the support of the Christian community. One of the fundamental contributions of Giussani's book is the education in the freedom required for the development of the religious sense. Freedom is not the solipsistic affirmation of an autonomous reason. Freedom is communion. Freedom is the intrinsic connectedness with fellow human beings that opens us to all dimensions of human experience. Hence the realistic sense of the past, the positive experience of the present, and the passionate and trustful projection into the future. I quote: "Today this destruction of the past has the audacity to present itself as an ideal. It is a generalized alienation."[4] Giussani retrieves the broad and rich heritage of the Christian metaphysical tradition. In reading him we find ourselves in the company of those who have forged the best expressions of the living tradition. Even if there are few explicit quotations, the spirit of the great masters emerges almost literally in the way he brings to life the universal thirst for truth and love. In Giussani's enthusiastic appraisal of reality, I see a firm and unambiguous stance concerning the intrinsic relationship between nature and grace, which prolongs the great moments of Christian tradition, namely, Augustine's confession of the human heart's longing for God, Aquinas' natural desire to see God, Pascal's affirmation of human transcendence over all cosmic threats, Newman's convergence of signs in assessing the "grammar of assent," Blondel's new apologetic, which overcomes from within the modern separation between faith and reason, de Lubac's conception of man as paradox, and Vatican II and Balthasar's Christocentrism as the ultimate key to fully reveal man to himself.

Reawakening the value of continuity with the past is one aspect of education in freedom; fostering the communital phenomenon is the other, and in fact both are connected. Continuity is thus diachronic communion and community is synchronic continuity. As Giussani puts it, "The most ferocious persecution is the modern state's attempt to block the expression of the communital dimension of the religious phenomenon."[5] Isolation kills freedom, because it oppresses the image of the Trinitarian God in us who reveals that in the end freedom and love are coextensive. Isolation paralyses the energy for decision making, while communion awakens the person and channels his or her energies towards a positive confrontation with reality. Chesterton's paradox expresses that very well: "Two is not twice one; two is two thousand times one."[6] As he quotes this paradox, Giussani recalls the genius of Christ, who identified his religious experience with the Church: "There where two or three are gathered together in my name, there also shall I be."[7]

All in all, I would say in conclusion that the Italian master does not add a new recipe, a magic formula for being happy and successful, or an esoteric teaching for sectarian purposes. He engages himself passionately for the redemption of human reason, for healing and promoting the religious depth of the human person. For this purpose he breaks away from modern rationalism and nourishes the reader and the disciple with the common heritage of Christian tradition. His philosophical stance retrieves the capacity for admiration, contemplation, and loving engagement when living the real. The spiritual vibration that runs through the book reveals without any doubt an experience of an encounter with the mystery. This shared encounter is contagious, liberating, energizing, and community building. Ultimately, *The Religious Sense* rests upon the presupposition of the biblical and traditional view of man created in God's image. The catechism of the Catholic Church states in this regard that "God thirsts that we thirst for him." While this doctrine is not given an explicit treatment in Giussani's book, it nevertheless shapes the horizon within which the religious question is raised and kept fully alive: "Life is hunger, thirst, and passion for an ultimate object, which looms over the horizon, and yet always lies beyond it. When this is recognized, man becomes a tireless searcher."[8] In honour of the poets so often called on stage as partners in this book, I want to conclude by quoting Claudel's drama *The Tidings Brought to Mary*, which sums up, quite well, the spirit of Luigi Giussani: "Is the object of life only to live ... It is not to live, but to die, and not to hew the cross, but to mount upon it, and to give all that we have, laughing! There is joy, there is freedom, there is grace, there is eternal youth ... What is the worth of the world compared to life? And what is the worth of life if not to be given?"[9]

NOTES

1 See F. Dostoyevsky, *The Brothers Karamazov*; cit. in L. Giussani,
  *The Religious Sense*, trans. John Zucchi (Montreal: McGill-Queen's
  University Press 1997), 79.
2 Giussani, *The Religious Sense*, 145.
3 Ibid., 106.
4 Ibid., 83.
5 Ibid., 131.
6 G.K. Chesterton, *The Man Who Was Thursday* (Middlesex, England:
  Penguin Books 1988), 88.
7 Mt 18:20.
8 Giussani, *The Religious Sense*, 51.
9 P. Claudel, *The Tidings Brought to Mary: A Mystery*, trans. Louise
  Morgan Sill (New Haven, CT: Yale University Press 1916), 157–8;
  cit. in Giussani, *The Religious Sense*, 77–8.

# 7 For Man

JORGE MARIO BERGOGLIO

When I gave the lecture on which this chapter is based during the presentation of the Spanish edition of Luigi Giussani's book *The Religious Sense*, I was not simply performing a formal act of protocol or acting out of what could seem to be simple professional curiosity about a work bringing into focus an explanation of our faith.[1] Above all, I was expressing the gratitude that is due to Msgr Giussani. For many years now, his writings have inspired me to reflect and have helped me to pray. They have taught me to be a better Christian, and I spoke at the presentation to bear witness to this.

Msgr Giussani is one of those unexpected gifts the Lord gave to our Church after Vatican II. He has caused a wealth of individuals and movements to rise up outside the pastoral structures and programs, movements that are offering miracles of new life within the Church. On 30 May 1998, in St Peter's Square, the Pope met publicly with the new communities and ecclesial movements. It was a truly transcendent event. He asked specifically for four founders from among the many movements to give their witness. Among these was Msgr Giussani, who in 1954, the year he began teaching religion in a public high school in Milan, initiated Communion and Liberation, which is present today in more than sixty countries in the world and is much beloved by the Pope.

*The Religious Sense* is not a book exclusively for members of the movement, however, nor is it only for Christians or believers. It is a book for all human beings who take their humanity seriously. I dare say that today the primary question we must face is not so much the problem of God – the existence, the knowledge of God – but the problem of the human, of human knowledge and finding in humans themselves the mark that God has made, so as to be able to meet with Him.

### FIDES ET RATIO

By happy coincidence, the presentation of Giussani's book was held the day after the publication of Pope John Paul II's encyclical *Fides et Ratio*, which opens with this dense consideration:

Moreover, a cursory glance at ancient history shows clearly how in different parts of the world, with their different cultures, there arise at the same time the fundamental questions that pervade human life: *Who am I? Where have I come from and where am I going? Why is there evil? What is there after this life?* These are the questions which we find in the sacred writings of Israel, as also in the Veda and the Avesta; we find them in the writings of Confucius and Lao-Tze, and in the preaching of Tirthankara and Buddha; they appear in the poetry of Homer and in the tragedies of Euripides and Sophocles, as they do in the philosophical writings of Plato and Aristotle. They are questions which have their common source in the quest for meaning which has always compelled the human heart. In fact, the answer given to these questions decides the direction which people seek to give to their lives.[2]

Giussani's book is in tune with the encyclical: it is for all people who take their humanity seriously, who take these questions seriously.

Paradoxically, in *The Religious Sense* little is said about God and much is said about human beings. Much is said about our "whys," much about our ultimate needs. Quoting the Protestant theologian Niebuhr, Giussani explains that "Nothing is so incredible as an answer to an unasked question."[3] And one of the difficulties of our supermarket culture – where offers are made to everyone to hush the clamouring of their hearts – lies in giving voice to those questions of the heart. This is the challenge. Faced with the torpor of life, with this tranquillity offered at a low cost by the supermarket culture (even if in a wide assortment of ways), the challenge consists in asking ourselves the real questions about human meaning, of our existence, and in answering these questions. But if we wish to answer questions that we do not dare to answer, do not know how to answer, or cannot formulate, we fall into absurdity. For man and woman who have forgotten or censored their fundamental "whys" and the burning desire of their hearts, talking to them about God ends up being something abstract or esoteric or a push toward a devotion that has no effect on their lives. You cannot start a discussion of God without first blowing away the ashes suffocating the burning embers of the fundamental whys. The first step is to make some sense of the questions that are hidden or buried, that are perhaps almost dying but that nevertheless exist.

## THE RESTLESSNESS OF THE HEART

The drama of the world today is the result not only of the absence of God but also and above all of the absence of humankind, of the loss of the human physiognomy, of human destiny and identity, and of a certain capacity to explain the fundamental needs that dwell in the human heart. The prevailing mentality, and deplorably that of many Christians, supposes that there is an unbreachable opposition between reason and faith. Instead – and here lies another paradox – *The Religious Sense* emphasizes that speaking seriously about God means exalting and defending reason and discovering its value and the right way to use it. This is not reason understood as a pre-established measure of reality but reason open to reality in all its factors and whose starting point is experience, whose starting point is this ontological foundation that awakens a restlessness in the heart. It is not possible to raise the question of God calmly, with a tranquil heart, because this would be to give an answer without a question. Reason that reflects on experience is a reason that uses as a criterion for judgment the measuring of everything against the heart – but "heart" taken in the Biblical sense, that is, as the totality of the innate demands that everyone has, the need for love, for happiness, for truth, and for justice. The heart is the core of the internal transcendent, where the roots of truth, beauty, goodness, and the unity that gives harmony to all of being are planted. We define human reason in this sense and not as rationalism, that laboratory rationalism, idealism, or nominalism (this last so much in fashion now), which can do everything, which claims to possess reality because it is in possession of the number, the idea, or the rationale of things, or, if we want to go even further, which claims to possess reality by means of an absolutely dominating technology that surpasses us in the very moment in which we use it, so that we fall into a form of civilization that Guardini liked to call the second form of unculture. We instead speak of a reason that is not reduced, is not exhausted in the mathematical, scientific, or philosophical method. Every method, in fact, is suited to its own sphere of application and to its specific object.

## EXISTENTIAL CERTAINTY

Concerning personal relationships, the only adequate method for reaching true knowledge is to live and live together a vivid companionship that, through multiple experiences and manifold signs, allows us to arrive at what Giussani calls "moral certainty," or even better, "existential certainty."[4] This is the only adequate method because certainty does not reside in the head but in the harmony of all the human faculties, and it is in possession at the same time of all the requisites for a real and a rational certainty. In its turn, faith is, precisely, a particular application of the method of moral or existential certainty, a particular case of faith in others, in the signs, evidence, convergences, witness of others. Despite this, faith is not contrary to reason. Like all typically human acts, faith is reasonable, which does not imply that it can be reduced to mere reasoning. It is reasonable – let us push the term – but not reasoning.

Why is there pain, why death, why evil? Why is life worth living? What is the ultimate meaning of reality, of existence? What sense does it make to work, love, become involved in the world? Who am I? Where did I come from? Where am I going? These are the great and primary questions that young people ask, and adults too – and not only believers but everyone, atheists and agnostics alike. Sooner or later, especially in the situations at the very edge of existence, in the face of great grief or great love, in the experience of educating one's children or of working at a job that apparently makes no sense, these questions inevitably rise to the surface. They cannot be uprooted. I have said that they are questions that even agnostics ask, and I would like to mention here, paying him homage, a great poet from Buenos Aires, an agnostic, Horacio Armani. Whoever reads his poems encounters a sage exposition of questions that are open to an answer.

### THE TOTAL RESPONSE

Human beings cannot be content with reductive or partial answers that force them to censor or neglect some aspect of reality. In fact, however, we do neglect some aspect of reality, and when we do so we are only running away from ourselves. We need a total response that comprehends and saves the entire horizon of the self and our existence. We possess within us a yearning for the infinite, an infinite sadness, a *nostalgia* – the *nostos algos* (home sickness) of Odysseus – which is satisfied only by an equally infinite response. The human heart proves to be the sign of a Mystery, that is, of something or someone who is an infinite response. Outside the Mystery, the needs for happiness, love, and justice never meet a response that fully satisfies the human heart. Life would be an absurd desire if this response did not exist. Not only does the human heart present itself as a sign, but so does all of reality. The sign is something concrete, it points in a direction, it indicates something that can be seen, that *reveals* a meaning, that can be experienced, but that refers to another reality that cannot be seen; otherwise, the sign would be meaningless.

On the other hand, to interrogate oneself in the face of these signs, one needs an extremely human capacity, the first one we have as men and women: wonder, the capacity to be amazed, as Giussani calls it, in the last analysis, a child's heart. The beginning of every philosophy is wonder, and only wonder leads to knowledge. Notice that moral and cultural degradation begin to arise when this capacity for wonder is weakened or cancelled or when it dies. The cultural opiate tends to cancel, weaken, or kill this capacity for wonder. Pope Luciani once said that the drama of contemporary Christianity lies in the fact that it puts categories and norms in the place of wonder. But wonder comes before all categories; it is what leads me to seek, to open myself up; it is what makes the answer – not a verbal or conceptual answer – possible for me. If wonder opens me up as a question, the only response is the *encounter*, and only with the encounter is my thirst quenched. And with nothing else is it quenched more.

NOTES

1 Translated by Susan Scott.
2 The presentation was for L. Giussani, *El sentido religioso*, revised ed. with notes, translated by José Miguel Oriol, in collaboration with Cesare Zaffanella and José Miguel García (Buenos Aires and Madrid: Editorial Sudamericana and Ediciones Encuentro 1998).
3 *Fides et ratio*, par. 1.
4 R. Niebuhr, *The Nature and Destiny of Man*, vol. 2, *Human Destiny* (London and New York: Nisbet 1943), 6.
5 L. Giussani, *The Religious Sense*, trans. John Zucchi (Montreal: McGill-Queen's University Press 1997), 19–21.

# 8 The Religious Sense and American Culture

DAVID L. SCHINDLER

Commenting on the cultural situation of the Anglo-Saxon world, the philosopher Alasdair MacIntyre once remarked that our "difficulty lies in the combination of atheism in the practice of the life of the vast majority, with the profession of either superstition or theism by that same majority. The creed of the English is that there is no God and that it is wise to pray to him from time to time."[1] Luigi Giussani's account of the religious sense, set forth in his book of the same title, helps us to see that this is the creed not only of the English but of Americans as well. Indeed, I believe the book's significance lies above all in its exposure of atheism – or, to put it in positive terms, the religious sense – as the fundamental cultural issue of our time.

Now the most obvious objection to any suggestion that America's fundamental cultural issue is atheism, or the lack of religion, is that it appears to run up against the facts. And so we need to set an American context for Giussani's argument. My proposal is that atheism is a phenomenon affecting the lives of the vast majority of Americans and that the theism characteristic of the lives of that same majority does not so much contradict atheism as coincide with it and, indeed, lend it support. The purpose of this chapter is to say a word about how this is so and about the meaning and significance of Giussani's proposal in light of this phenomenon.

Regarding the religiosity of Americans, the positive evidence seems abundant. Wendy Kaminer, for example, writing in *The New Republic* in 1996, insists that the problem in America is not too little religion but too much – that what America in fact needs is *more* atheism, because of the anti-intellectual habits bred by religion.[2] Kaminer cites the statistics with which we are all familiar: 95 percent of Americans profess belief in God or some universal spirit, and 76 percent imagine God as a heavenly father who actually pays attention to their prayers. Catholic sociologist Andrew Greeley, echoing many others on all sides of the religious spectrum, interprets the same polling data positively, arguing that the history of American culture refutes the conventional wisdom that modernization inevitably leads to secularization. In fact, says Greeley, in some countries, like "the United States [and Ireland], religious devotion may be higher than it has ever been in human history."[3] In *The People's Religion* George Gallup Jr and Jim Castelli state that "the baseline of religious beliefs [in America] is remarkably high – certainly, the highest of any developed nation in the world."[4] And the *New York Times Magazine*, recording the same figure of more than 95 percent professing belief in God, reported a year ago that, statistically, Americans remain one of the most religious peoples on earth.

Many who hold this (empirical or sociological) view that religion is thriving in America tend as a consequence to "regionalize" the phenomenon of unbelief, restricting it mostly to a certain sector of our society, such as the educational, journalistic, and political elite – for example, what has been called by Peter Berger the "new knowledge class." For this first group of thinkers, in short, atheism (or secularism: I leave the two terms undifferentiated, for reasons that will become clear later) in America is not a pervasive phenomenon but is limited to the secular elites who contrast sharply with the mostly religious masses.

Now MacIntyre's statement quoted at the outset hardly disputes the existence of widespread belief in God; on the contrary, that is what it affirms. But of course it does so in a paradoxical way that requires explanation. The paradox is not unlike that focused on by Will Herberg in his classic *Protestant Catholic Jew* of the mid-1950s. As is well-known, Herberg argues that the peculiarity of America's religious situation consists in the fact that religion and secularism are basically two sides of the same coin. Coincident with its intentional sincerity and moral generosity, the religion of Americans contains within it a largely unconscious logical framework consisting of notions of the self, of human being and action, drawn mostly from post-Enlightenment, democratic-capitalist institutions. Herberg summarizes the coincidence of religion and secularism in terms of what he calls "secularized Puritanism" or "the American Way of Life."[5]

The same paradoxical coincidence of religion and atheism is also made clear in the larger context of modern culture by Friedrich Nietzsche. Recognizing widespread profession of belief and, indeed, relatively full churches, Nietzsche insisted nonetheless that God was dead. Provoking much laughter as he ran into the marketplace crying "I seek God! I seek God," and asking "Whither is God?" Nietzsche's Madman answers his own question: "I will tell you. *We have killed him* – you and I. All of us are his murderers ... What were we doing when we unchained this earth from its sun ... Are we not straying as through an infinite nothing ... Do we smell nothing as yet of the divine decomposition ... God is dead. God remains dead. And we have killed him."[6]

Theologian Michael Buckley rightly points out in his comment on this passage that "the difference between the Madman and the market crowds was not that one believed in the reality of god and the other did not. Neither believed, and god died in the event of his own incredibility."[7] But the Madman alone knows what they have done and what they have lost. Nietzsche, then, is not really surprised by the crowds' laughter: "The event [of God's death] is far too great," he says, "too distant, too remote from the multitude's capacity for comprehension even for the tidings of it to be thought of as having *arrived* yet. Much less may one suppose that many people know as yet *what* this event really means – and how much must collapse now that this faith has been undermined because it was built upon this faith, propped up by it, grown into it; for example, the whole of our European morality."[8] The death of God does not imply for Nietzsche that the market crowds were evil, however. Such a moralistic simplification misses Nietzsche's subtlety. Indeed, as he says in *The Will to Power*, "corruption is not the cause of the advent of nihilism [nihilism: see "straying as through an infinite nothing"]. Ours [in fact] is the most decent and compassionate age."[9]

We can summarize the distinctiveness of modern atheism, then, in the words of Buckley: "What began in the Paris of the Enlightenment has become a religious phenomenon which Western civilization has never witnessed before. It is critical to notice the historical uniqueness of the contemporary experience: the rise of a radical godlessness which is as much a part of the consciousness of millions of ordinary human beings as it is the persuasion of the intellectual. Atheisms have existed before, but there is a novelty, a distinctiveness about the contemporary denial of God both in its extent and in its cultural establishment. The recent judgment of John Paul II coincides with [the judgment of those who insist that our culture is characteristically 'the age of atheism']: 'Atheism is without doubt one of the major phenomena and, it is necessary to say, the spiritual drama of our time.'"[10]

It is beyond my purposes to sort out the differences between authors like MacIntyre, Herberg, Buckley, and, indeed, Nietzsche on the issue before us. I wish only to suggest, in the light of their arguments, that the claim of an atheism present throughout all sectors of society does not entail a denial that religion is also, in some obvious sense, thriving in those same sectors. On the contrary, all four authors show the possibility of affirming the near coincidence of atheism and theism. My first contention, then, is that this is the case in contemporary America, that the difference between our two groups of authors, accordingly, turns in the first instance not on the *fact* of a widespread, indeed almost pervasive, profession of religious belief in America – which neither group disputes – but rather on their divergent understandings of what suffices as an authentic religiosity, or as the integrity of the religious sense. The second group alone sees in America's virtually omnipresent religion – I emphasize, sees already *in* this religion – the seeds of a-religion, the beginnings of God's incredibility, of God's death.

But it is crucial to understand properly what is meant by God's death, and so I move on to my second proposal. As Buckley rightly insists, the modern death of God is not merely about God's cultural disappearance, as if the content of belief in God or of the idea of God remains essentially healthy and only the practice of religion is unsatisfactory – as if America is theoretically religious and only practically atheistic.[11] Any such reading of the death of God blunts the seriousness of what is really at stake, for it is the idea of God itself – in this sense God himself – that has become unbelievable. It is the content of American religion itself that is already atheistic, and this content comprehends both theory and practice. What is peculiar about America's religious situation, in a word, is not that Americans are theoretically theistic but fail practically to live up to their theism (which would in fact amount to a rather banal claim, since no one in the history of the world, save Jesus's mother, Mary, has practised completely faithfully what he or she has professed); rather, what is peculiar is that the theism practised by Americans is already theoretically atheistic and they do not know it. Americans explicitly intend to practise religion faithfully even as this intention and practice are mediated implicitly by a theory of theism that already contains the seeds of atheism.

Thus my second contention regarding religion in America: America's religious theory inclines toward atheism at the same time as it wills or intends the contrary. Now, to explain this proposal, I could draw further here (inter alia) on Buckley's analysis of what may be called the Christian contribution to atheism in modern culture, on the arguments of Herberg regarding "the American Way of Life," or, indeed, on elements of Max Weber's classic study of the inversion of American Puritanism into a rationalized notion of worldly order and activity and, indeed, into a kind of Pelagian consumerism.[12] However, for present purposes I will draw mainly from the argument of James Tunstead Burtchaell in his recently published study of the history of church-related higher education in America.[13]

Burtchaell describes this history largely in terms of a gradual transfer of identity of church-related colleges and universities from the church to nation and guild. But the theoretical core of Burtchaell's argument as it affects my context is to be found in his summary claim that "the critical turn of allegedly Christian colleges and universities in the United States has been a modern rerun of the degradation of an unstable pietism through liberal indifferentism into rationalism."[14] Pietists thought that all those quarrels over the *homoousios* and *homoiousios*, Communion from the cup, predestination, and so on, were unresolvable quarrels because they could appeal to nothing stronger than unverifiable opinion. Thus the credibility vacuum created by pietism came naturally to be filled by rationalism, which proffered a more peaceable life by refusing to discuss anything beyond what could be resolved consensually by appeal to empirical evidence. "Rationalism ... out of little more than habit ... provided itself with Deism, the religious equivalent of safe sex ... For those who liked their Deism in costume, there was Freemasonry."[15]

Burtchaell's point is nicely summarized when he writes that religion's move to the academic periphery was not so much the work of godless intellectuals as of pious educators who, since the onset of pietism, had seen religion as embodied so uniquely in the personal profession of faith that it could not be seen to have a stake in social learning. The radical disjunction between divine knowledge and human knowledge had been central to classical Reformation thinking, and its unintended outcome was to sequester religious piety from secular learning. The older, pre-Reformation view, that faith was goaded by revelation to seek further understanding and that learning itself could be an act of piety – indeed, the form of piety proper to a college or university – succumbed to the view that worship and moral behaviour were to be the defining acts of a Christian academic fellowship. Later, worship and moral behaviour were easily set aside, because no one could imagine they had anything to do with learning.[16]

The heart of Burtchaell's argument is thus that an understanding of Christianity that separates divine knowledge from human knowledge leads to a disjunction between the realms of piety and knowledge, which in turn invariably paves the road for a secularistic reduction of knowledge: pietism, in short, inverts inevitably into rationalism. My contention is that it is just this dualism between divine and human knowledge, and in turn between piety and knowledge, that undergirds and most adequately explains America's coincidence of theism and atheism: the pietistic will (voluntarism) making up America's religion inverts into and indeed continues to coexist peacefully with the rationalized intelligence (mechanism) that lies at the heart of America's a-religion. Pietistic religion or explicitly theistic will, in short, gives rise to implicitly a-theistic intelligence and order. Thus, if I may anticipate the terms of Giussani, the subjectivist-sentimentalist-pietist reduction of Christianity eases the cultural slide into (naturalism and) rationalism – that is, into the primacy of Power – which makes up the content of what Giussani calls de facto, or "constructed" (i.e., artificial), atheism.[17]

But before taking up discussion of Giussani's analysis of religion, it is important to add a clarification here that consists in a friendly amendment to Burtchaell's lengthy and convincing argument. Burtchaell rightly notes how the "radical disjunction between divine knowledge and human knowledge had been central to classical Reformation thinking, and [how] its unintended outcome was to sequester religious piety from secular learning."[18] At the same time, he says that Catholics entered within the ambit of pietism and onto the road to rationalism beginning mostly in the 1960s, due to the crises following the Second Vatican Council.[19] Notable in Burtchaell's account, therefore, is how the Protestant entry into pietism has a significant theological origin, whereas the Catholic entry seems much more cultural and indeed motivational in nature, the result, mostly, of fallout from the council. It seems to me crucial to see that the dualism between pietistic religion and rationalized intelligence undergirding America's distinctive coincidence of theism and atheism has a significant theological tradition in Catholicism as well. Otherwise, the problem identified by Burtchaell is likely to be construed as it affects Catholics as a matter mostly of "restoring" the historical-cultural conditions prevalent in American Catholic academies before the council. I mean to imply not that Burtchaell would necessarily disagree with what I am proposing here but only that he himself does not really address the issue of preconciliar Catholic dualism as it pertains to his overall argument.

Evidently, the story of the development of this dualism in Catholic theology is a long and complicated one that cannot be fully rehearsed in the present forum. As Hans Urs von Balthasar has insisted, the split between theology and sanctity, or again between dogmatic theology and "Christian piety," is of fundamental importance for a proper reading of our contemporary situation.[20] This dualism of theology and piety had its origin already in the pre-Reformation period, in the emergence of philosophy as a separate discipline alongside theology. (Indeed, it could be argued that this bifurcation of theology and piety helped to prepare the way for the Reformation itself: but that is for discussion elsewhere.) For von Balthasar, it is not at all the case that the philosophical concept of truth did not have a certain legitimacy in its own sphere. The difficulties began to emerge when the "philosophical propaedeutic came to be considered a fixed and unalterable basis, whose concepts, without the necessary transposition, were used as norms and criteria of the content of faith, and therefore set in judgment over it. Teachers [began to behave] as though man knew from the outset, before he had been given revelation, knew with some sort of finality what truth, goodness, being, light, love and faith were. It was as though divine revelation on these realities had to accommodate itself to these fixed philosophical concepts of philosophy and their content, before going on to their application in theology."[21] Thus there emerged a double movement: a separation of philosophy from theology (dualism), coincident with what then became the pressure to reduce theological truth to philosophical truth (rationalism).[22]

In any event, it was the epoch following Bonaventure and Thomas, says Balthasar, that saw the completion of the split between theology and spirituality. "Spiritual men were turned away from a theology which was overlaid with secular philosophy – with the result that alongside dogmatic theology, meaning always the central science which consists in the exposition of revealed truth, there came into being a new science of the 'Christian life,' one derived from the mysticism of the Middle Ages and achieving independence in the *devotio moderna*."[23] Thus, in sum, according to Balthasar modern Catholic thought developed too much under the influence of a double extrinsicism: between the order of nature and the order of revelation and between the true and the good. This double extrinsicism had fractured the unity of knowledge and life required by Catholic faith itself, resulting in formalistic intelligence and voluntaristic piety. As the great Thomist historian of philosophy, Etienne Gilson, put it, "a flat rationalism that fits every kind of deism" grew up in modern Catholic thought, which succeeded in pushing mystery and the life of faith to the margins of intelligent order.[24]

The point, then, is that there is a Catholic version of the problem described by Burtchaell. Catholics as well Protestants have participated in the dualism between piety and knowledge, or in the religious positivism (positivism: extrinsicism between the orders of nature and revelation) that spawns America's distinctive atheism. To be sure, Protestant and Catholic pietisms took on very different forms: for example, a tendency toward biblical positivism, on the one hand, and a tendency toward magisterial positivism, on the other. My point is simply that there was a tradition showing an intrinsic link between pietism and rationalism also in the Catholic intellectual tradition.

I conclude my argument regarding the religious situation in America, then, by defining America's religion, or indeed its coincidence of theism and atheism, with the following summary. America's religion is essentially positivistic, by which I mean that its doubtless, sincere piety carries a de facto relegation of God to the margins of intelligent order. Against the background of a double dualism between nature and the Trinitarian God revealed in Jesus Christ and, within nature itself, between the orders of being and truth, on the one hand, and love, on the other, American religion has developed a relation to God that is without mind (fideism, pietism) and, therefore, a mind that is without real relation to God (atheism, mostly implicit). But this divorce between the mind and the life of the spirit that is the essence of what I am calling positivism entails, in turn, a reduction of intelligent order (including the order of civilization and culture) to the relations of power manifest in a machine and a reduction of love to what now becomes simply voluntaristic – or arbitrary – movement. In technical theological terms, intelligent order within a positivistic framework is best defined as an ontological Pelagianism and nominalism, according to which being and knowing are made up of relations (between creatures and God, among creatures) that are primarily external in nature and most basically power-driven (Bacon: "knowledge is power").

My proposal, in sum, is that religion in America, because and insofar as it is positivistic and voluntaristic in nature, reveals – in ways evidenced in abundance by Burtchaell – an inversion into what is, de facto, an a-theistic mind and, consequently, an a-theistic cultural order.

I have described the American religious situation at some length because I believe that it highlights the significance of Giussani's account of the religious sense and, at the same time, suggests where controversy is most likely to emerge in any American engagement with that account. With the foregoing sketch of this situation in hand, let us turn to Giussani's proposal. To go directly to the heart of the matter, Giussani says, in words taken from Romano Guardini, that "In the experience of a great love, all that happens becomes an event inside that love."[25] These words provide the proper context for understanding Giussani's insistence on the "totalizing" nature of the religious sense, which he considers the latter's most relevant and, indeed, most profound feature. The religious sense is described as totalizing because the creatures' relation to God, which is constitutive of the creatures' being, affects all things at all times and from the depths of what they are. God, in other words, is not relevant only at discrete moments when, say, he engages our will or affections (pietism and voluntarism); on the contrary, he always affects the *meaning* of everything from top to bottom, thereby ruling out any cession of intelligent order in the cosmos or in culture to the Pelagian and nominalistic mind of rationalism.

Giussani's insistence on the totalizing nature of the infinite thus cuts to the core of what I have been calling religious positivism. It helps us to *see* this positivism and, at the same time, exposes its (implicit) atheism. It suggests, in fact, that any religiosity whose God does *not* affect the basic meaning and order of being is just so far atheistic, since a God who does not affect everything all the time is finite, and a finite God is in the end no God at all.[26] But in perceiving the atheism implicit in America's positivist religiosity, we also see the roots of a profound anthropological crisis. Since only the totalizing infinite can give creatures their own centre and their integrity, creatures that are outside of a realized encounter with God at the heart of everything lose the centre, become fragmented, and remain floating on the surface of things. At stake in any recovery of a totalizing relation to the infinite in the context of America's implicit atheism is nothing less than the integrity of the creature as such.

The meaning and significance of Giussani's claim here is thus perhaps best understood in light of what Pope John Paul II has stated is likely the most important teaching of the Second Vatican Council: the integration of theology (Trinitarian Christology) and anthropology summed up especially well in *Gaudium et Spes*, 22, which reads, "in his very revelation of the Father and his love, Jesus Christ reveals man to himself."[27] Later in the same paragraph 22, the Pope stresses that human nature is assumed and not absorbed by its union with the divine nature in Jesus Christ. But what this assumption – rightly interpreted – implies is that human nature is now revealed in its fullest integrity, *precisely as human nature*, in Jesus Christ and hence, in turn, in the *communio sanctorum*. And if the integration of the divine with human nature does not reduce or suppress the latter but on the contrary releases it into its deepest integrity, precisely as human, then this integration alone permits human nature and activity its rightful distinctness or "legitimate autonomy."[28]

So far, I have argued that it is only such an *integration* of the divine or the supernatural and the human, of theology and anthropology, to which Giussani's religious sense gives profound expression, that permits us to go to the root of the problem of our peculiarly American atheism. But of course it is just this claim of totality, or integration, that is likely to arouse the most strenuous objections, given America's religious tendencies delineated earlier. The question that will be asked, in other words, is how Giussani's emphasis on integration can avoid becoming "integralist," and hence, in turn, also sectarian.

Here I can only suggest the direction of a response. Properly understood, integralism is a program for effecting a (religious) unity, or wholeness, arbitrarily and through relations of power. Such an integration will by definition exclude those who do not share the same arbitrary relation to God: integralism is the progenitor of sectarianism. Now, such a unity is rightly experienced as one that does not resonate with my deepest being but instead is imposed arbitrarily and from the outside, as it were. Insofar as nature and culture are presumed to function (logically) on their own, in abstraction from God, any attempt to bring religion into their inner workings, any dynamic for integration, will be understood to be what it now is – and logically must be – given such abstraction from God, namely, an imposition of arbitrary unity: integralism.

The point I wish to make here should be obvious. Religious integration reduces to integralism and sectarianism only on the basis of a prior assumption – conscious or unconscious – of a positivist conception of religion, such as I have said has prevailed in America. Any charge that Giussani's religious sense is in principle integralist, in other words, presupposes just the religious positivism that it is the burden of that religious sense to challenge and that alone finally makes integralism possible. (Note that both integralists and anti-integralists can and generally do share this positivist presupposition. Those who wish to integrate religion into life and who do not break cleanly with religious positivism will invariably fall into integralism. But those who wish to keep religion out of life, on the assumption that integration in principle entails integralism, just so far presuppose – from the opposite direction – the same religious positivism as the integralists).[29]

My point, in sum, is that Giussani's religious sense indicates neither integralism nor sectarianism but the opposite of these. Indeed, only something like Giussani's sense of religion will enable us, while avoiding the integralism and sectarianism that are the risk of all positivistic religion, to foster instead the genuine integrity of the human. For only something like Giussani's sense of religion presupposes a religious wholeness that already comprehends – grounding, securing, and informing – the integrity of creaturely nature and freedom.

I will now move on to note quickly what seem to me some of the main features of Giussani's proposal in light of the American situation as I have described it. The list will of course be incomplete, both for reasons of space and because I will restrict myself mostly to *The Religious Sense*, with help from his important text "Religious Awareness in Modern Man."[30] My basic question, in light of the foregoing discussion of integration, and indeed of America's religious horizon, is

how the religious sense as understood by Giussani liberates the whole
of the human in its integrity. What does this mean?

Of fundamental importance is that reason and freedom are now
defined most profoundly in terms of their movement toward reality in
the totality of its factors.[31] Reason and freedom are best understood
as capacities for the infinite, for the infinite God. For Giussani, this
means, on the one hand, that reason is opened up to mystery from its
very core. The empiricist notion of reason prevalent in much of contemporary culture is revealed for what it is: a rationalist reduction of
reason. (Indeed, the primacy accorded poll-taking in religious matters
in the present situation is on Giussani's terms already an important
sign of an attenuated religious sense!) On the other hand, Giussani's
conception of freedom places the capacity for infinity, for God, anterior
to and therefore as the always already intrinsic context for freedom as
a matter of choosing this or that.

Consequently, for Giussani reason and freedom in their interrelation
are always dramatic and never neutral. They are never neutral because
they always imply God, imply an engaged relation to God that may
be positive or negative but that remains in any case a relation. Passion
is thus restored to the core of human life, that is, not as a moral but
precisely as an ontological category, which means that the individual's
capacity for God goes to the depth of his or her being and comprehends the orders of both reason and freedom. Here, then, we might
ponder the implications of the non-neutrality of reason and freedom
against the backdrop of the dominant liberal claim that these ideas
can be empty – that is, sufficiently neutral with respect to God that
they can construct institutions that would, in principle, be themselves
religiously neutral. On Giussani's view, this is ontologically impossible.
Indeed, such a claim of neutrality implies just the religious positivism
that is the beginning of atheistic order.

The structural openness and non-neutrality of human beings with
respect to the infinite God imply that their activities of reason and
freedom can never be accounted for exhaustively in terms of the finite.
The person's restlessness for the infinite does not disappear when he or
she denies or ignores or is unaware of the true infinite. The restlessness
for what is truly infinite, if it does not resolve itself in God, will construct for itself other infinities. Giussani's proposal thus helps disclose
the proper meaning of America's widespread consumerist and empiricist mentality – twin shoots of the positivist trunk – as a "bad infinity"
(this term has a Hegelian origin but not a Hegelian meaning as I use
it here). Both consumerism and empiricism consist in an endless, suc-
cessive preoccupation with finite entities. The consumerist seeks meaning and fulfillment through the acquisition of one *thing* after another.

The positivist thinks along the (empirical) surfaces of *things*, gathering meaning through the endless addition of finite bit to finite bit. Both disperse the true ("vertical") Infinite at the heart of things into an endless ("horizontal") succession of finite entities, thus losing, in the words of Giussani, the "relationship with (the) 'beyond' ['vertical infinity,' ... which] ensures the adventure of the here and now."[32]

The consumerist and empirical-positivist patterns of thought and life characteristic of America are thus revealed as forms of atheism or nihilism. "Bad infinity" is, in fact, simply a way of emptying the reality of the Infinite *as infinite*, turning the infinite thereby, however unconsciously, into "nothing." Atheism of this consumerist, positivist sort is boring – nihilism with a whimper – in contrast to what Giussani notes as the atheism of the anarchist who remains alive to the infinite at the heart of the finite and is thus much closer to the authentically religious person. (The loss of ontological seriousness is what constitutes the profound difference between, say, Richard Rorty and Nietzsche.)

In light of what I have said, we can now approach the proper meaning of what Giussani terms the "heart," or the "elementary experience," which is the criterion for judgment that is the beginning of the human being's liberation. For Giussani, the heart, or "elementary experience," is "the original impetus with which the human being reaches out to [the whole of] reality."[33] The elementary experience is not something other than reason but rather the whole person inclusive of reason – reason being defined, again, as the capacity to become aware of reality in all of its factors.[34] The criterion for judgment is thus carried within our elementary experience of reality: within our *heart*. This criterion does not free us entirely from the circularity of inquiry, even as it suffices nonetheless to make our judgments reasonable, that is, "objective." On the one hand, we do not break out of the circle: the elementary experience is always already an engaged disposition of the whole person toward and with the whole of what is. On the other hand, the judgment of what Giussani calls "correspondence" (between the judging person and reality), when it occurs, is not merely "subjective," for an engaged disposition of the whole person toward and with what is reveals the truth of being, namely, that being is "presence," hence just this dynamic event of encounter between subject and object.

Giussani's "resolution" of the problem of "realism" therefore consists in what we may call a new integration of subjectivity and objectivity. On the one hand, every engagement with reality is just that: a drama that always presupposes the immanence of freedom in every reasonable approach to reality. At the same time, that engagement always discloses at its core the presence of an other (always, at least implicitly, the Other: as Aquinas said, "every knower knows God implicitly in all that he or she knows") – a presence best defined in aesthetic terms.[35]

Giussani's approach thus offers a challenge to two dominant characteristics of post-Enlightenment culture. On the one hand, it replaces the idea that knowledge is power (Bacon, and Descartes also) with the idea that knowledge is more basically – both in terms of the knower and of what is known – a matter of love. On the other hand, it replaces the moralism that fails to see that our engagement with the other is not primarily a construction of the self consisting in the manipulation of the other but rather a being drawn out of one's self by the beauty or attractiveness of the other (the moral is always already included in the aesthetic). To put this point in theological terms: the self's relation to the other is not Pelagian but first a matter of grace (understood aesthetically as the appearance of the gratuitous love of the Other).

It should not be necessary, in light of all that I have said, to point out that Giussani's radical approach to questions of meaning and existence does not for all that signify what is often called a root-and-branch critique of modernity. First of all, integration properly understood can never be reactionary, since it must – at least on Giussani's reading – always take account of the truth of the other, which cannot but be in some way always historical and new. Second, and in this light, the substance of Giussani's proposal consists precisely in taking over modernity's subjectivity and freedom, transforming these in a way intended not to reject them but to deepen them, by reintegrating them into the fullness of their creaturely being, hence into their constitutive relation to God. Indeed, it is precisely because Giussani does not wish to deny but to secure and deepen modern subjectivity and freedom that he is compelled to reject the fragmented liberal (i.e., Pelagian and nominalist) reading of them that has prevailed in much of modernity.

So far, I have said nothing explicitly about what Giussani calls the hypothesis of Christian revelation.[36] I will say a word here about this crucial notion only insofar as it helps clarify Giussani's response to the religious positivism I have insisted is prevalent in America. It is important to see, first of all, that for Giussani this "hypothesis" has nothing to do with what is arbitrary and distant and could therefore reasonably be ignored. If it did, Giussani would himself slip into the very positivism that his religious sense – as I have interpreted it – is meant to counter. The apparent dilemma therefore is this: on the one hand, if Christian revelation is proposed to us as a purely accidental or arbitrary fact that, accordingly, is not experienced as the very truth of our being, we are left by definition with positivism – that is, with some variant of fideism or pietism. If, on the other hand, Christian revelation is proposed to us simply as the truth of our being, we lose the essential mystery and gratuitousness of that revelation and, accordingly, fall into some variant of rationalism.

Giussani's hypothesis thus must be interpreted in terms of paradox. On the one hand, the truth of our being is always already – hence, from its beginning – a restlessness that can neither conceive nor produce what it nonetheless somehow anticipates and hopes for. It is a restlessness, in other words, that must be patient, that, structurally, must wait for the Infinite Other to reveal his existence. On the other hand, precisely in the surprise of God's revelation to me, which is actualized first and essentially in the sacramental conversion, or reversal, called Baptism, we experience the truth of our being. We experience the "correspondence" with what we were all along and from the outset of our existence desiring, albeit unknowingly.

Both the simultaneity and the asymmetry indicated here are crucial: it is precisely *in* the conversion, or reversal, which includes most fundamentally the Cross and Eucharist of Jesus Christ, that I experience the truth of what I had desired all along, in other words, the truth of my being. Indeed, if the truth of creaturely being did not resonate precisely in the reversal of the Cross and the Eucharist, Giussani's attempt to redress the problem of positivism would only embrace the opposite side of the positivist coin, thus falling into rationalism.

To be sure, this raises profound issues that need further unpacking. I would only conclude my comments regarding Giussani's position on the hypothesis of the Christian Fact by suggesting that it is best interpreted in light of the great Augustinian (and Thomistic) tradition, which insists that our hearts are restless until they rest in the God of Jesus Christ, and that this God, in his infinite transcendence, is at the same time *interior intimo meo* (Augustine) – more intimate to me than I am to myself. Here, then, is the answer to America's religious positivism, which gives us a transcendence conceived as mechanical exteriority without real immanence. For the proper response to positivism's transcendent God consists in countering it, not with a simply immanent God (pantheism) but with a God who is radically immanent precisely because he is infinitely transcendent. In thus recalling to us the way of the Christian God of love, who is so Other that he acts in us as though he were the non-other (Nicholas of Cusa), Giussani overcomes America's religious positivism – its atheism – without succumbing to integralism: God's entry into us comes from infinitely outside of us, but it comes in the immanent, and hence freeing, manner of love.

I conclude this section regarding the religious sense with a summary of the method by which Giussani means to propose it to others. Citing the text from 1 John about how the eternal life present to the Father became visible to us in Jesus Christ, Giussani says: "Here is the answer: the presence of the Christian Fact lies in the unity of believers. Here is the most telling phenomenon. This is the miracle, the sign. That which is humanly impossible – the abolition of estrangement and the birth of a new fraternal bond, which does not spring from the flesh but does involve the flesh – Jesus understood as the evidence of his divinity: 'As you, Father, are in me, and I in you, I pray that they may be one in us, that the world may believe that you sent me'" (Jn 17:21, cf. Gal 3:26–9).[37]

Thus we see the method, characteristic of that Fact, for "converting" the world: that this unity be made visible everywhere. In the absence of this unity, no Christian religiosity can stand. Paul VI strongly affirmed this: Where is that "People of God" of which so much has been said, and of which so much is said now – where is it? This *sui generis* ethnic reality which is distinguished and qualified by its religious and messianic (or priestly and prophetic, if you will) character, which entirely converges on Christ as its central focus, and which derives entirely from Christ – how is it structured? What characterizes it? How is it organized? How does it exercise its ideal and invigorating mission in the society in which it is immersed ... We know well that the people of God now has, historically, a name which is more familiar to everyone: the Church ... This is not an esoteric theology, inaccessible to the common mind-set of the faithful People; it is indeed the highest truth, but open to every believer and capable of inspiring that style of life, that "communion of spirit," that identity of sentiment, that feeling of mutual solidarity, which pours forth into a "multitude of believers a single heart and a single soul," as it was at the dawn of Christianity. That sense "of community, of charity, of unity, that is, that sense of the one, catholic – or universal – Church, must grow in us. The awareness of being not only a population with certain common characteristics, but a People, a true People of God, must assert itself in us." Bringing out the unity of believers in the place where the believer finds himself: this is the revelation of 'communion' that will have as its fruit a 'liberation' that can be humanly experienced, that is, a humanization of the environment which is more adequate to the person's destiny.[38]

To sum up: the significance of Giussani's religious sense for our present situation consists in its essentially ontological, dramatic, and aesthetic character. For Giussani religion comprehends the order of being in a way that integrates the true, the good, and the beautiful. His religious sense at its core thus indicates a new culture in which being takes precedence over having, and the significance of this becomes particularly clear in light of Pope John Paul II's discussion of a growing battle between a culture of life on the one hand, and a culture of death on the other[39]. For at the heart of the culture of death lie the problems of abortion, poverty, and homelessness, and so on, all of which derive from the primacy of having and the relations of power bound up with this primacy.

It is, on the other hand, the renewed sense of God and of the being of the true, the good, and the beautiful that makes possible and demands and, indeed, constitutes the priority of being over having that is the essence of the culture of life. The claim is stunning: America's most serious social problems are problems most fundamentally of the existence and nature of God and, consequently, of the reality of creatureliness, and the task of eliminating them is, anteriorly and most fundamentally, the task of retrieving a renewed sense of the intrinsic truth, goodness, and beauty of all creatures, of the entire cosmos. The Christian's missionary task, in other words, is spiritual and ontological before it is moral or political or, in terms of John Paul II's "new evangelization," it is social *precisely as theological*. Or so, at least, this is how I read Giussani.

In a word, Giussani's religious sense reintroduces a sense of being as gift that is summed up in his assertion that "prayer is the only human gesture which totally realizes the human being's stature."[40] The religious sense, in short, consists most fundamentally in reinserting the order of being into prayer. It is just here, in the reintegration of the orders of being and knowing – and not only the order of willing – into prayer that the problem of peculiarly American atheism is met, the atheism that, as Pope John Paul II puts it, constitutes the spiritual drama of our time.

NOTES

1  A. MacIntyre, *Against the Self-Images of the Age* (New York: Schocken Books 1971), 26.

2  W. Kaminer, "The Last Taboo," *New Republic*, 14 October 1996.

3  Cited in T.C. Reeves, "Not So Christian America," *First Things* (October 1996): 17.

4  G. Gallup Jr, and S. Castelli, *The People's Religion: American Faith in the 90s* (Garden City, NY: Doubleday 1989), 20.

5  W. Herberg, *Protestant Catholic Jew* (Chicago: University of Chicago Press 1983).

6  F. Nietzsche, *The Gay Science*, n. 125.

7  M. Buckley, *At the Origins of Modern Atheism* (New Haven: Yale University Press 1987), 29. See Nietzsche, *The Gay Science*, n. 343: "The greatest recent event – that 'God is dead,' that the belief in the

Christian god has become unbelievable – is already beginning to cast its shadow over Europe."

8 Nietzsche, *The Gay Science*, n. 343.

9 Nietzsche, *The Will to Power*, bk. I, 1.

10 Buckley, *Modern Atheism*, 28.

11 Whether this is the view implied in MacIntyre's statement above need not be resolved here.

12 Buckley argues that in order to defend the existence of God, Christian theologians in the modern period developed a philosophical apologetics that precluded any primary appeal to intrinsically religious experience or evidence. Thus, unwittingly and contrary to their own intentions, these theologians set in motion a process that led to false notions of God that eventually resolved themselves into a negation of God. As for Weber, he traces the inversion of the religious belief of American Puritans into a kind of rationalized notion of worldly activity. By virtue of their religious ideas of salvation and Church and sacrament – that is, by virtue of their fear of damnation, coupled with the absence of a sacramental Church (e.g., no sacrament of penance) – the Puritans' sense of *Deus solus* drifted of its own internal logic into a kind of Pelagian sense of human activity that over time took on a consumerist hue. On Weber, see my "Reorienting the Church on the Eve of the Millennium," *Communio* 24 (winter 1997): 762–5.

13 J.T. Burtchaell, *The Dying of the Light: The Disengagement of Colleges and Universities from their Christian Churches* (Grand Rapids, MI: Eerdmans 1998).

14 Ibid., 843: "The Pietists propounded the primacy of spirit over letter, commitment over institution, affect over intellect ... invisible church over visible" (839). "So they begot piety ... without theology, preaching without sacrament, community without order" (841). "People determined to persevere as Christians developed a liberal piety whose wisdom had to be framed so broadly as to lack all depth. It had all the pungency of a cliché" (841).

15 Ibid., 841–2.

16 Ibid., 842.

17 See L. Giussani, "The Religious Awareness in Modern Man," *Communio* 25 (spring 1998): 115, 129.

18 Burtchaell, *The Dying of the Light*, 842.

19 Ibid., 705–71.

20 See H.U. von Balthasar, "Theology and Sanctity," in *Explorations in Theology*, vol. 1 (San Francisco: Ignatius Press 1989), 181–209. Van Balthasar notes how the dualism indicated here is linked with several dualisms characteristic of modern thought: "between spirit and life, between the theoretical and practical reason, between Apollo and

Dionysus, idea and existence, between [a] conception of the spiritual world as valuable but impotent, and of the practical world as one of power but spiritual poverty" (193–4).

21 Ibid., 186. Again, this does not mean that philosophical truth does not have its own natural integrity. It means only that philosophy's (method-ological) abstraction from theology – the light of faith – can never pro-ceed in a neutral fashion relative to the fact that nature is created in the image of the concrete trinitarian God revealed in Jesus Christ, and that nature and reason have been wounded by sin. Pope John Paul II's recent encyclical, *Fides et Ratio*, provides a rich discussion of these issues.

22 Ibid., 180.

23 Ibid., 187.

24 Evidently, much detail and nuance needs to be added to this brief over-view of the Catholic problematic, but this suffices for the present context.

25 See R. Guardini, *L'essenza del Cristianesimo* (Morcelliana: Brescia 1981), 12. Original edition: *Das Wesen des Christentums* (Wurzburg: Werkbund-Verlag 1949).

26 Giussani explains: "If a God who became one of us … did not tend to shape our every thought, plan, and sentiment, if he were not under-stood in this all-embracing way, he would cease to be God" ("The Religious Awareness in Modern Man," 137). Giussani insists that "totalizing" involves neither a theological reduction nor the claim that the Gospel provides "a ready-made formula for every last detail of life" (ibid., 137). It nonetheless does imply "the radical transformation of every last detail of life through the total engagement of a subject who dwells in the atmosphere of a perturbing fact. Faith impacts on the subject, and in changing him it tends to change every detail of his existence" (ibid., 137).

27 See also the *Catechism of the Catholic Church*, 1701–2, regarding the primary content of the creaturely *imago Dei*.

28 *Gaudium et Spes*, 36, 59.

29 It is instructive here to note the contrast between Giussani's view and the view of some strands of evangelical Christianity in America that seek to penetrate human culture with the religious sense *but that do so all the while continuing to assume the dominant positivism of Ameri-can religious history*. These two contrasting modes of penetrating cul-ture give rise to profoundly different sensibilities with regard to the integrity of the human – and consequently with respect to the nature of evangelization – which sensibilities I cannot discuss in detail here. Suffice it to say only, for example, that Giussani's approach entails a different inclusion of the moral within the "aesthetic" – within the beauty that is the most proper language of love.

30 L. Giussani, *The Religious Sense*, trans. John Zucchi (Montreal: McGill-Queen's University Press 1997); "The Religious Awareness in Modern Man," 104–40.

31 Giussani, *The Religious Sense*, 12.

32 Ibid., 133.

33 Ibid., 9.

34 Ibid., 12.

35 This is not the place to attempt to resolve the more technical ontological and epistemological issues brought into play here. Giussani's proposal, for example, implies a different sense of what suffices as "scientific demonstration," or "proof," in its conventional, post-Enlightenment sense, at least as far as the fundamental questions of the meaning of existence are concerned, but this is for discussion on another occasion.

36 Giussani uses the term "hypothesis" in a sense different from the more conventional meaning in English: "hypothesis" for him has nothing to do with what is arbitrary and distant and of little consequence – for example, as in "if it rains tomorrow ..." On the contrary, "hypothesis" in Giussani's sense is rather a matter of urgency, literally of life and death, and it just so far poses an "obligatory" question, one emerging from the heart of the experience of being. Giussani's interpretation, as ontological rather than pragmatic, should therefore also not be confused with American philosopher William James's understanding of hypothesis and experiment in the matter of religious belief: but that must be shown elsewhere.

37 Jn 1:1b-2.

38 Giussani, "Religious Awareness in Modern Man," 139. See Paul VI, Wednesday general audience, 24 July 1975.

39 See *Evangelium vitae*, 28.

40 Giussani, *The Religious Sense*, 106.

# PART THREE

# The Christian Event: Life in the Church

# 9 Mystery Incarnate

## JOHN O'CONNOR

*At the Origin of the Christian Claim* is a difficult book, and difficult, as well, for me to introduce.[1] How can one get at the very subtle, complex mind of Msgr Giussani? He does wonderful work with Communion and Liberation and is a straightforward, ordinary person to meet. But he writes with extraordinary subtlety and in a very compressed fashion. This time – and I say this with great respect – he has outdone himself in density, even in turgidity. And if you want to grasp this book, you really have to work at it. Even though it is little more than a hundred pages in length it is not for summer reading at the beach.

*At the Origin of the Christian Claim* is mostly an inquiry into Christ's incarnation in which Giussani examines Christ's claim to identify himself with the Mystery that is the ultimate answer to our search for the meaning of existence. Giussani argues that if we accept the hypothesis that the Mystery entered the realm of human existence and spoke in human terms, the relationship between the individual and God is no longer based on a moral, imaginative, or aesthetic human effort but instead on coming upon an event in one's life. Thus the religious method is overturned by Christ, and Christianity is no longer the person who seeks to know the Mystery but the Mystery that makes himself known by entering history. Now, admittedly, this is virtually a paraphrase of Msgr Giussani's words, but the arguments that he offers, especially the arguments on comparative religions in the earlier part of the book, are, as I said, very subtle indeed. So I shall first provide a very brief context for looking at the book itself, a context developed from other works that are, at best, analogous to his. The concepts are not identical, but at least they are analogous.

In a fascinating book called *The Unknown God*, which was published in 1934, Alfred Noyse points out that

the bewilderment of the contemporary mind groping blindfolded after some ultimate belief upon which it can support its own highest values or reasonably sustain even its most necessary codes of right and wrong is continually illustrated by flashes of disaster in the world around us. A great change is working through our western civilization and none can foresee the outcome. There are vast forces moving, not upon the face of the deep, but below the surface, out of sight, and neither men nor nations can tell where we are all drifting. "Drifting" is the word for an ultimate goal and purpose in our lives, no longer believed discernible by the human intellect. The task of keeping afloat a partially wrecked hulk so closely engages the greater part of the population that we've come to look upon the steering gear as a relic of a superstitious age ... it is not merely that the gear itself seems to be worn out [there is no] fixed star, no invariable compass and no ultimate end at which to aim. The authority of conscience that philosophers were prepared to revere, if it might be called the "categorical imperative," has lost its weight for a great part of the contemporary world.[2]

Although Noyse's argument is only partially similar to Giussani's, I think that he would agree with what Noyse had to say.

St Paul writes to the people of Philippi that God emptied himself (*exinanivit seve ipsum*) taking upon himself the form of a slave. This great *kenosis*, this great emptying, is what seemed to be demanded of God himself if he was to become one of us, and I think Giussani would say that it is demanded of us if we are to become one with God, if we are truly to have a Christian experience. I would like to refer, as well, to *Neuroses and the Sacraments* which was written by an English Franciscan, Father Keenan.[3] His theme is a simple one, but it is a theme once again of Giussani – a theme of his later years. Keenan writes that Christ is the norm, that Christians meet Christ in the sacraments to the degree that we are most attuned to the sacraments – to that degree we are closest to Christ. And since we are fashioned in accordance with the image of Christ, Christ is the model of our normalcy. We are truly normal, in the quintessential sense of the term, to the degree that we are fashioned after Christ. As we read in the prologue to the Gospel of St John, "In the beginning was the Word and the Word was with God, and the Word was God. All things were made through him." The Greek is *dia autou*, not "by him" but "through him." He was the pattern, he was the model, and so Keenan makes the point – and I think Giussani would agree – in that to the degree that we approximate the likeness of Christ, to that degree we are achieving our destiny; indeed, to that degree we are achieving normalcy.

I turn now to a book that has recently appeared, Reynolds Price's *Letter to a Man in the Fire*, which is subtitled *Does God Exist and Does He Care?*[4] That question is one that Giussani might ask. Price's book was reviewed in the *New York Times Book Review* (23 May 1999) by a Professor Hirsch, who is Jewish. (Price is a strongly believing Christian.) That review, again, helps us to understand the context of Giussani's approach to Christ. Hirsch says:

I admire the large and benign ecumenical spirit that Reynolds Price brings to his inquiry, the generosity with which he responds to a man crying out from the fire. This is a man with cancer and in horrible, horrible pain. Reynolds Price himself had gone through a horrifying form of cancer that he calls his *elenkos* (trial). I admire the generosity with which he responds to a man crying out from the fire, even though I cannot share his Christian answers or sensibility. As a Jew I simply do not believe the same things the author does. In a way, Jesus interposes himself between this book and me, and I find myself wrestling with the faith of a man whose writings I greatly appreciate but whose belief system seems greatly distant and even alien to me. What I can participate in is the spirit of his quest, the way he turns to old artistic texts, to wise literature for guidance. His perception of poetry as a move into sacred space, his trust in epiphanies and visionary influxes of being, in what Wordsworth called "those fleeting moods of shadowy exultation." His intuition is of an order beyond ourselves.

This passage could be a superlative description, as far as it goes, of Giussani's *At the Origin of the Christian Claim*.

Finally, I would like to mention an example from the Hasidic literature that I personally love. The following tale reminded me of myself when I finished reading Giussani's book:

Once upon a time there lived an absent-minded man. So absent-minded was he that he would forget in the morning where he had put his clothes in the evening. He would spend hours looking for them, which made him late for work, late for meals, late at meetings. One day a friend gave him this excellent advice. "Why trust memory? Write down everything." That very evening he took a piece of paper and he jotted down, "My jacket is on the chair, my shoes are under the chair, my hat is on the table and I am in my bed." That night he slept well, peacefully. He rose early as always and was lucky enough to find the piece of paper. Quick! Where's the jacket? On the chair. The shoes? Under the chair. In a matter of minutes he had located everything. He was happy. He felt like screaming with joy. He wanted to let the entire world know that he had finally found the solution to all of his problems. He was about to sing and dance when his eyes fell on the last lines, "and I am in my bed." He was seized with horror when he looked around and found that he was not in bed. He was not even under the bed. In a frenzy he began searching the room and the next room in vain and he became once more intensely sad and one heard him whisper, "and I, where am I?"

This is a basic question for Giussani. He tells us in *At the Origin of the Christian Claim* – and it is a significant thrust of his theme – that the Mystery has entered into this world. But where are we in relation to the Mystery? That is the question he is really asking, and the third book of the trilogy (*Why the Church?*) will address it in great detail and intensity.[5] Giussani has satisfied himself and expresses that satisfaction in *At the Origin of the Christian Claim* that the Mystery came into the world by way of the Incarnation. But he would ask, But I? Where am I in relation to the Mystery? and this question would return us to the idea that the closer we come to modelling ourselves on the incarnate Christ, the more normal we are, the more human we are.

I turn now to Giussani's book itself and look first at the foreword by David L. Schindler, who is also a contributor to this volume (chapter 8). Since Schindler begins with a very brief exploration of John Paul II's phenomenological personalism, which is part of all of his writing and part of his very being, to understand Schindler's foreword, one must first read John Paul II's *Redemptor hominis*, his seminal work, written when he first became Pope. In that work a key sentence is repeated: "Man is the way. Man is the way that we must follow to make any sense out of anything."[6] But why? Because humankind is made in the image and likeness of the incarnate Christ. John Paul II states that the basic human drama is the failure to perceive the meaning of life – to live without a meaning. He goes on to say that this failure indicates a failure to know the totality of the human person's resources, those of an external nature, those of human nature itself, and finally the supernatural resources open to the person in Jesus Christ. Schindler says of this that "It's difficult to exaggerate our need today for pondering anew the basic human drama as identified by the pope. Does life have a meaning – in the here and now, and ultimately? Does this meaning have the depth and breadth to make sense of everything: to breathe hope into life's most painful moments and significance into its apparently most trivial moments?" He goes on: "In *At the Origin of the Christian Claim*, Giussani treats the religious sense essentially in two stages. First, building on his earlier work *The Religious Sense*, the first volume of his trilogy, he shows how the dynamism of human intelligence and freedom leads the person in the end to recognize his or her insufficiency in the face of ultimate meaning and destiny ... In the second stage, Giussani proposes that this mystery has become a 'Fact' incarnate in our midst. His proposal changes the method for approaching the 'hypothesis' of revelation and the change is decisive."[7] Schindler goes on to say that the apostles asked the question of Christ, "Who are you?" I am a little puzzled by this, because it was Christ who asked the apostles the key question, "Who do men say that I am?" And after they had shuffled their feet for a while and come up with embarrassing answers, because they apparently did not want to face it, he pinned them down; he said, "but who do you say that I am? Who do you say that I am." Then Peter cried out, "Thou are the Christ, the son of the living God." and that changed everything. Schindler says that perhaps the simplest way to summarize the method of Giussani is in terms of the eighth chapter of St John. Jesus said to those who had begun to believe in him that if they abode in his word they would be his disciples, they would then know the truth and the truth would make them free.

In *At the Origin of the Christian Claim* Giussani shows that the religious sense is not simply a matter of morality or even piety but of an ontology that gathers up and integrates every last bit of what is true, good, and beautiful. He thereby responds profoundly to the core problem of our consumerist culture as noted by John Paul II – its widespread suffering induced by meaninglessness and by a boredom that is often frenetic. The problem, however, is that so many people today have never been exposed to ontology and ontological thinking. This has been lost, even in the study of philosophy in many universities, in part because of what began in the Wiener Kreis (Vienna Circle). In Vienna in the late 1920s people like Schlick and Wittgenstein, who were members of the circle, sowed the seeds of what was later to become, in Cambridge, logical positivism and operationalism; and ontology – the study of being in itself – was cast aside. But without an ontological background it is difficult to understand Giussani. After all, when God asked Moses to tell the Egyptians to release God's chosen people, Moses said, in essence, "I'm nobody. Who shall I say sent me?" And God said: "Tell them I am who am." *He who is*: this is an ontological definition of God to the degree that God can be defined.

I turn now to page sixteen of Giussani's book. I find the passages here very revealing, whether I always agree with Msgr Giussani or not. He ranges from John Paul II and phenomenological personalism to Teilhard de Chardin (without mentioning him) to people like Nietzsche and Dostoevsky, to Paul's Letter to the Romans, to the Gospel of John, and so on. The study of comparative religions, very briefly given here, is difficult to grasp because it is so very subtle, except when he devotes a couple of paragraphs to Islam and to Israel and Judaism. Then he becomes very crisp and clear and very laudatory, because both religions are crisp and clear and laudatory in their monotheism. But then, at page twenty-eight, Giussani comes to the heart of the matter when he says that "Within the freedom and variety of attempts that are made and messages conveyed, a religion may commit only one crime: to say 'I am *the* religion, the one and only way.' And this is precisely what Christianity claims. This constitutes a crime, the moral imposition of its own expression on others. So there is nothing wrong in feeling repelled by such an affirmation. What would be wrong would be to leave unquestioned such an affirmation, the reason for this great claim."

Giussani makes a very good point. And even though he calls it a crime, he does not back down from his belief in the uniqueness of Christianity and the uniqueness of Christ. He says, but in philosophical parlance, that it would be a crime to argue that Christianity is the truth and the only religious truth, ultimately, but he also says that for him the real crime would be to leave such an affirmation and the reason for this great claim unquestioned:

If Jesus is what he claimed to be, no time and no place can possibly have a different center from this one. "How, then, are we to account for the irresistible impression, felt by non-Christians especially, that Christianity is an *innovation* in relation to all previous religious life? To a Hindu who is sympathetic to Christianity, the most striking innovation (apart from the message and the divinity of Christ) is its valorization of Time – in the final reckoning, its *redemption* of Time and of History ... Time turns into *pleroma* [fullness] by the very fact of the incarnation of the divine Word: but this fact itself transfigures history. How could it be empty and meaningless – that Time which *saw* Jesus come to birth, suffer, die and rise again? How could it be reversible or repeatable *ad infinitum*?"[8]

Giussani says that there is an "instinctive resistance" to the consequences of the Christian Event in the human heart: "Man, in all the ages of history, resists the consequence of the mystery made flesh, for, if this Event is true, then all aspects of life, including the sensible and the social, must revolve around it. And it is precisely man's perception of being undermined, no longer being the measure of his own self, that places him in the position of refusal, on the pretext that he does not want to see the clouds lifting off the inaccessibility of the mystery obscured, he does not want to render the idea of God impure with anthropological notions, he wants freedom respected, and so on."[9]

In the history of religions, the fact of the Incarnation also constitutes a divide. The historian Mircea Eliade describes this fact well and then discusses a subject I have already mentioned with reference to St Paul, the great emptying on the part of the Christ. Giussani does not refer explicitly in the following passage to St Paul's epistle to the Philippians, but I think that is what he is referring to.

The fact of the incarnation, this inconceivable Christian claim, has remained in history in its substance and entirety: a man who is God – who thus knows man – and whom man must follow if he is to have true knowledge of himself and all things.

The task of the Christian is to fulfil the greatest function in history – to announce that the man, Jesus of Nazareth, is God ... But the task is also the most tremendous in history because it is destined to provoke unreasonable reactions; yet it is supremely reasonable to face and to verify an hypothesis on its own terms, and here the issue is precisely an event which happened in history. The struggle against the fact of the incarnation, the dogma of the Church, triggered a tenacious counter-dogma over the centuries which, presuming to be able to set the limits on God's action, proclaims that it is impossible for God to become man. From this derives the modern dogma of the whole enlightenment culture which, unfortunately, has had such a strong impact, thanks in part to its influence on the so-called Catholic "intelligentsia": the dogma of division between faith and the reality of all of the world with all of its problems. This attitude precisely mirrors man's childish prohibition against God intervening in his own life. This is the ultimate boundary of this idolatrous claim – the claim to attribute to God what pleases reason and what reason decides.[10]

With this passage Msgr Giussani concludes his book. It is in the latter portions of the book, as I have said, that I find his dense and extremely subtle inquiry most readable and convincing. His fascinating contribution is to be recommended to those capable of distinguishing between God's presence in the world and sheer pantheism, and I would strongly recommend a careful, prayerful, studied reading.

NOTES

1  L. Giussani, *At the Origin of the Christian Claim*, trans. Viviane Hewitt (Montreal: McGill-Queen's University Press 1998).
2  A. Noyse, *The Unknown God* (London: Sheed and Ward 1934).
3  A. J. Anthony Keenan, *Neuroses and Sacraments* (London: Sheed and Ward 1950).

4 R. Price, *Letter to a Man in the Fire: Does God Exist and Does He Care?* (New York: Scribner 1999).

5 L. Giussani, *Why the Church?* trans. Viviane Hewitt (Montreal: McGill-Queen's University Press 2001).

6 See *Redemptor Hominis*, 14.

7 D.L. Schindler, foreword to Giussani, *At the Origin of the Christian Claim*, vii–viii.

8 Giussani, *At the Origin of the Christian Claim*, 104.

9 Ibid., 105.

10 Ibid., 107–8.

## 10 The Christian: Subject of a New Culture

JAVIER PRADES

### THE CONTEXT OF *GENERARE TRACCE NELLA STORIA DEL MONDO*

The purpose of this essay is to present faith as a new principle of knowledge and action and, thus, as the source of a new culture. My point of departure will be *Generare tracce nella storia del mondo* (1998), which gathers together the main lines of a reflection on Christian experience developed by Msgr Luigi Giussani over the last several years.[1] The systematic character of this book allows for a meaningful reflection on the problem of faith, a problem that lies at the very heart of human life and of the life of the Church.

#### The Beginning of Novelty in the Realm of Knowledge

The point of view from which I approach *Generare tracce nella storia del modo* was suggested to me by reflections Msgr Giussani himself offers in his book *L'uomo e il suo destino*, where he claims that "Change cannot help but begin from knowledge. Change in the 'I' depends upon some knowledge into which the 'I' is thrust, into which it is introduced."[2] In another passage of the same text he adds this additional word of emphasis: "I would have liked to tell you about ... a phrase of St Gregory of Nyssa I read two or three days ago: 'Ideas create idols, only wonder leads to knowing.' This remark really struck me since it is the same as the conception of getting to know Christ, of acknowledging Christ, found in our texts, in our language. How can we define the motivation for saying yes to Christ? The motivation for saying yes to something that enters into our life defeating all preconceptions, is beauty ... Faith – which is the affirmation of a fact, of the objectivity of a fact, Christ – gives rise to an aesthetics, namely, to an evocativeness, which reveals an adequate reason that is truly active. It is an adequate reason that brings about aesthetics in a relationship."[3] Further on he adds, "Only wonder convinces, that is to say, 'leads to knowing' ... to the point of generating conviction."[4] What, then, is this true knowledge, born of wonder, of the evocativeness of the fact of Christ that marks the beginning of the change that leads ultimately to conviction? What consequences does such knowledge entail for our understanding of reason and affection? What type of humanity is born from this new knowledge? With these questions in mind, let us look more closely at *Generare tracce*.

### Theology of Faith as a Context for Understanding a Theological and Methodological Novelty: From the Second Vatican Council to Fides et ratio

Before plunging directly into the book, it will be useful to touch very briefly on some elements in the panorama of the theology of faith that provide a context for a better understanding of the richness of *Generare tracce*. Contemporary theology of faith owes a great deal to the Second Vatican Council. In fact, one of the points that the dogmatic constitution *Dei Verbum* placed in the forefront was the nexus between faith and God's self-revelation in Jesus Christ. Faith is examined in section 5 of chapter 1, which is dedicated to the nature of Revelation; the section immediately follows the proclamation (in paragraphs 2–4) that Christ is its mediator and fulfillment. The council presents revelation as a historical Event in the person of Jesus Christ: "The most intimate truth which this revelation gives us about God and the salvation of man shines forth in Christ, who is himself both the mediator and the sum total of Revelation."[5] It goes on to say that "Jesus Christ, sent as 'a man among men' 'speaks the words of God' and accomplishes the saving work that the Father gave Him to do. As a result, He himself – to see Whom is to see the Father – completed and perfected Revelation and confirmed it with divine guarantees. He did this by the total fact of His presence and self-manifestation – by words and works, signs and miracles, but above all by His death and glorious resurrection from the dead, and finally by sending the Spirit of truth."[6] In the next section faith appears as the response to this Event of human freedom, since correspondent to this revelation of God is "the obedience of faith," by which "man freely commits his entire self to God, making 'the full submission of his intellect and will to God who reveals' and willingly assenting to the Revelation given by Him."[7] Starting with this intrinsic bond between faith and the Event of God's self-revelation, we can reflect in an adequate way upon the characteristics of the Catholic faith.

The newness of *Dei Verbum* lies not simply in its proposal of a personalistic, or dialogue-centred, vision of revelation, as a dialogue of an "I" and a "you" between God and man. Undoubtedly, this is an essential dimension of the act of faith and is understood as such in the council documents. In this way, *Dei Verbum* manages to overcome, on the one hand, an intellectualistic, or abstract, vision of revelation, almost as though it were a set of doctrinal precepts and moral norms, while, on the other, it widens the horizon from an analysis excessively centred upon the act of faith in and of itself, considered almost exclusively in terms of the spiritual dynamism of the subject, as was the case with the old apologetics in its study of the "analysis fidei." In line with such great figures as J.H. Newman (with his theory of antecedent probabilities)[8] and Pierre Rousselot (with the thesis of the synthetic activity of reason)[9] who were already moving in a new direction by underlining the integral character of the human response to God and the value of reasonableness as a factor that is internal and not merely anterior to the act of faith, contemporary theologians such as Hans Urs von Balthasar have also reaffirmed the character of faith as the experience of a personal encounter between human beings in their totality and the living God.[10]

But the renewal made possible by *Dei Verbum* would stall midway if one did understand that the presentation of revelation as the Trinity's self-communication *ad extra* has a more radical goal: showing humankind the beginning and meaning of all things. Therefore, we are dealing here not only with an opening to a personalistic or existentialistic sensibility but, more deeply still, with a presentation of revelation as a living communication of the truth about man, the world, and God.[11] Here, then, is the true significance of the texts of *Dei Verbum* just cited. In fact, the conciliar document insists that truth reveals itself in the person and history of Jesus of Nazareth, because in Him the triune God self-communicates to men.[12] *Dei Verbum* liberates us from a reductive preconception of the nature of truth (as though it were a set of notions) and reproposes it as a historical Event, which surely also implies a doctrinal dimension.[13] There enters into human history that singular fact that discloses as a definitive and unsurpassed promise the eschatological accomplishment of God's truth for humankind and the world. For every man, therefore, the question of truth is determined in relation to Christ, who is the fullness of truth in its historical form of realization and who requires in reply the totality of the human being, including his or her reason and his or her liberty. Within this presentation of revelation one can understand the novelty of the council's comprehension of faith as the response of reason and freedom – by grace – to the truth, which reaches out to human beings through God's initiative. This approach retains the classical elements of the act of faith (rationality, freedom, supernaturality) but overcomes the traditional dichotomy between *fides quae* and *fides qua*, which guaranteed the objective content of the faith and its gratuitous character but underemphasized faith's historicity and the totalizing character of the human response.

It would be superfluous to add that in order to be able to speak of Christian faith at all, it is necessary that the Christian Fact be continually present in history: today it is the ecclesial Body, just as two thousand years ago it was the humanity of Christ. The assent of faith, as *Dei Verbum* teaches[14], implies that the object of such assent is present in space and time. This intrinsic reference of faith to living revelation makes the Christian faith specific and renders it radically different from both natural religiosity and from a faith generically conceived as belief.[15] There is no doubt that the human opening to Mystery is the highest expression of our dignity, as the council itself reminds us[16], but it is equally certain that between natural religiosity and Christian faith there is an insurmountable difference: one cannot speak of faith in the Christian sense if not as the response to the historical Event of Jesus Christ, mediator and fullness of Revelation.

## THE JOURNEY TO A NEW AWARENESS

If we read *Generare tracce* with the concern I noted at the beginning, we can trace in the first three chapters the following points: the concept of faith as a belonging to an Event (chapter 1), the transformation that faith and baptism bring about in reason and affectivity (chapter 2), and finally, a new culture that leads to mission and ecumenism (chapter 3). We will be able to see the continuity between these three chapters and at the same time see how each enriches its predecessor by always maintaining the same leitmotif for understanding this new mentality that is born of the encounter with Christ. Indeed, in those who encounter Christ is born the faith that elicits in them a new awareness and a new affection, thus making them protagonists of a new culture, of an ecumenical attitude.

I will attempt to map out a few steps along this journey, while emphasizing that the factor I have underlined is only one of several that are necessary for an adequate understanding of the book: it must be integrated with many other perspectives, as well as with the numerous consequences that the text identifies (for memory, offering, morality), consequences that I will not outline here. My readers should understand that this chapter is intended primarily as an invitation to a personal reading of *Generare tracce nella storia del mondo*.

### Faith as a Part of the Event: The Loving Acknowledgment of an Exceptional Presence

In chapter 1 of *Generare trace* Giussani addresses the question of faith, after having described in the preceding pages what an Event is and the physiognomy of the Christian Event as an encounter.[17] Later, he presents faith as part of that Event and describes its principal characteristics. A few salient elements of this description can be highlighted: faith is brought about by the intervention of Christ himself, who reaches out to human beings; faith is an acknowledgment, that is, an act of reason; this acknowledgment is loving, free, and simple.

The Intervention of Christ. "Faith is part of the Christian Event because it is part of the grace that the Event represents, of that which the Event is."[18] This is the first great statement about the nature of faith. In fact, the possibility that human beings can acknowledge the presence of Christ exists only because "it is Christ himself who wins over the individual." This factor is absolutely necessary for faith to come about in human beings and in the world; it is something new, something prior, and it is a grace, a pure grace. From the grace of His presence in the world comes the possibility of acknowledging and following Him, a possibility that no attempt of human reason by its own strength can obtain. As the text states, "faith, inasmuch as it is a loving acknowledgement of something exceptional, is a gift." Christ reveals himself to us in a present Event – and this is a pure grace – and with the same gesture, enlivens the capacity in us to understand Him and acknowledge Him in His exceptionality. These two dimensions are part of the moment in which the Lord, through the strength of His Spirit, reveals himself to us; they are part of the moment in which the Event of Christ enters into our life. It should be noted that the gratuity of faith not only is explained as an interior gift of the Holy Spirit (which is evidently an undeniable factor) but is closely linked to the historicity of a human presence. As it emerges in these pages, the original nexus between the gratuity and historicity of faith in the Event offers a unified starting point that strikingly surpasses the weakness of other conceptions of faith, which are forced to juxtapose these factors according to an unresolved and unconvincing dialectic.

An Act of Reason. The gift of faith entails in the person who is struck by the Encounter an attitude of acknowledgment, which is an act of reason, a judgment, and not a mere feeling or state of mind. In this sense one can understand the rationality of faith as an intrinsic fulfillment of human reason, because it brings it to an understanding of reality with respect to its ultimate horizon, that is, to an acknowledgment of what everything depends upon. Again in this second factor, the fulfillment of human rationality, gratuity, and historicity begins in an intimate unity, as born of the same origin: "It is only by something that has happened, by the Event of God made man, by His gift, that our renewed comprehension can acknowledge Him and touch Him. In this way faith grasps a culmination beyond reason."[19] The exceptional character of the object recognized (up to the point that reason alone is unable to accept it) is never affirmed as irrationality or arationality but, on the contrary, as the fulfillment of reason, because of the total and original correspondence of this presence with the deep expectations of the person, of his heart.

The Loving Character of Faith. The last factor contributing to a unitary description of the act of faith is its intrinsically loving character. Faith cannot be a knowledge of just any type but is precisely a loving knowledge, that is, a knowledge that "lets itself be determined entirely by the object. It is a knowledge that is simple, without equivocation, which involves attachment."[20] The words "sincerity" and "simplicity" are used as analogous in *Generare tracce* to indicate that we need to look at the Event for what it says, for what it communicates to reason, without introducing extraneous factors to evaluate it, without introducing "buts," "ifs," or "perhaps." Therefore the morality of knowledge emerges at this point as the constitutive factor of the knowledge of faith, which is rooted in the unity of the whole "I" as reason and affection, to the point of free adherence. In fact, sincere acknowledgment, full of love, leads to a self-donation to Christ in original simplicity.[21] Therefore, one can well understand how faith can never be reduced merely to an intellectual assent to revealed truths but rather demands, in its very constitution, the completeness of the subject's movement to the point of free adherence, which is expressed in asking and in offering.[22] It is not by chance that the Second Vatican Council speaks of faith as obedience to God.

Implied by this vision of faith is a conception of reason that is poles apart from modern reason, which is "ab-solute," in the etymological sense of the latin *ab-solutum*, that is to say, detached from the "I's" relationship with reality and conceived as a totalizing measure.

## The Birth of a New Mentality: Reason and Affection

Those who have met Christ and been incorporated into the Church by baptism become the subjects of a new consciousness and a new affection. Detailed explanation of the nature of the change of these typically human spiritual energies is found in chapter 2 of *Generare tracce*.[23] The preceding sections of the book develop baptism as the birth of the new creature and indicate that belonging is a dimension of the "I," of the new creature. Immediately thereafter begins a consideration of the effects of this new birth on human reason and affection.

The claims advanced in the first chapter are taken up again and deepened here, made existentially closer to us and thereby made more readily identifiable by the reader. In this way, the claim that faith is an expansion of reason is not left in a generic, indefinite, or vague form, and a similar process obtains for affection. The new awareness or new mentality implies having "a capacity for gazing at and for understanding reality that others do not have. A new affection means a capacity for an adherence to the real, to that which is other than self, which is not even imaginable."[24]

How is this mentality born? It is born of adherence to an Event to which one says yes, of adherence to a particular fact that carries a claim to all-encompassing meaning. Here we find one of the factors that make this conception of reason profoundly different from that of modern reason. For the dominant mentality, which is born of an absolute conception of reason, the road of knowledge subsumes particulars into an abstract universal, whereas this new mentality is not born of deduction from certain principles but from an Event, from something that happened and happens, from a present reality concretely given in history; it is born of experience. It is not "ab-solute" reason – which, as mentioned, is reason detached from any relationship with reality – but rather reason as the capacity to relate to the real and, more concretely, to relate to a particular history that is born of the Event that has evoked faith. Jean Guitton used to say, "The reasonable man is one who submits reason to experience."[25] Clearly, Christian faith requires a conception of reason that is in accord with affection, of reason that allows itself to be moved, touched, provoked by reality in a present relationship. In fact, we are relational in our very constitution: it is reality as given in our experience that initiates and nourishes our reason. The culmination of reality is properly a person. Therefore, it is in the relationship with other human beings that one can perceive more clearly this character of human reason.[26]

Two conditions are necessary for the birth of this new mentality. The first is to "be contemporary with the Event that generates it and continually sustains it."[27] This requirement is the logical consequence of the fact that the origin of this mentality is not another idea but precisely a place, a living reality. Therefore, it is necessary to be in a continuous relationship with this reality, that is, with the human company that carries on the initial Event in time. Just as the Event continues through history, so too does the origin of a new judgment. Therefore, one can add here as a corollary that the method of remaining in a continuous relationship with the Event is defined by the word "gaze," inasmuch as this word expresses a remaining in the presence of the Event one has met, not a severing of fidelity to the relationship at some point or other in order to affirm one's own wishes or wants out of an interest that is extraneous to the original source of the newness.[28]

The second condition that is necessary for the birth of this new mentality is that of being continually engaged in comparing present events with this Event.[29] Inasmuch as it is born in the here and now, this new awareness judges the present; if this were not the case and it did not enter into present experience, the new knowledge would not exist but would remain an abstraction. Perhaps one can find the deep motive for this second condition in the unitary characteristic of the new knowledge that is born of faith: it requires not merely an abstract judgment deduced from some principle but an acknowledgment of the real in experience that does not stop until it arrives at affection. Since this is the unitary movement of any genuine knowledge, one can understand that a mentality that is not involved in the events of the present mortifies such knowledge and makes it sterile, separating it from reality. The biblical expression that best summarizes this dynamism of the new mentality, inasmuch as it is born of belonging to a present place and can be assessed with every aspect of present reality, is found in Saint Paul's letter to the Galatians: "The life I now live in the flesh I live in faith: faith in the Son of God who loved me and who sacrificed himself for my sake."[30] In this quotation one can in fact acknowledge that, on the one hand, Christians must never renounce anything but must change their way of relating with everything, because "living in the flesh" means living every human circumstance: one's girlfriend, family, work, illness, and so forth. Living one's life "in the faith in the Son of God" means belonging to an Event that makes me capable of this new and truer understanding of all my life's circumstances, which become signs through which I am invited to follow in the flesh the being of things, to enter thoroughly into the reality of things to the point where things are made. In this sense, Paul's words appear as "the definition of the profound change of human intelligence and human expression" that are born with the new mentality.[31] It is here that one finds the way that enables us to overcome the dualism of reason and faith, the terrible consequences of which are all too evident in the life of the Church and the world.[32] Only a conception of faith based on this idea of reason can acknowledge the rationality of a gaze that is able to grasp the true meaning of life's circumstances in their relationship to human destiny. For this reason, to be a believer does not mean to be a visionary; believers are reasonable human beings who grasp the real in its most profound unity.

### The Birth of a New Culture: Mission and Ecumenism

The last step on our itinerary – the birth of a new culture and an ecumenical attitude – is found in chapter 3 of *Generare tracce nella storia del mondo*.[33] The chapter begins by drawing upon what I have said so far. Belonging to an Event "changes the self-consciousness of our person in such a way that the principle of action is no longer the 'I' but a 'You' … [the result is] this new knowledge, which judges all relationships in life and enables us to love every little scrap of truth left in anyone with a positivity and an acuity unknown to the world."[34] We can already see the new content that this third moment introduces to the previous ones. The new creature, transformed by a new awareness, becomes the subject of a different human stance within the world, capable of opening himself or herself to everything and everyone.

The four most important steps in this process are as follows. First, the Encounter and baptism draw forth a new person who participates in the mission of Christ. Second, this new person is defined by a new principle of action: obedience. Third, the new culture is identified with the genesis of a changed "for whom": the new person now lives for a "You." Finally, the most fulfilled and original expression of this cultural process is found in the word "ecumenism."

The Encounter with Christ. From the Encounter with Christ and the objective gesture of baptism is born the Christian's participation in the person and mission of Christ, who makes us different from what we were before: "we are another thing, which comes from the Father and is for the human glory of the Son."[35] The existential aspect of this awareness of belonging to the person and mission of Christ is illuminated by a quotation from the second letter to the Corinthians: "The love of Christ impels us who have reached the conviction that since one died for all, all died. He died for all so that those who live might live no longer for themselves, but for Him who for their sakes died and was raised up."[36] The first part of the quotation indicates above all else that the radical change in the content of self-consciousness flows from the experience of being overwhelmed by the thought of how Christ loved us (here again is the wonder expressed by Gregory of Nyssa). It is really a passion, a yearning, which means no longer remaining indifferent but being moved by the memory of the love of Christ, by the awareness of His Presence. Together with Gal 2:20, which we have already examined, this Pauline quote becomes one of the leitmotifs for understanding the originality of the cultural position advanced by *Generare tracce*. This step is made possible by a love of childlike simplicity, being "poor in spirit."

A New Principle of Action. The loving and simple wonder becomes the source of action. The new subject of action is one who lives obedience, that is to say, one whose point of departure is not what s/he thinks or feels, his or her claims or illusions but the consciousness that the ultimate ground of reality is a "You," affirmed with gratuity and simplicity. Whereas normally the principle of action is the "I," here it becomes the "You." "It is a real 'metanoia' [change of mind] which arrives at the point that 'You,' rather than 'I,' is the content of self-consciousness,"[37] as is shown admirably in the yes of Peter to the Lord.[38] Obedience brings into existence a concrete method in history, the relationship with Mystery lived as friendship – that communion with being (lived as reason and affection) that satisfies the structural need of the human heart. The person who is shaped by the Encounter to the point of obedience of heart becomes creative, capable of new construction, of embracing the real in all its circumstances. Inasmuch as this person "demonstrates" this obedience before others, s/he becomes a witness to the Lord. Only in this way is the reasonableness of faith attested to, going against every eschatologicalism that by its nature is fideism.

Living for Another. Thus one can affirm that the cultural power of the Christian Fact is in a vision and in a sentiment about the world defined by "living for Another." If culture is a unitary way of seeing, of judging everything, then the cultural dynamic of Christianity is characterized by living totally in the flesh according to all the degrees of experience of being human, with a criterion of judgment based on faith in the Son of God. The change occasioned by the Encounter, in fact, is attested to in the fundamental change in "for whom" one lives, a change that is understood as the synthesis of a cultural position: while before one lived for one's self, now one lives for He who was dead and is now risen. We can draw two corrolaries from this conception of the new culture. First, the new culture generated from the Encounter with Christ and from participation in His person makes us capable of "not taking on the mind of the world," as Saint Paul says in his letter to the Romans (12:1–2 and as J. Zverina maintains magnificently.[39] If we do not take on the mind with which the dominant mentality would have us confront every aspect of reality (women, sex, bioethics, politics, art, and so forth), the only possible way to treat people and things in a nonschematic way – that is to say, in a way that is not extrinsic to them – is to participate in the one interior reality of which people and things are made: Jesus Christ. "Culture is not an empty schema when its beginning is something that has happened to us and from which we cannot take our eyes, a unique living reality": Christ as expression of the Father's plan.[40] Only if we penetrate ever more deeply into that reality of which all other realities are made will it become possible for us not to treat them according to extrinsic and insufficient models but to discover them in their newness.

The second consequence of the new culture is also methodological: the new awareness of self generated by the Encounter with and incorporation into Christ also requires a different awareness of our common path and implies a new morality. The "metanoia" that brings us to live no longer for ourselves but for Another causes us to become conscious of other human beings whom Christ has also called into baptism, to the point of acknowledging ourselves as one with them. "Thus arises a real communionality which ... expands as the whole subject of society, of the world, of the history of humankind, of the entire universe: the Church as the Body of Christ."[41]

Ecumenism. The complete expression of the transformation I have been describing is found in the Christian term "ecumenism" in its original derivation from *oikumene*. "This means that the Christian's gaze vibrates with an impetus that makes him capable of exalting all the good that there is in all he meets, inasmuch as this gaze makes him acknowledge his participation in the plan that will be fulfilled in eternity, and that has been revealed to us in Christ."[42] I will limit myself to highlighting a few characteristic factors of this conception of ecumenism. As should be evident from my description of the process of change, a truly ecumenical stance originates in the Event of Christ, inasmuch as it is the Event of the truth of all that is contained in history. Only by participating in the Event of truth in history can one understand how men and women have been made capable, not of a generic tolerance, but precisely of a love of the truth that is present in the real, contrary to the predominant tendency in the field of ecumenism. One can say the same of the possibility of experiencing a true criticality and affirming a universality that is not generic. In fact, insofar as one is convinced that one participates in the truth of Christ, one can be unequivocably positive and can use reason not as a measure that quickly denounces the limitations of things but rather as an openness, which in the face of the value of the present reality, howsoever little or great it may be, remains in wonder. For this very reason, whoever participates in the unique source of an absolutely positive gaze upon everything (namely, the gaze of Christ) can go beyond an attachment to partial apprehension of the truth and be open to everything and everyone, in all the most exquisite particularity of things and persons.

It is truly meaningful that the end of our journey, which began with the Encounter with a man, Jesus of Nazareth – a historically contingent and particular fact (just as the Enlightenment thinkers used to fulminate against the Christian claim to be universal)[43] – should be an exciting proposal for an openness and an embrace that "makes us feel at home wherever a scrap of truth is conserved, at ease anywhere."[44] Thus, I conclude this section with quotations from *Generare tracce* that are among the most persuasive concerning the kind of affinity with the real that is sustained by a truly Catholic experience: "*The Imitation of Christ* says 'Ex uno Verbo omnia et unum loquuntur omnia, et hoc est Principium quod et loquitur in nobis.' (From one Word all things, and all things one Word proclaim, and this Word is the Principle that also speaks in us). It is not possible to find another culture that defines everything with such a unitary, powerful and inclusive embrace. Jacopone da Todi, in the thirteenth century, used to say that everything happens in order that we might all go together to the 'regno celesto che compie omne festo / che 'l core ha bramato' (the heavenly reign that fulfils all the joy the heart has been longing for). And again, in the most beautiful verse in Italian poetry, he says: 'Amor, amore, omne cosa conclama.' The word amore (love) must be understood here in its ultimate meaning, that is, as a synonym for Christ, the God who bent over us and embraced us."[45]

## A SYSTEM OF THOUGHT BORN FROM THE FACT OF COMMUNION

The last part of this chapter will serve as a summary, but one that does not simply repeat the most important points of my journey but touches instead on my experience of preparing *Generare tracce*.

In the process of drafting *Generare tracce*, I could see a way of conceiving things that developed precisely from reality as grasped in lived experience. The days spent with Msgr Giussani at Cobacha (Spain), the work sessions in Milan, and a memorable evening at the Milanese restaurant Laghetto all provided opportunities to "reason in the making," beginning with the Event of Christ in relation to present events. I will be forever grateful for the opportunity I had over these years to experience the communal genesis of understanding. I am not claiming an undue role, since the origin of this text has been the fruit of a collaboration. I wish rather to acknowledge the power of a unity of conception, directed both in its organization and in every particular.

To conclude, I wish to emphasize once again the link between truth and beauty. One is struck first sight by the systematic structure of this book, which surely expresses a powerful dimension of Msgr Giussani's thought. Still, I was really impressed by the fact that the originality of his thought is reflected not only in its logical consistency but also in the very splendour of its truth, that is to say, in the engaging beauty of certain pages, which reawaken wonder and so allow one truly to know.

## NOTES

Translated by Sheila Beatty

1 L. Giussani, S. Alberto, and J. Prades, *Generare tracce nella storia del mondo* (Milan: Rizzoli 1998).

2 L. Giussani, *L'uomo e il suo destino* (Genoa: Marietti 1999), 150.

3 Ibid., 151.

4 Ibid., 154.

5 See DV 2–4, in *Vatican Council II: The Conciliar and Post-Conciliar Documents*, volume 1, ed. Austin Flannery, O.P. (New York: Costello Publishing, 1984) 751

6 Ibid., DV 4, 751–2

7 Ibid., DV 5, 752

8 J.H. Newman, *Fifteen Sermons Preached before the University of Oxford*, 1826–1834 (London: SPCK 1970); *Essay in Aid of a Grammar of Assent* (1870; London: Longmans, Green 1947).

9 P. Rousselot, "Les yeux de la foi," *Recherches de Science Religieuse* 1 (1910): 241–59, 444–75.

10 Hans Urs von Balthasar, *Herrlichkeit*, vol. 1: *Schau der Gestalt* (Einsiedeln: Johannes Verlag 1988), 211–24.

11 See G. Colombo, "Grazia e libertà nell'atto di fede," in *Noi crediamo: Per una teologia dell'atto di fede*, ed. R. Fisichella (Rome: Dehoniane 1993), 39–57; *La ragione teologica* (Milan: Glossa 1995).

12 See also *Fides et Ratio* 80.

13 See DV 6, in *Vatican Council II: The Conciliar and Post-Conciliar Documents*, 752. See also H. de Lubac, *La révélation divine* (Paris: Cerf 1983), 36–60.

14 Ibid., 752

15 In the sense in which, for instance, Hume explains our "belief" in the existence of an external world and of our self.

16 See GS 19, 21; NA 1, 2.

17 Giussani, Alberto, and Prades, *Generare tracce nella storia del mondo*, 28–34.

18 Ibid., 31.

19 Ibid., 32.

20 Ibid., 33.

21 See ibid., 32.

22 See ibid., 34–5.

23 Ibid., 74–8.

24 Ibid., 74.

25 J. Guitton, *Arte nuova di pensare* (Cinisello Balsamo: Edizioni Paoline 1991), 71. Original edition: *Nouvel art de penser* (Paris: Aubier 1946).

26 On being in relationship as a constitutive character of human beings, see, among others, Hans Urs von Balthasar, *Theodramatik*, vol. 2/1: "Die Personen des Spiels: Der Mensch in Gott" (Einsiedeln: Johannes Verlag 1976), 355–61. It was L. Feuerbach who in the modern age recovered the essential communitarian character of human beings, in opposition to an individualistic subjectivism of a rationalistic mould. In *The Essence of Christianity* he writes resolutely, "Where there is no you, there is no I" (L. Feuerbach, *Samtliche Werke*, (Stuttgart-Bad Cannstatt: Hrsg. Bolin-Jodl 1959), 6, 111.

27 Giussani, Alberto, and Prades, *Generare tracce nella storia del mondo*, 75.

28 See ibid., 76.

29 Ibid.

30 Gal 2:20.

31 Giussani, Alberto, and Prades, *Generare tracce nella storia del mondo*, 78.

32 See *Gaudium et Spes* 43; *Evangelii Nuntiandi* 20; *Veritatis Splendor* 88; *Fides et Ratio* 45.

33 Giussani, Alberto, and Prades, *Generare tracce nella storia del mondo*, 144–61.

34 Ibid., 144.

35 Ibid., 145.

36 2 Cor 5:14–15.

37 Giussani, Alberto, and Prades, *Generare tracce nella storia del mondo*, 146.

38 See Jn 21:15–17.

39 See J. Zverina, Lettera ai cristiani di occidente, in *L'esperienza della Chiesa* (Milan: Jaca Book 1971), 177–8.

40 Giussani, Alberto, and Prades, *Generare tracce nella storia del mondo*, 153.

41 Ibid., 149.

42 Ibid., 157.

43 See, for example, G.E. Lessing, *Uber den Beweis des Geistes und der Kraft* (1777), *Lessings Werke* (Frankfurt: K. Wolfel, 1967). This objection has very ancient roots. See, for instance, the argument between Origenes and Celsus in which Celsus, defends the conception of an immutable God who cannot debase himself to the point of assuming a mutable, passible, contingent humanity. Origen, *Contra Celsum* 4, 14–15. trans. Henry Chadwick (Cambridge: Cambridge University Press 1953).

44 Giussani, Alberto, and Prades, *Generare tracce nella storia del mondo*, 160.

45 Ibid. See *Imitazione di Cristo*, I, 3, 8; Jacopone Da Todi, *Cantico de la natività de Iesù Cristo*, Lauda 64, in *Le Laude*, (Florence: L.E. Fiorentina 1989), 218; *Como l'anema se lamenta con Dio de la carità superardente in lei infusa*, Lauda 90, *Le Laude*, 318.

# 11 Toward Human Flourishing

RALPH DEL COLLE

I do not claim to be an expert on the thought of Msgr Luigi Giussani or even on his trilogy – *The Religious Sense*, *At the Origin of the Christian Claim*, and *Why the Church?* – although I have read them and taught a class using the first two. In fact, I had heard of Communion and Liberation but did not know the he was the founder, nor had I any first-hand contact with CL. It was Robert Gotcher who introduced me to Giussani's books when I was his faculty observer for a course he was teaching at Marquette University. In looking at Robert's syllabus I noticed the books of Giussani that he was using and then decided I wanted to read them and then use them for my own course the following semester. Hence my introduction to Msgr Giussani. Providential? After reading his books, I am sure that he would say yes. For the God of Jesus Christ is one who is present and active in history. But enough of introductions, now to the heart of the matter.

Giussani's trilogy is representative of a theological genre in fundamental theology, what used to be called apologetics, that is familiar. There one explores three basic claims that are intended to demonstrate the truth of Christianity. Those three claims narrow from the more universal to the more particular. One begins with establishing either the truth of the existence of God or that the human being is fundamentally religious – hence, *The Religious Sense*. Second, one seeks to persuade the thinking and good-willed person that Jesus Christ is indeed the revelation of God – hence, *At the Origin of the Christian Claim*. Third, one validates the necessity of the Church, specifically the Catholic Church, in order for the first two claims to properly find their terminus – hence, *Why the Church?* I initially said "fundamental theology," which is now sometimes called foundational theology, because the discipline is fundamental, or foundational, for all subsequent theological claims in the Christian tradition. In systematic theology, fundamental theology comes first, then dogmatic theology, in which the various Christian doctrines are explored and interpreted.

In recent years and in such notable Catholic theologians such as Karl Rahner and Hans Urs von Balthasar, the strict separation of the two disciplines has been questioned. The issue is, can one examine these three basic claims without speaking from these claims and from within their horizon to begin with? Giussani's trilogy presents an interesting case study for this issue and also for the more robust effort at constructing an apologetics rather than just doing fundamental theology. Perhaps this is due to his own position as founder of an ecclesial movement, where the task of evangelization is more pressing than it is for someone who just holds an academic post. In this chapter I would like to examine Giussani's trilogy as Catholic apologetics in the context of this related issue about the relationship between fundamental and dogmatic theology.

Of course, it is clear that Giussani writes as a committed Christian for whom Jesus Christ is the truth of humanity, the cosmos, and God. The announcement of such a commitment is the stuff of Christian proclamation, and it proceeds from divine revelation. Human beings will not flourish unless they accept and enter into the truth of this revelation. Yet while there are elements of proclamation in the trilogy and while it is certainly the goal to which it points and even the presupposition out of which it operates, the overarching style of the trilogy is one of argument – slow, patient, and intended to be convincing. The arguments are indeed demonstrative of Christian truth, but they proceed with the deliberation of persuasion. Overriding throughout is the firm Catholic conviction that grace perfects nature and that reason and revelation are not contradictory but complementary. In other words, faith is reasonable. In fact, it the most reasonable choice that a person can make. What we have before us is an old-fashioned apologetics, but one that is robust and confident. Eminently reasonable individuals ought to see the truth of the Christian faith without loss to their humanity. To help them see, Giusanni enters into the world of human culture – from the inside, so to speak – as few have. From within this world the door gradually cracks open to God, Christ, and the Church without ever contradicting our fundamental human impulse to truth and the good.

On the surface, then, it would seem that Giussani presents us with a fairly standard, although intriguing, apologetics. He encourages us to be truly reasonable. Along the way, in fidelity to reason, we will encounter Christ. Better yet, Christ will illuminate the path of reason such that the truth that is Jesus Christ will be seen to be the most reasonable choice we could make. If we are successful in this endeavour, the unfolding of the mystery by Christian dogmatics would be the natural second step. Catechesis and mystagogy, the stuff of dogmatics, would then follow this apologetics of evangelization.

If I am accurate this is no small feat. As with all good apologetics, it will ground the believer – and I suspect it will be primarily believers who read and ponder these texts – in a substantial appreciation of the human person and will equip him or her to wage the battle of truth with integrity and faithfulness. An understanding of the human will be promoted that does justice to the Gospel but that also captures what is best in human culture, philosophy, and religious aspiration. False paths and shortcomings will be flagged to make way for the truth of the fuller and more penetrating Christian truth about the human being. Such is the stuff of apologetic argument, and Giussani does not shrink from the task.

So it would seem that I am making a case for the first option that I presented, namely, apologetics first, then the explication of the faith in dogma. Persuade the person that the truth is Christ, and then Christ will become the truth of that person in Christian life and discipleship. As I have already stated, this is no mean task and if it does not actually serve as an instrument of evangelization, it can certainly still bolster the faith of believers whose faith is constantly challenged by the culture – also an important and too-often neglected service of teaching in the life of the Church.

Are there any drawbacks to this approach? Only for the unskilled. Giussani's trilogy is no formula for the apologist-cum-evangelist – some very sophisticated Catholic equivalent of the evangelical protestant "four spiritual laws." One could easily be in over one's head if, armed with the trilogy, one attempted a frontal assault on the bastions of secularity. The temptation would be to think that if I am reasonable and faithful to the arguments of the trilogy, all should and will believe, excepting their ignorance or ill will. I think that would be a misreading of Giussani. Something more subtle is taking place in these texts, and so I return to my original query about the relationship between fundamental and dogmatic theology.

The real issue in the integral relation of the two disciplines – and here I must come clean: I favour such integration – is the presupposition that the actuality of God's grace is operative at both levels. One does not simply want to persuade the unbeliever by the natural light of reason and then let grace kick in with the advent of supernatural revelation. The danger here is not just that the powers of reason are confirmed – although in fact I would not necessarily identify this as a danger – but also the presupposition that the sufficiency of reason, along with a virtuous will, is sufficient for living the Christian life. Rather I think that Giussani in this trilogy, and I trust in the movement of Communion and Liberation, is concerned with what Cardinal Ratzinger mentioned in his 1998 Pentecost address to ecclesial movements in the Church: they signify a "deep personal encounter with Christ" and they engender a consequent following of Christ (*sequela Christi*) that they promote and embody.[2] Such is grace proceeding from within the horizon of Christian faith and illuminating the path to Christ and his Church.

In my reading of Giusani's trilogy I would identify his pedagogy as the most important element. By this I mean that what he introduces in the very first chapter of *The Religious Sense* as an "ascesis for liberation" is absolutely decisive for all three volumes.[3] Arguments to expand our notion of reason – to argue against all reductive forms of reason; to explore the ultimate question and our evasions of it, to make way for revelation and then to illustrate its truth from above, to carefully examine our premises for the truth of Christianity and then to unpack them from within the communal horizon of Catholic ecclesial life and practice – are all intended to expose one to the ever-increasing pedagogy of grace. This I take to be at the heart of his trilogy.

Perhaps a phrase from each of his volumes can illustrate this point and give a taste of this "ascesis for liberation," wherein we need to be attuned to our subject matter, the ultimate object of the human quest for truth, goodness, and beauty. From *The Religious Sense*: taking in the affirmations of God whether in the negative terms that God is infinite, im-mense, im-measurable, in-effable or in the positive ones that God is goodness and love, Giusanni states that "they are expressions that intensify the way we relate to, draw closer to the Mystery. They are openings to the Mystery."[4] From *At the Origin of the Christian Claim*: in identifying the pedagogy of Christ's self-revelation, Giussani states that "Jesus gradually places himself at the core of man's affections and freedom."[5] And in *Why the Church?* in explicating the constituent factors of ecclesial life and truth Giussani states that "The gift of the Spirit makes it evident that we are immersed in that new flow of energy generated by Jesus; it shows us that we are part of that new phenomenon."[6]

Here we have it. The grace of God at work! Openings to Mystery, Jesus at the core of our being, immersed in the gift of the Spirit! Such is the truth to which Christianity bears witness. Such is the truth that Christianity is. In this respect we can be grateful to Msgr Luigi Giussani for not only illuminating the way to Christ but for also revealing the possibilities of the human being in Christ, on the road of discovery, in the encounter with Jesus, and in the life of his Body, the Church.

## NOTES

1 L. Giussani, *The Religious Sense*, trans. John Zucchi (Montreal: McGill-Queen's University Press 1997); *At the Origin of the Christian Claim*, trans. Viviane Hewitt (Montreal: McGill-Queen's University Press 1998); *Why the Church?* trans. Viviane Hewitt (Montreal: McGill-Queen's University Press 2001).

2 "The Theological Locus of Ecclesial Movements" was published in *Communio* 25 (1998): 502.

3 Giussani, *The Religious Sense*, 10–11.

4 Ibid., 119.

5 Giussani, *At the Origin of the Christian Claim*, 64.

6 Giussani, *Why the Church?* 91.

# 12 Against the Theological Prejudices of the Age

RODNEY HOWSARE

While I was finishing my dissertation during the spring of 1998, the chair of the theology department at Marquette University gave me the opportunity to teach two upper-division courses in the fall of 1999 called Explorations in Theology. The course is one of the systematic theology electives in Marquette's undergraduate program. Since I was just about done with my dissertation and had not yet found full-time employment, I jumped at the chance. I had been eagerly reading the first volume of Giussani's trilogy, *The Religious Sense*, and was thinking how much fun it would be to read it with a group of questioning young students. Because time to order books for the next semester had already come and gone, I quickly put in my order for the first two volumes of the trilogy, the third not yet being in print.[1] In the middle of the summer, however, I was offered a full-time position at another college and so had to inform Marquette that I would not be able to teach the expected class, even though it was now in fact full.

The situation was quickly remedied when a friend of mine agreed to make my place. I would often get e-mails from him regarding the difficulties he was having "translating" Giussani to American undergraduates, even the fairly gifted ones at Marquette. Anyone who has read him will acknowledge that his writing can be demanding, and very European. Yet, aside from the practical question whether these texts are appropriate for undergraduates with relatively little theological background, there remains the question why I thought these books would be good for undergraduates in the first place. And it is that question that I would like to address.

I should begin by saying that I have found my undergraduate students in theology, both the students I taught at Marquette and those I currently teach at DeSales University, to be a microcosm of the culture in which we live. As such, their theology – and they do have a theology, whether they are aware of it or not – is the theology, for the most part, of that culture. It is important to realize, in short, not only that theologians have a theology but furthermore that the relationship between the theology of the average theologian and that of the average American is a reciprocal one in many respects. Indeed, I consider it part of my task as a theology professor to get my students to face up to the fact that they do have a theology, implicit or otherwise, and that the less thought they have given to their theology, the more likely it is to be a reflection of the prevailing prejudices of their culture.

But why choose Giussani to aid in such a task? I think there are two particularly pervasive modern tendencies that, if left unchecked, pose a real threat to authentic Christian thought. The first I will identify as dualism. The second, and for Catholic theology, at least, more recent one, I will call reductionism. The great twentieth-century Catholic theologian, Henri de Lubac, in fact, spent most of his theological career fighting against one or the other of these tendencies, first the dualist one and then the reductionist one.[2]

In one of his most influential works, *The Mystery of the Supernatural*, de Lubac explicitly excoriated the tendency of preconciliar theology to isolate the realm of nature from the realm of grace.[3] According to this theology, human beings have two distinct ends, one natural, which they can reach through their natural powers, and one supernatural, which requires the assistance of grace. Reason and the natural law were sufficient to aid human beings in terms of their natural end; revelation and grace were required if they were to reach their supernatural end. The difficulty with this approach, in de Lubac's view, is that it facilitates, even if unwittingly, the removal of the Christian faith from the ordinary affairs of the workaday world. Or, to say the same thing in more technical, theological terms, it makes it possible to devise an ethics and an anthropology without recourse to Christology. De Lubac's response to this older dualism was based on his fresh reading of Thomas Aquinas and the Church Fathers. For Aquinas, de Lubac insisted, human beings are really ordered to only one end, and that end is the beatific vision. To put it somewhat more pointedly, one cannot fully understand humanity apart from Jesus Christ. Those who are familiar with the encyclicals of John Paul II will notice that in every encyclical he quotes the following passage from *Gaudium et Spes*, paragraph 22: "The truth is that only in the mystery of the Incarnate Word does the mystery of man take on light. For Adam, the first man, was a type of him who was to come ... Christ the Lord. Christ, the new Adam, in the very revelation of the mystery of the Father and of his love, fully reveals man to himself and brings to light his most high calling ... He who is the 'image of the invisible God' ... is himself the perfect man who has restored in the children of Adam that likeness to God which had been disfigured ever since the first sin."[4] This quote is a testimony to the new, Christocentric approach initiated by de Lubac.

In the end, de Lubac's battle against the older dualism held the day, and this result is reflected throughout the documents of Vatican II, the just-mentioned quote from *Gaudium et Spes* being a case in point. But it was not long after the council that de Lubac and others, Karol Wojtya among them, began to see another danger with regard to the same issues. As de Lubac put it in the preface to *The Mystery of the Supernatural*, originally written in 1965,

On the one hand, though the dualist – or, perhaps better, separatist – thesis has finished its course, it may be only just beginning to bear its bitterest fruit ... While wishing to protect the supernatural from any contamination, people had in fact exiled it altogether – both from intellectual and social life – leaving the field free to be taken over by secularism. Today that secularism, following its course, is beginning to enter into the minds even of Christians. They too seek to find harmony with all things based upon the idea of nature which might be acceptable to a deist or atheist: everything that comes from Christ, everything that should lead to him, is pushed so far into the background as to look like disappearing for good.[5]

In short, the older dualism had unwittingly turned this world over to secular reason, and now secular reason, was coming home to roost.

But what does any of this have to do with my undergraduates or with Giussani, for that matter? Typical undergraduates have been influenced by both these tendencies and adhere to them in an uneasy tension. On the one hand, they are dualists in that they believe that Christianity is relevant only as a matter of private choice and only as having to do with things that are "spiritual" or "other-worldly." Christianity is what some people – those who go in for such things – do in church or when they pray; it has little or nothing to do with how one approaches and organizes the prosaic world. The "real" world – this world, that is – is run by technology, science, politics and money. Who do they turn to, for instance, when they need advice about sex? MTV's Dr Love, a scientist of sex.

And so, they are dualists. But they are also affected by what I am calling reductionism, or the second of de Lubac's theological temptations for moderns. In other words, when I ask them what Christianity is really about, they reply very much the way that C.S. Lewis guessed they would. In *Mere Christianity* Lewis says that: "when you get right down to it, is not the popular idea of Christianity simply this: that Jesus Christ was a great moral teacher and that if we only took his advice we might be able to establish a better social order and avoid another war?"[6] Distinctively Christian beliefs – such as the divinity of Christ, the idea that Christ's death somehow effects our salvation, or that sacraments convey the grace they signify – appear to them as mere distractions. Christianity is really reducible to the acknowledgment of some spiritual dimension and the improvement of our moral behaviour.

Notice that this view is not like the older, dualistic view and that it even in some ways contradicts it. Rather than push the distinctively Christian into a realm where it cannot touch the ordinary day-to-day world, this view wishes to reduce the distinctively Christian *to* the ordinary. Jesus Christ becomes just another great teacher; salvation becomes a turn from self-centredness to others-centredness; the liturgy becomes an event in which we celebrate our common humanity; and so on. This explains my students' almost unanimous support for the pluralist approach to the world religions. Because all religions are really just about making us into decent people, it follows that one religion is just as good as the next. The world religions become virtually interchangeable. Giussani's work is valuable in this context, because it serves as a guard against both the older dualism and the newer reductionism. In the face of the former, Giussani insists that the religious dimension is not just an add-on to the ordinary dimension; instead, the religious dimension touches this world at its very core. The entire first part of *The Religious Sense* sets out to show how eminently reasonable and natural it is to be open to the Supreme Reality. Indeed, to refuse to ask the big questions is to cease to be fully human. As Giussani himself puts it, "the religious factor represents the nature of our 'I' in as much as it expresses itself in certain questions: 'What is the ultimate meaning of existence?' or 'Why is there pain and death, and why, in the end, is life worth living?' Or, from another point of view: 'What does reality consist of and what is it made for?' Thus the religious sense lies within the reality of our self at the level of these questions: *it coincides with the radical engagement of the self with life, an involvement which exemplifies itself in these questions.*"[7] It is our *nature* to seek out the ultimate, according to Giussani.

Because my students are dualists, they fail to see that the organizing principle – the Why? – behind one's day-to-day choices is one's god. Giussani is relentless in his insistence that one cannot even choose not to decide in such matters. If we fail to ask these big questions explicitly, we will still answer them implicitly in the manner in which we live from day to day. With T.S. Elliot, Giussani insists that modern people have not ceased to believe in gods; they have simply replaced the older gods with the newer ones of money, sex, and power. He quotes the following passage from Elliot's "Choruses from 'The Rock'":

> But it seems that something has happened that has never
>     happened before: though we know not just when, or why,
>     or how, or where.
> Men have left GOD not for other gods, they say, but for no god;
>     and this has never happened before
> That men both deny gods and worship gods, professing first
>     Reason,
> And then Money, and Power, and what they call Life, or Race, or
>     Dialectic.
> The Church disowned, the tower overthrown, the bells up-turned,
>     what have we to do
> But stand with empty hands and palms turned upwards
> In an age which advances progressively backwards?
>
> ·  ·  ·  ·  ·  ·  ·  ·  ·  ·  ·  ·  ·  ·
>
> Waste and void. Waste and void. And darkness on the face of the
>     deep.
> Has the Church failed mankind, or has mankind failed the
>     Church?
> When the Church is no longer regarded, not even opposed, and
>     men have forgotten
> All gods except Usury, Lust and Power.[8]

The first movement, then, of Giussani's *Religious Sense* is to show that human beings are by their very natures oriented to an explanation of the whole. They seek ultimate answers; and when they deny the legitimacy of such a search, they are being unreasonable, are being, in fact, less than human.

Another way of saying the same thing is to point out how modern people so frantically try to fill up every empty moment of their lives with activity, with distractions. Giussani quotes Kazimierz Brandys's "Defense of Granada" accordingly,

In the streets of our city the crowd moves along the widened sidewalks under buildings taller than they have ever been. In a deaf and sorrowful disquietude, it seeks out the flavour of the present day. Thirsty for strong excitations, it turns to the cinema, the stadiums, the taverns. The crowd is unsatisfied by the social motivation for existence, even though it ought to recognize the logic, pointed out every day with a thousand arguments. Generally these arguments are convincing: the crowd is not made up of madmen: it has understood the importance of work in life, it takes seriously organized effort, it feels respect for material energy, the source of future successes. All this, however, does not disperse its uneasiness. The principles and the goals do not appease its yearnings. Tormented by a confused desire, longing to forget the program for its realization, the crowd wants to discover the flavor of life, which allows it to taste the pleasure of the space of existence. The crowd is not exacting in all of this, it takes that which is given it. Alcohol contains the most secure guarantee of reconciling one's self with the present, a half-liter bottle contains the desired percentage of the irrational.[9]

The longing for the ultimate, which is in the soul of every person, is filled in the modern world by an endless pursuit of distractions.

A longing for the ultimate, for the final answers, seems to be built into the very heart of human existence; and if one does not artificially short-circuit this search, one can get a glimpse of the infinite, can gain a sense, that is, of the Supreme Being. This explains, according to Giussani, the universality of the religious sense. However, there is a snag in all of this, and it leads directly to the second movement of Giussani's work. In order to combat the modern tendency toward dualism, Giussani has emphasized the fact that human beings by their very nature tend toward the absolute, toward some ultimate destiny. But this tendency, if it solves the older problem of dualism, brings with it the second of modernity's temptations, namely, the equation of the ultimate with what can be grasped by reason or nature. At this point Giussani goes into a brilliant analysis of the story of Ulysses from Dante's *Inferno*.

Dante encounters Ulysses in his tour through Hell, raising the logical question of what Ulysses did to get there. Ulysses is presented as a man who was relentless in his pursuit of the unknown. Incorrigibly curious, Ulysses pursues every part of the globe, fearless in the face of people's warnings and previous failures. But at one point he reaches the Pillars of Hercules, which mark the end of the explorable world, the point where what is open to human exploration and what lies beyond human capacities meet. Guissani goes on accordingly, "But he, Ulysses, precisely because of that same "stature" that had driven him all over the *Mare Nostrum* (the Mediterranean), felt not only that the Pillars of Hercules were not the end, but that they were, in fact, the moment of the unleashing of his true nature. And so he smashed to smithereens this wisdom and went on."[10]

The reader might be immediately inclined to think that Ulysses' error consists precisely in his hubris in the face of the humanly impossible. But, Giussani insists, this is not the case. Indeed, not only is Ulysses' decision to push beyond the Pillars of Hercules not his mistake, it is actually his advantage over the modern, positivist mindset that tells us that we can never venture beyond what is humanly calculable. This narrative, then, calls attention to the first temptation in the face of the religious sense: the temptation to reduce all of reality to what can be grasped by instrumental reason. This temptation is distinct from – but not unrelated to the older dualism, in that it dispenses with the supernatural altogether.[11] But this is rarely a direct temptation for the theologian or for the vast majority of my students, for that matter.

Ulysses does not succumb to this temptation, however, and for this he deserves our admiration. But he does succumb to the second temptation in the face of the ultimate mystery: the notion that one can navigate this "beyond" with the ordinary tools of sailing. Again, Giussani:

By nature, the human being intuits the Beyond. However, because of an existential condition, he does not hold up, he falls. Intuition is like an impulse falling off due to some sad and malignant force of gravity. Ulysses and his men were mad not because they sailed on past the Pillars of Hercules, but because they claimed to identify the meaning, that is, to sail the ocean beyond the Pillars, with the very means they used to sail the "measurable" shores of the *Mare Nostrum* ... Reality is a sign, and it awakens our religious sense. But it is a suggestion that is misinterpreted. Existentially, the human being is driven to interpret it poorly; that is to say, prematurely, with impatience. The intuition of our relationship with mystery becomes degraded into presumption.[12]

The last line is of basic importance: because we have become aware of transcendence, we think that we can determine our relationship with it on our own terms and by our finite powers.[13]

I will now tie this into what has gone before. I began by stating that we moderns are inclined to two theological errors: the dualist and the reductionist. In order to combat the dualist temptation, both Giussani and de Lubac point to the innate human tendency towards the absolute: Augustine's "restless heart." This means that what God offers us in Jesus Christ is not an extrinsic addition to human nature but something that actually fulfills what human beings innately desire. But the danger of this position has always been its tendency to threaten the gratuity or the newness of grace, its "from above" nature. The older dualism, for all of its problems, at least insured the gratuity of grace. Has this newer position, on the other hand, not made it almost incumbent upon God to give us the grace that he designed us for in the first place? Or, even worse, has the newer theology not made it possible to deny the need for something from above, something supernatural? It might seem that our innate tendency toward the absolute is impetus enough to push us right up to the possession of what we long for.

It is time to make a couple of final points and to answer how Giussani guards not only against the dualistic tendency but also against the more recent, reductionist tendency. There has been a tendency in the theology since the Second Vatican Council to reduce Christianity to what it has in common with general humanitarianism. This tendency is the result of an abuse of Karl Rahner's assertion, itself ambiguous and subject to misinterpretation, that love of neighbour *is* love of God. Such theologizing has generally resulted in a tendency to treat the particulars of the Christian faith – the sacrificial nature of the death of Christ, the Trinity, the efficacy of the sacraments, the sacramental role of the Church, and the like – as extrinsic, even if ultimately desirable, add-ons to basic human religiosity. This is why, as I said before, my students are so naturally inclined to the pluralist view of the relationship between Christianity and the world religions. I note also, and only in passing, the outcry over the recent Vatican document *Dominus Iesus*.

Giussani militates against such reductionism by calling attention to the precarious position to which our religious awareness leads us. Humanity's inherent sense of the divine, possessed in the form of asking ultimate questions, leads it to dizzying heights. At this point frustration sets in, for the very powers that got us to the brink of the ultimate mystery are insufficient to navigate the mystery at hand. This result reminds me very much of de Lubac's paradox, taken from Aquinas, that human beings are the only creatures who are directed to an end that surpasses their natural capacities. And with this paradox both Giussani and de Lubac avoid the reductionism of which I have been speaking. If we are to come to know the mystery to which our natures point us, that mystery is going to have to come to us. Giussani calls this the "hypothesis of revelation." What it means for theology is that revelation does not comes to us from the outside as something extrinsic to our nature. Indeed, it is, to repeat, something to which our natures themselves point: "Our hearts are restless until they rest in Thee." But at the same time, our natures are radically unequal to the task before them. And this is the punch line: Jesus Christ is that place where humanity's religious search is met by God's search for humanity, so that the hypostatic union of the two natures in Jesus

Christ make him uniquely capable of saying, "I am the way." And this conclusion takes us back to the quote from *Gaudium et Spes*: "Only in the mystery of the Incarnate Word does the mystery of man take on light."


NOTES

1 L. Giussani, *The Religious Sense*, trans. John Zucchi (Montreal: McGill-Queens Press 1997); *At the Origin of the Christian Claim*, trans. Viviane Hewitt (Montreal: McGill-Queens Press 1997); *Why the Church*, trans. Viviane Hewitt (Montreal: McGill-Queens Press 2001).

2 It might be of interest to the reader to note that C. S. Lewis also saw the danger of these two tendencies in modern theology. In fact, I read Lewis' theology as being very much in line with the instincts of de Lubac, von Balthasar and others. Anyone who has read Lewis' first, postconversion book, *The Pilgrim's Regress* (Grand Rapids, M: Eerdmans 1981), will notice these two tendencies in his depiction of the Northern and Southern territories. In intellectual terms, the North and South represent two different rejections of what Lewis calls "romantic longings": the Northern rejection is based upon a kind of rationalistic rejection of all "immortal longings" and the Southern rejection is not so much a rejection as an acceptance of everything – and therefore nothing. Lewis describes it this way: "The Northerners are the men of rigid systems whether sceptical or dogmatic, Aristocrats, Stoics, Pharisees, Rigorists, signed and sealed members of highly organised 'Parties.' The Southerners are by their very nature less definable; boneless souls whose doors stand open day and night to almost every visitant, but always with readiest welcome for those, whether Maenad or Mystagogue, who offer some sort of intoxication. The delicious tang of the forbidden and the unknown draws them on with fatal attraction; the smudging of all frontiers, the relaxation of all resistances, dream, opium, darkness, death, and the return to the womb." He goes on to say, rather strikingly, that in theology there is also a North and a South. "The one cries 'Drive out the bondmaid's son,' and the other 'Quench not the smoking flax.' The one exaggerates the distinctness between Grace and Nature into a sheer opposition and by vilifying the higher levels of Nature (the real *praeparatio evangelica* inherent in certain immediately sub-Christian experiences) makes the way hard for those who are at the point of coming in. The other blurs the distinction altogether, flatters mere kindliness into thinking it is charity and vague optimisms or pantheisms into thinking they are Faith, and makes the way out fatally

easy and imperceptible for the budding apostate" (afterword to the third edition, 206–7, emphasis omitted). It will be helpful to keep these two extremes in mind in what follows.

3 H. De Lubac, *The Mystery of the Supernatural*, trans. Rosemary Sheed (New York: Herder and Herder 1967).

4 *Vatican Council II: The Conciliar and Post-Conciliar Documents*, ed. Austin Flannery, O.P. (Northport, NY: Costello 1977), 922.

5 De Lubac, *The Mystery of the Supernatural*, xii.

6 C.S. Lewis, *Mere Christianity* (San Francisco: Harper Collins 2001), 155.

7 Giussani, *The Religious Sense*, 45.

8 L. Giussani, "Religious Awareness in Modern Man." *Communio* 25 (spring 1998): 105.

9 K. Brandys, "Obrona Grenady" (The Defense of Grenada), in *Czerwona Czapeczka* (The Little Red Hat) (Warsaw: Panstwowy Institut Wydawniczy 1957), 308, quoted in Giussani, *The Religious Sense*, 65.

10 Giussani, *The Religious Sense*, 133.

11 It could even be argued that it was the older dualism that made this positivistic mindset possible. Once this world is turned over to secular reason, it should come as no surprise when that reason decides that this world is all there *really* is.

12 Giussani, *The Religious Sense*, 140.

13 It may be imagined that because Giussani is so interested in "apologetics," his approach to theology would go directly against the grain of that of, say, Karl Barth or his many "unapologetic" or "post-liberal" followers. But I would like to suggest that this would be a superficial reading of *The Religious Sense*, especially if one reads the next volume in the trilogy, *At the Origin of the Christian Claim*. Even the first volume makes it very clear that in spite of the fact that our nature itself points to the infinite, it is by no means capable of grasping this infinite. Furthermore, in the second volume Giussani draws especial attention to the "event character" of Christianity. It is precisely because the God of Christianity cannot be grasped by our reason that He has to come to us in an Event: the incarnation. It is that Event that ultimately stands in judgment over the religious sense, even if it fulfills it without destroying it. Giussani's theology could, just so far, be described as "revelocentric."

# 13 The Only Point of View

CARLO CAFFARRA

Saint Robert Bellarmine writes that when seen from the valley, the mountains appear extraordinarily big and the stars extraordinarily small. However, if we could place ourselves in the heights of the firmament, the stars would seem extraordinarily huge and the mountains, even the loftiest, so small as to be almost invisible. A question of our point of view? the great theologian asks himself. A question of our point of view, contemporary nihilists undoubtedly affirm. Christianity affirms that we have come to know God's "point of view" and thus that this point of view is the *only* true one, that is, the only one that makes us see reality as it is. How has God made known *His* point of view and thus the only point of view for us? In a shocking way: by making Himself man, incarnating Himself. This Event is simply, purely, the foundational charism of Msgr Giussani, reminding us that only one true point of view exists for knowing the value of every reality: Jesus Christ, the Word made flesh. "We place in the center of our life this Presence that explains everything, that is at the origin of all we are and do, within our self-awareness and our action. And this Presence is precisely the man Jesus, born of a woman."[1] This discovery evokes amazement because everything comes down to it, everything is explained by it, everything is built upon it: *gaudium de veritate* (Saint Augustine). Giussani's book *Porta la speranza* is evocative precisely because it shows this experience, this intuition at its birth: it is already there in its entirety; the subsequent years are nothing more than a coherent development of this seed. Giussani writes: "Remember that everything is the glory of God, everything is done for an ultimate context, for an ultimate plan, of which you are a part, into which you are grafted, into which you are assimilated ... It is the knowledge of this ultimate context, that Jesus Christ came to bring ... This is the Gospel: the good news that life has a meaning, a great destiny, a greater context that gives me worth. This is what Jesus Christ came to bring."[2]

Today we discover more clearly how this foundational charism, like every foundational charism, has been given to the Church for the salvation of man. This testimony to the "only true point of view," to the "greater context that bestows worth," is opposed by the nihilist affirmation that wreaks ever-increasing devastation on us today, that says this point of view does not exist, simply because no point of view exists that can make us understand mountains and stars, no "Archimedean point to which we can appeal to be able once again to name the whole."[3] We are forced to continuously make and unravel the same cloth, since we have lost the right to hope for the return of a Presence. Msgr Giussani's response to this challenge, already found embryonically in *Porta la speranza*, is wonderful.

The rejection of the "only point of view" is in reality our rejection *of ourselves*: "He who denies it, does so because he denies something of his life."[4] In what sense? A text of Thomas's is in singular agreement with what I am saying. He writes: "Another reason also exists (for which it is convenient that Revelation exists), the defeat of presumption, mother of error. In fact there are persons who presume so much of their intelligence that they think they can measure all things with their reason (*ut totam rerum naturam se reputent suo intellectu posse metiri*): that is, they hold true all that which seems such to them and false all that which seems thus to them."[5] What decides the destiny of human beings is their way of relating themselves to being, their attitudes (*intentio*, Thomas would say) towards reality. It must be one of the two: either human reason is the measure of being or being is the measure of reason; either being reduces itself exhaustively to the consciousness of being, or being is the intelligible light ("full of love") that awakens consciousness. This is the only true alternative upon which human destiny is decided. If you put yourself at first place, inevitably you *opt* for a limiting point of view, exclusive and excluding, not ecumenical: you will not see all of reality. If you put yourself at second place, you *remain* in the only limitless, all-encompassing, ecumenical point of view. You opt, you remain: the first case, in fact, deals with a decision that goes against our constitutive *desire*, leaving our own home, the home of being; in the second case reason is simply itself, faithful to itself deep down, and remains home.

There is a reciprocal indwelling of *ratio in desiderium* (reason in desire) and of *desiderium in ratio* (desire in reason), in which the entire human event is built, as Thomas explains (1.2, q.3, a.8). Thomas thinks of the life of the created person as life that springs from a desire that does not demur until "restat sibi aliquid desiderandum et quaerendum" (something is left to be wished for and sought after). It is this desire that evokes *inquisitio*, which does not "quiescit, quosque perveniat ad conoscendum essentiam causae," does not rest until it discovers the entire intelligibility of the real.

The central intuition of the charism of Msgr Giussani is that in the encounter with the Word, humanity can possess *in hope* this interpretive key to the whole: "Thus in education to hope one penetrates the experience of the Redemption."[6] Deep down, only individuals who have not limited the measure of their desire can meet Christ and in Him *every* reality, known in its truth, loved according to the measure of its goodness, enjoyed according to the splendor of its beauty. The incarnate Word is the one true point of view, because it is the only point of view that excludes nothing of all that exists: "Through Him all things came into being, not one thing came into being except through Him."[7] The prophetic testimony of Msgr Giussani has posed the supreme question, the one true ultimate challenge to thoughtless and merry contemporary nihilism: in reality human beings want not more power but a whole realization of their being, not an incessant increase in possibilities, but "to be capable of all the existence allowed by [their] own essence."[8] Therefore, the affirmation of the "only point of view" that is Christ and the affirmation of all the human stand hand in hand. *Simul stant; simul cadunt.*

The most distinctive characteristics of Giussani's proposal derive from this point. Here I can only list them.

- This charism places the act of education at the centre of its proposal: to educate means precisely to introduce to all of reality, offering an interpretive hypothesis for the whole. And from this perspective one sees the inconsistency of an "educational neutrality."
- This charism is congenial to the ecumenical-missionary dimension: *nihil humani a me alienum puto* now takes on meaning, an absolutely new weight.
- This charism regards culture as a necessary expression of faith: faith shapes the entire human, expressing him or her in the splendor of its truth.

"It is an error to hold that man still has a content or should have one … in fact man no longer exists, only his symptoms still exist."[9] This is the final result of a process that has rejected the only true point of view.

A true prophet has called us to remember the one Event that, making itself present in human existence, not only blocks us from reducing human beings to a symptom of something that no longer exists but gives us the fullness of life.

NOTES

Translated by Sheila Beatty.

1 "Se non fossi tuo, mio Cristo, mi sentirei creatura finita," talk given at La Thuile, 17 August 1997, supplement to *Litterae Communionis – Tracce*, no. 8, September 1997, 22.

2 See L. Giussani, *Porta la speranza* (Genoa: Marietti 1997), 186.

3 F. Volpi, *Il nichilismo* (Bari: Laterza 1996), 117.

4 See Giussani, *Porta la speranza*, 186.

5 SCG I, section 5, 31.

6 See Giussani, *Porta la speranza*, 162.

7 John 1:3.

8 F. Balbo, quoted in V. Possenti, *Il nichilismo teoretico e la "morte della metafisica"* (Rome: Armando Ed. 1996), 133.

9 G. Benn, *Lo smalto sul nulla*, ed. L. Zagari (Milan: Adelphi 1992), 264.

# PART FOUR

# At Home with Truth: Ecumenical Perspectives

# 14 Ecumenical by Its Nature

## NIKOLAUS LOBKOWICZ

I must begin by expressing my gratitude to Msgr Giussani. Even though when I first became acquainted with Communion and Liberation, I was too old to be able to actively participate, in the true sense of the expression, his thoughts have decisively changed my way of conceiving what it means today for a lay person to be a disciple of Christ. I met him for the first time in Milan in the autumn of 1984 and asked him to help me liberate the University of Eichstätt, the only Catholic University in Germany, from a Catholicism devoid of joy: he spontaneously offered to send me a few young people whose presence would testify to how beautiful it can be to be Catholic. At times I have the impression that my decision back then to come from Eichstätt to Milan was the only truly sensible thing I did in my twelve years at the University of Eichstätt. In fact, the students whom Msgr Giussani sent in 1985 changed my university, my work as president, and, not least of all, the world of my dreams in a way I will now describe.

We live in difficult times for the Church – to speak in the language of the world – and in German-speaking countries the times seem even more difficult than elsewhere, for various reasons. I will limit my analysis to Germany, one of the first European countries to see the birth of an important Catholic lay movement, which began in the 1930s. This movement was clearly influenced by the circumstances of the times. Except for Bavaria, Germany considered itself officially Protestant, above all in the Prussian territories, which at that time included the Rhineland. Because Catholics were a minority discriminated against by the state, they made a conscious decision to build Catholic organizations and institutions.

The movement was very successful and bore good fruit until the Second World War. But later, after the last Vatican Council, it became clear that even the best beginnings can go off track if they do not respond to the "signs of the times." This was the case in Germany after 1945, for three reasons. First, because of the waves of refugees coming to Germany immediately after the Second World War, few regions were still univocally Protestant or Catholic. Catholics found themselves living with Protestants and vice versa. Thus the efforts of committed German Catholics to affirm themselves in the country's Protestant milieu became anachronistic. Second, the Christian original-ity of the numerous Catholic associations and organizations had paled; not infrequently their Catholicity was reduced to merely having a priest as an assistant and meeting in the churches on festive occasions for solemn liturgies. Third and above all, instead of going out into the world beyond the church doors, various arganizations built a kind of Catholic "parallel world." For every association or organization present in society there was another Catholic one, often in open contrast with the corresponding Protestant structures, and its Christian spirit in the face of progressive secularization was no less feeble and no less super-ficial and focused on appearances.

Consequently, after the Second Vatican Council the work of genera-tions of courageous Catholics collapsed almost instantaneously, in what was a specifically German variation of the so-called postconciliar crisis: Catholic educational structures and channels of communication, which had been built laboriously over a long time, broke down unexpectedly. German Catholicism, till then faithful to Rome in a way that would have been difficult to find elsewhere, developed anti-Roman sentiments (as did Dutch Catholicism) and became at the same time "liberal" in an entirely singular way. The council wanted a renovation, a Christian dialogue with the modern world that started from the roots of faith and evoked a spirit open to the desires of the world but that was at the same time ever closer and more faithful to the Lord. In Germany, and not only there, this objective had a strange consequence: on the one hand, Catholics gathered around the altar even more fearful than before, while on the other hand, in the circle around this altar one could find all the confusions and the ideologies of the world. This led to intra-ecclesiastical conflicts between conservatives and progressives, discord that compromised the unity of the Church. And the contending factions clung ever more often to questions of secondary importance.

I therefore find Msgr Giussani's movement to be of obvious contem-porary relevance. I am certainly not mistaken in saying that he has taken up an idea that Saint Augustine captures with the expression *exspoliatio Aegyptiorum* (the despoliation of the Egyptians). Drawing from the *Book of Wisdom*, Augustine uses this idea (whose significance was understood by Hans Urs von Balthasar) to refer to what happened during the Exodus after the miracle of the Red Sea.[1] The sea had swallowed up Pharaoh and his army, and when it withdrew again the Israelites collected all the valuables that remained but did not bring them into their tents, gathering them instead as if they belonged to God. Thus the image of the despoliation of the Egyptians indicates that everything of value comes from God and belongs to Him, even if it is found in the hands of adversaries and enemies; one must only carefully collect it and use it. The tragedy that Paul VI deplored as the modern abyss separating Church and culture consists substantially of the fact that for too long the Church did not know that what came to it from the world in the process of secularization were fragments of its inheritance: the Church battled what came to it only because it came from those who – rightly or wrongly – seemed like its enemies. Aside from a renewal and a deepening of the faith, the true direction inaugurated by the council and prepared by theologians like von Balthasar and de Lubac can be summed up more or less as follows: Do not fear what blows towards you from a world that is ever more secularized; a large part of it is authentic and could even very well suit you as disciples of Christ. You need only to recover it and understand it correctly.

It seems to me that this message has been taken up by Giussani in a particularly fascinating way, especially for youth. Like no other theologian of our time, he has understood that the Christian announcement can find a positive echo only if it does not stand defensively against the world – thus also against the current one – and if it appropriates all in the world that indicates the future and leads it to the Christian Fact. Naturally, this way of proceeding involves risks, but, Giussani tells us, if we do not succeed in showing that the desires that move human beings today have their answer in Christ and ultimately in him alone, almost no one will listen to us anymore. The faith and the human life determined by it should be understood and interpreted as a response to the questions that move us; the faith and the following of Christ in the Church planted in the world should not both be misunderstood as tradition exempt from verification and ultimately detached from the world; instead, they are founded on a happening that corresponds to us as nothing else in the world: it responds to our most secret questions and satisfies our desires.

Theologians have long spoken of a *desiderium naturale Dei*, a natural yearning in humanity for completion in God. Saint Thomas noted that not only does the supernatural presuppose nature (as has been often said) but that grace also responds to what nature desires in the depths of its being. However, to a certain degree Christianity has been unsuccessful, or has succeeded only here and there, in translating this thought into an anthropology that would render it existentially reasonable. Instead, Christianity has too often presented itself only as the conveyor of knowledge of what one should or should not do. We should not be surprised that, on the one hand, following Christ became for many an annoying, almost even dark, inconvenience and, on the other hand that many looked fondly at what the Church rejected. Would we not have more freedom, it was asked, if we did not listen to the orders and the prohibitions of the Church?

Msgr Giussani seems to respond to this and similar questions as follows: Run the risk of immersing yourself in a tradition that will teach you what freedom truly is. Acknowledge in Christ the friend who shows you already in this world how you can find what you desire; and recognize in the Church, even with all its imperfections, the road He indicates to you for this. The consequence of this announcement is a new openness to all that is usually presentted, in contrast to the Church, as *the* world: instead of *reducing* humans to Christian beings, I was almost about to say, this announcement shows that following Christ, verifying each and every thing in the light of the faith in Him, brings with it an incredible openness to the world that almost inevitably flows into a great creativity. No more fear, then, of educating men and women for freedom and for the achievement of what they have always desired; no more fear, then, of seeking among those who think and believe differently for truths that we ourselves so far have been unaware of. One of the most surprising effects of the patrimony of thought of Giussani's movement is its willingness to enter into dialogue with anyone, without any reserve. It is by its nature ecumenical, without in the least falling into an erroneous liberality.

But, one could ask, how can this new openness to the world avoid ceding to the world in the end? What or, rather, who is the anchor that keeps the ship steady, so that it does not capsize in the storm? Giussani's response is clear: this anchor can only be Christ and our faithfulness to Him. But he has added a dimension as unexpected as it is traditional, one that goes back to antiquity. The longest chapter of the oldest masterpiece of Western ethics, the *Nichomachean Ethics* of Aristotle, is dedicated to the virtue of friendship. The Christian tradition, which generally drew willingly from classical antiquity, was not able to do anything with this virtue; even in Saint Thomas it pales into a generic love of neighbour. Without perhaps thinking much about Aristotle, Giussani has conferred a new face on this virtue: in order to be well anchored, he seems to say, you must be in a community in which you live with all your heart; you must form a community whose members are reciprocally friends in the deepest and, at the same time, most natural and thus most spontaneous sense of the word. At the Last Supper Christ himself spoke to his disciples as "his friends,"[2] and in his Letter to Titus, Paul speaks of "the kindness and love of God our Savior for humanity."[3] In a way until now unusual in the Church, Giussani invites us therefore to acknowledge Christ himself as our most faithful friend I myself experienced this acknowledgment a meeting of the leaders of Communion and Liberation, and I have never forgotten it.[4]

What do friends do? They are near us even in difficult times, and we can speak to them of anything that interests us; we do not even need to fear that their friendships have ulterior motives, as if people were our friends only to obtain something. Giussani understood that the Church's new openness to the world can succeed only with the birth of communities of friends who help each other to deal with all they meet in life in the light of faithfulness to the Lord, friends who regularly share their experiences and interpret them – experiences of the individual and those of the community – in the light of their experience of Christ. The friendship of the members of Communion and Liberation, which is visible even from outside, is infinitely more than simple Italian warmth; for the newcomer it is perhaps the most fascinating aspect of Msgr Giussani's movement (of course in its essence it has been for some time infinitely more than a simple movement). The young people say privately, "I have always desired friends like these." They come, they participate, and they soon recognize that their friendship is not that of any club but that of men and women who regularly help each other reflect on how they can better serve the Lord and his Church where they find themselves living. And it is precisely because of this idea of friendship, not least of all because of "the kindness and love of God our Savior for humanity," that the expression *exspoliatio Aegyptiorum* lacks any note of triumphalism in Giussani. It reminds us only very tenderly that in all the complexity of our life's journey we are all creatures whom the Lord accompanies with the concern and loving care of a shepherd; it also almost secondarily reminds us seniors – and in a certain way the entire Church – that important works of culture call us to our destiny, even if the author or artist is a pagan or an atheist. Who would not want to follow a Lord who is such a friend, even of sinners, as Giussani presents him to us?

In this way Giussani has by now reached several generations who live exactly what the council called the vocation of the laity: ordering the things of the world with the gaze directed towards what God wants from us – groups of friends who silently, but with constancy, counsel each other about what God wants from them and trust that the Lord, as friend of them all, will show them the road. Some have become priests or joined orders, but they were originally lay people; in fact, we all are born lay people and are baptized as such. As members of this community, which year by year ever more evidently has come to form one international community, they are immune to what I would call the German temptation to avoid going into the world as Christians and to gather assiduously around the altar, almost like priests, and then to expect that, in the end, the altar will look different. They are immune because they know that the Church is more than the work of human beings; because they consider the tradition of the Church as the road that, even through all its imperfections, God indicates; because they experience daily Revelation as something joyously new, which for this reason never bores them; because they understand that it is the external world, which opens out before the doors of the church, and not the altar that must be transformed.

I imagine that Msgr Giussani, looking back over his work, at times marvels with gratitude that what he began and has accompanied for years has not failed. It has not failed surely because it was the right response to a contemporary need, because it pleased the Lord and because the Lord gave his grace to the work of Giussani. But the risk was and continues to be great. Christians truly risk something when they go into this confused world and place themselves in front of its confused desires. However, as I have said elsewhere, Giussani's work has not failed because he places great faith in *magnanimitas*, the magnanimity, of young people. Everyone complains that the young do not want to follow the old paths. (Even Plato complained in this way.) But Giussani realized from the beginning that these complaints are mistaken. It is necessary only to indicate the right road to the young and then leave them free to follow it. However, in order to awaken their magnanimity, it is necessary also to show them what our destiny is, the meaning of our life here on earth. If in addition one succeeds in showing them that the path to the realization of our destiny may at times involve great efforts but that it is a path of joy that renews itself daily – and Giussani has succeeded in an extraordinary way – they will set aside any skepticism or cynicism that the world counsels them to feel, and they will set off on their journey.

At times I feel sorry that I did not meet Msgr Giussani earlier, when he was beginning and I was a bit less hardened than I am today. My life would have been different in many ways, and I would have been able to avoid many wrong turns, as well as many fears. Thus careful attention to the announcement of Msgr Giussani will reveal that it is not intended only for young people with romantic sentiments. The path it indicates is no different from the one Christianity has always travelled – the path of "making yourself available to the Savior." But in his old age Giussani continues to present this path with a happy passion that would suit someone younger. I myself have been motivated by this impassioned joy for what Christ has given us as truth and liberty, and I want to thank Msgr Giussani publicly for it.

NOTES

Translated by Sheila Beatty

1 See St Augustine, *Conf.* 7.9, 15; *De Doct. Christ.* 2.40, 60; *C. Faust.* 22.72; 83 *Quaest.* 53.2; *En. Ps.* 104, 28.
2 Jn 15:14 ff.
3 Ti 3:4.
4 The author refers to an international meeting of Communion and Liberation that took place at Corvara, in the Northern Italy, from 25 to 30 August 1987.

# 15 A Presence That Can Be Touched

GILBERT MEILAENDER

In the first chapter of the Gospel of Mark, in the New Testament, shortly after having called his first disciples and performed several healings, Jesus goes off by himself to a lonely place away from the crowds and prays. The disciples come looking for him "And Simon and those who were with Him pursued him, and they found Him and said to Him, 'Every one is searching for you.'"[1]

That verse is not a bad summary of Msgr Giussani's understanding of the Event that lies at the heart of the Christian claim and of the human longing that Event answers. Everyone is searching for Jesus. I read a story once about some parents whose little four-year-old daughter was terrified of the dark. When they put her to bed at night, they would always reassure her that God was watching over her. But one night, after they had themselves gone to bed, the mother felt a soft tap on her shoulder. "Mommy," the little girl's voice said, "I know God's in there with me, but I need somebody with skin." Giussani thinks we all do – and Jesus is the Event in which God himself encounters us as somebody with skin.

And yet, if we take Giussani seriously, I think we have to say that this Event – the revelation of God in Jesus of Nazareth – is not simply an answer to the question lurking in the whole of human experience. Even as the Event of Jesus fulfils that human longing, it also overturns, reshapes, and restructures it. No longer are we permitted to contemplate a God who is simply humanity writ large, who exists to satisfy us, or who is merely a projection of human wish and desire. Instead, we must find a way to come to terms with "the decisive Fact of all time." As Giussani writes, "If God had manifested a particular will in a particular way in human history, if he had charted a pathway of his own leading us to him, the central issue of the religious phenomenon would cease to be man attempting to imagine God, even though this attempt is the greatest expression of human dignity; instead, the whole issue would lie in freedom's pure and simple gesture of acceptance or rejection. This is the overturning of the [religious] method."[2]

That is, the question no longer is whether our search – the religious method – will find an answer. The question is whether we will learn to trust the answer that has been given. I said that this Event that lies at the origin of the Christian claim overturns, reshapes, and restructures our understanding of the religious sense of humanity. For this Event – when in Jesus God takes human life into his own divine life – is not the conclusion of our search, nor is it the conclusion of a philosophical argument. It is simply there

for us to reckon with. Thus, for example, in his *Confessions*, St Augustine seems to be – and perhaps at first he thought that he was – recounting the story of his own religious quest, a quest that culminated in finding God. But, in fact, it turns out that the truth is almost the other way round, and Augustine has to say, "It was you, Lord, who with your most tender and merciful hand gradually laid hold upon my heart."[3] Rabbi Abraham Joshua Heschel said something similar: "The Bible speaks not only of man's search for God, but also of God's search of man ... The way to God is a way of God. Unless God asks the question, all our inquiries are in vain."[4] For Giussani that is why the encounter with Jesus of Nazareth is so crucial: it is the Event in which God himself makes the way to God for us. Thus, St Augustine says that for all the help the Platonists had been to him along the way, it turned out that they did not know that one Fact that made possible the reorientation of his life: that, as the Gospel of John puts it, the Word was made flesh. They could not, Augustine says, tell him of "the face and look of pity, the tears of confession, your sacrifice."[5]

If Msgr Giussani is right, several important things follow about how human beings – ourselves included – might respond to this Fact. First, although the presence of God in Jesus is "the decisive Fact of all time," no one should be compelled to acknowledge it. For what is offered here on Giussani's account is the possibility of being human, of acquiring a human face.[6] Drawn into personal relationship with Jesus, as were the first followers, we ourselves become fully human for the first time. This change cannot be coerced or demanded, however. It can only be offered, an invitation can only be extended. If Christians have sometimes forgotten this, Msgr. Giussani has not. If what the God who has encountered us in Jesus desires is the loving response of our hearts, then "He cannot ravish. He can only woo."[7]

What also follows is equally important. Not only can we not be compelled to acknowledge this Fact, no one is irrational who declines the offer. Because what is offered is a personal relationship, something more than reason and logic is required, namely, trust. C.S. Lewis makes the point nicely:

There are times when we can do all that a fellow creature needs if only he will trust us. In getting a dog out of a trap, in extracting a thorn from a child's finger, in teaching a boy to swim or rescuing one who can't, in getting a frightened beginner over a nasty place on a mountain, the one fatal obstacle may be their distrust ... We ask them to believe that what is painful will relieve their pain and that what looks dangerous is their only safety. We ask them to accept apparent impossibilities: that moving the paw farther back into the trap is the way to get it out – that hurting the finger very much more will stop the finger hurting – that water which is obviously permeable will resist and support the body – that holding onto the only support within reach is not the way to avoid sinking – that to go higher and onto a more exposed ledge is the way not to fall. To support all these *incredibilia* we can rely only on the other party's confidence in us.[8]

Giussani has, I think, something similar in mind. If it is a personal bond into which we are called, then the very logic of personal relationships teaches us that it can not be created or sustained without trust. Evidence alone will never settle the matter. Suppose a man loves a woman but wants to be certain that she too loves him before he commits himself and makes himself vulnerable. What possible evidence could provide such certainty? What could assure him that he was not overly gullible, a dupe, or a fool? There is no such evidence. Could two people become close friends if they were not willing to reveal something of their hopes and dreams before they were absolutely certain the other person could be trusted with such revelations? What possible evidence could assure them that they would not end up looking foolish? There is no such evidence. In the logic of personal relations, therefore, something more is needed than evidence. The Christian claim that God meets us in Jesus is not, first of all, an argument that demands our assent. It is a person who asks for our confidence. Across the centuries – and even into a new millennium of human history – he comes in search of us. He is not imprisoned in the past; he is not one whom we can only know about indirectly. Msgr Giussani makes a similar point I take it, when he writes of "a knowledge that cannot be reached by deduction."[9]

In any case, the Christian claim is that Love has become one of us and that we are called, therefore, to entrust our lives to this Love. No one should be compelled to offer such trust, and no one is simply unreasonable who declines to do so, just as no one can be compelled to fall in love or be charged with irrationality for failing to do so. But at the same time, we must say that, if I never fall in love, if I can never leap the chasm that separates trust from mistrust, certain great human goods will simply be unavailable to me.

There will, therefore, on Giussani's account, always be something a little mysterious about our response to the Christian claim that emerges in and from the Event of Jesus. No single way to leap the chasm from mistrust to trust can be delineated, but Giussani's comments about Jesus' first followers are nevertheless instructive. The call to follow involves – in different ways for different people – the necessity of renunciation and the necessity of public acknowledgment. That is, if we have found someone truly worthy of our trust, sooner or later we will want others to share that trust. "No relationship is complete and true if it is not strong enough to be revealed in public."[10] And, interestingly, given the way I have described the necessity of trust for the logic of personal relations, when he makes this point about public acknowledgment Giussani quite naturally turns to a similar example: "A girl might have a relationship with a boy for some time until, at one point, perhaps at her parents' prompting, she says to him: 'Come to my house. They want to meet you.' As long as the boy procrastinates, saying: 'No, let's wait a while,' and as long as he hesitates to acknowledge his relationship with her in front of his friends, the girl will rightly feel insecure and uneasy."[11] These are the first steps – somewhat different in each person's life, no doubt – on the other side of the chasm, within the life of trust.

There is at least one further aspect of Giussani's depiction of the Christian life that deserves mention here. The trust I have described involves a total giving of the self. The whole of one's life is seen as dependent on God, and "religiosity, insofar as it aims to make all actions depend on God, is called morality."[12] This gets us out of our own skins. It frees us from the great modern god of human autonomy, delivers us from the delusion of supposing that the only thing that counts in action is my own sincerity and authenticity. "To identify duty with one's own conscience," Giussani writes, "is a subtle form of imposing oneself on others, whereas conscience is the place where we perceive dependence, where the directive of Another emerges."[13] And this, contrary to what the modern world has for several centuries tried to teach us, is true freedom – freedom from bondage to our own wishes and desires, freedom *to respond* to Another."[14]

I have said that according to Giussani the Event at the origin of the Christian claim overturns, reshapes, and restructures our understanding of the religious sense of humanity. There is a further consequence of this teaching. A casual reader of *At the Origin of the Christian Claim* might suppose that the presence of God in Jesus is presented simply as the answer to a generalized religious quest that marks human life. And in some respects it is. But given that Event and given its continuing presence in our world through the life of the Church, it now gives us the very terms with which to articulate our quest. It helps us to understand what it is, in fact, that we actually desire – to trust with our whole heart Somebody with skin. Everyone is searching for Jesus. Ultimately, it is only in light of the answer that we learn how to ask our question. That, at any rate, is what Msgr Giussani believes we can learn at the origin of the Christian claim.

## NOTES

1 Mk 1:36f.
2 L. Giussani, *At the Origin of the Christian Claim*, trans. Viviane Hewitt (Montreal: McGill-Queen's University Press 1998), 31.
3 St Augustine, *Confessions* 6.5.
4 A.J. Heschel, *God in Search of Man*, quoted in L. Giussani, *The Religious Sense*, trans. John Zucchi. (Montreal: McGill-Queen's University Press 1977).
5 St Augustine, *Confessions* 7.21.
6 See Giussani, *At the Origin of the Christian Claim*, 86.
7 C.S. Lewis, *The Screwtape Letters* (New York: Macmillan 1961), 38.
8 C.S. Lewis, *The World's Last Night and Other Essays* (New York: Harcourt Brace Jovanovic 1960), 23.
9 Giussani, *At the Origin of the Christian Claim*, 85.
10 Ibid., 63.
11 Ibid.
12 Ibid., 87.
13 Ibid., 88.
14 Ibid.

# 16 Common Root and Christian Claim

## NEIL GILLMAN

I have learned a great deal from Msgr Giussani's two volumes *The Religious Sense* and *At the Origin of the Christian Claim,* and they have stimulated a wide range of reactions, unfortunately only very few of which I can describe here.[1] I read the books and speak to you now as a committed, believing, and observant Jew, a rabbi, and a Jewish professor of theology. At the core of my religious identity is the conviction that God's covenant with Israel is eternal, unshakable, and irreplaceable. I must say this as candidly and forcefully as I can, at the very outset, because it will inform everything else I have to say: I am a Jew who reads Giussani's writings through Jewish spectacles. That reading may resonate for some or many, or it may not, but that is all I can do.

My very first reaction upon reading the two books is to recall the writings of my late teacher, Rabbi Abraham Joshua Heschel. Heschel wrote a great deal, but his central theological message is contained in two books: *Man is Not Alone,* published in 1951, and *God in Search of Man,* published in 1956. The first book is subtitled *A Philosophy of Religion* and the second, *A Philosophy of Judaism.* Note the parallel with Giussani's two volumes: first *The Religious Sense* and then *At the Origin of the Christian Claim.* In each case the first volume deals with the religious claim in general, and the second, with a particular religious claim, the Jewish or the Christian.

But the parallel between the two authors goes far deeper. I read *The Religious Sense* with amazement because it was immediately apparent to me that Giussani's understanding of the religious experience is identical to Heschel's. In fact, I checked a few of his footnotes to convince myself that he was not quoting Heschel himself, so familiar to me was the language and mode of inquiry. There is one quotation from Heschel in chapter 10 of *The Religious Sense*, but there could have been three dozen of them. The book is totally Heschellial in its style, in its language, and also in its anthropological thrust. Heschel and Giussani share the notion that there is a human drive to receive God's presence and that it is there that religion begins.

Sometimes the language does differ. What Giussani calls the religious sense, Heschel calls "radical amazement," a term that Giussani also uses in his discussion. Heschel's version of the religious experience is a human encounter with what he calls "the meaning beyond the mystery" that pervades all things, to use his most striking definition, the mystery of the fact that there are facts in the first place. For Heschel, the mystery is nothing less than God's *pathos*, a term Heschel garnered from his study of the Prophets; it signifies God's ongoing reaching out – in nature, in history, and in the human experience – God's emotionally charged concern, God's aggressive pursuit of human acknowledgment. The encounter between our radical amazement and God's pathos is the heart of the religious experience. It is a momentary, ineffable (that is, beyond the powers of human conceptualization and human speech), preconceptual, presymbolic, intuitive sense of God's presence in and beyond all things, God's demanding presence in and beyond all things. And it can neither be confirmed nor denied; it can just be ignored or acknowledged. It is, Heschel claims, "an ontological proposition." To ask for proof is to concede that one has not had the experience in the first place. If you have had the experience, you know. This conceptualization is precisely Giussani's as well. Finally, it is accessible to all human beings simply by virtue of their common humanity. (Parenthetically, my reading of Giussani helped me understand why Heschel is so widely read in Christian circles.) Giussani's concluding chapters in his second volume – preeminently his chapter on prayer – also echo Heschel's superb phenomenological description of the act of prayer in Judaism.

And finally on this theme, one of my favourite Hasidic remarks from the Rabbi of Kotz was his answer to the question "Where is God?" which was, "Where you let Him in." Where the two thinkers – Heschel and Giussani – part company is in what comes between his first volume and the conclusion of his second. Giussani's second volume is devoted to demonstrating that Christianity represents the supreme exemplar of God entering into the realm of human history. Heschel's goal is to demonstrate the enduring power and relevance of the Jewish claim that it is God's relationship with Israel that serves as the exemplar of God's pathos. More significantly, they also part company on what Giussani claims is the "crime" – his word – that rests in the Christian claim that "I am the religion, the one and only way." Heschel never makes this claim for Judaism, nor does Judaism require him to make that claim. For Heschel, as for all authentic Jews, any authentic believer in the God of Israel will share in God's age to come.

What both thinkers do in their respective second volumes is to clothe that original primary human encounter with God in specific symbols, myths, narratives, rituals, liturgies, and institutions. (I use the terms "symbols" and "myths" here advisedly because of Giussani's many references to the writings of Mircea Eliade who pioneered our understanding of religion as symbolic and mythical.) Myths and symbols form the decisive point where religion ends and religions begin. Judaism and Christianity differ in the symbolic systems they use to reflect, concretize, and institutionalize our common experience of God in the world. For Heschel, for example, the ritual observance of the Sabbath – what he calls in one of his most memorable metaphors a "cathedral in time" – serves to create a certain sensibility, an openness, a receptivity to the very possibility of experiencing God's presence. The only way I can convey that to you is to urge you to observe one Sabbath as the traditional Jew observes the Sabbath to understand the openness that the ritualization of the day creates in us.

For Giussani the primary and ultimate site of God's revelation is in the person of Jesus. He traces, with great precision, the gradual emergence of Jesus' own answer to the question Who am I? Who is he? Only shortly before his death, does he identify himself as son of God. It was this identification that, according to Giussani, shocked the Jewish leadership of that time and led them to brand him a blasphemer. That claim, that Jesus was the son of God, Giussani insists, is "incomparable."[2] Through Jesus, the Infinite has entered into history as a presence that speaks to us as one of us.[3]

But I would reply that it is very much comparable. It is in fact a version of a much earlier claim made by the Hebrew Scriptures, that God did intervene in history, first in God's creation of the world and of human beings; later in God's choice of Abraham and his posterity as witnesses to his presence; then in the Exodus from Egypt and at Sinai, where God's presence was witnessed by six hundred thousand Israelites; then through the Prophets and through Am Yisrael, the collective Israelite community and the Temple, the place where God's glory dwelled and where the centre of Jewish corporal life served as the visible sense of God's presence in the world. As Giussani claims about Jesus, the Sinai revelation and the building of the temple also took place in space and time, in the full flowering of human life. The Bible seems to say, would you want to see God, look at Israel! Look at Torah! Look at the Temple! Even more, as Heschel used to say, look at every human being who was created in the image of God!

Early Christianity wrote a *midrash* on that claim, substituting the single person, Jesus of Nazareth, for collective Israel. That is the dispute about the Servant Psalms in Isaiah, who was the suffering servant. The early Church understood itself as the new Israel, Jesus as the new Torah, and the Gospels as the record of the new covenant. But this Jew must ask, What then was added to God's dispensation that was not already fully present in the older one?

There are two very interesting passages: one is Psalm 91:15 and the other Isaiah 63:9, in which the authors portray God as suffering with God's people. Psalm 91:15 says, "I am with him in his pain." It sounds a little Clintonesque, but this is before Clinton. And Isaiah 63:9 says, "In all of their pain, God, He is pained." The portrayal of God, then, is not the portrayal of the philosophers, not the transcendent God who has got it all together but, rather, a vulnerable God. Heschel used to say that everybody thinks this God is omnipotent. But this God got nothing that he wanted. In the entire history of humankind, the entire history chronicled by the Bible, he is never successful; he is a total failure. He has never succeeded in producing a generation of faithful, righteous people, and he shows himself in the Bible as being terribly vulnerable. So the whole notion of the God who is vulnerable, who suffers, led the rabbis later to portray God as being in the slavery camp of Egypt. Where was God when our ancestors were in Egypt? God was building bricks. And where was God in all the series of later traumas? God was in Auschwitz, with my ancestors. Now there is not a big stretch from that notion of God to saying, in fact, "God died." Very few Jews would make that claim, although it has been made in a number of post-holocaust Jewish theological statements. That God could suffer, that he was vulnerable, is a classically traditional Jewish claim, and it is there, I think, that the Christian notion of God, a human being who dies, finds its ultimate source.

The claim that God revealed himself in space and time, at a particular moment and to a particular community, as a Fact (to use Giussani's term), is quite properly scandalous. We call it the "scandal of particularity." We who are trained in Western philosophy are uncomfortable with the notion that God works within particular historical moments. God is supposed to be above all of that. However, it was not Christianity that first invoked the scandal of particularity but rather Israel. Giussani thinks that my ancestors of old were concerned that Jesus' claim would dilute the purity of their monotheism. The claim, Giussani believes, disturbed "the very idea of God which they honoured and defended against any equivocation, against anything that could falsify and adulterate their pure conception of Yahweh."[4] That statement is unbelievably on target but unbelievably wrong. Surely, this is not the case.

Israel knew that this transcendent God must appear in human images. The primary examples are the Torah and the Temple. But Jews never worshipped the Torah, nor did they worship the Temple. That is precisely why Judaism thrived for two millennia without a Temple. They simply substituted the Synagogue for the Temple. The difference between these two images and the golden calf was that Jews did worship the calf – and thus tumbled into idolatry. These symbols are supposed to be transparent, not opaque; they are windows through which we approach the transcendent. But they are not God and should not be worshipped in and of themselves. An absolutely superb contribution to the theological debate on this role of the symbol, the image in religion, was the Metropolitan Opera's staging of Arnold Schönberg's Moses and Aaron in the autumn of 1999. It was an unbelievably powerful theological experience that centred around the debate between God and the images of God. To quote Paul Tillich, "the task of theology is to preserve God from the aspirations of God's images."[5]

In short, what troubles me about Giussani's discussion of the emergence of the Christian claim is that it posits an overly sharp distinction between the two faith traditions, too early. There were many Judaisms abounding in first-century Palestine. One of those was a reading of Judaism that thoroughly maintained its Jewish character but also acknowledged that with Jesus something new had entered the world. But Jesus himself was a Jew, as were all his early followers. Jesus spoke of familiar Jewish things to his community. They did not perceive him – at least not until some decades later – as introducing a schismatic community. His goal was to bring Jews back to God. That role was perfectly familiar to his contemporaries; he was a prophet, he believed that God intervened in history, he may even have called himself Messiah – all of this was familiar to his Jewish contemporaries. That he was the "son of God" was also familiar to them from 2 Samuel 7:14, where God identifies himself as father and King Solomon as "a son to me." Little of this would have overly disturbed my ancestors. Jesus' death was his apparent defeat, which the early Church transformed into his ultimate victory. But that was much later.

And that transformation led, tragically, to the doctrine of Christian supercession, which has haunted the Jew throughout our history. I notice also, parenthetically, that Giussani relies a great deal on John. And it is, of course, the passion in the John version that is read in church on Good Friday, and it is precisely this reading that led to countless persecutions of my ancestors throughout the Middle Ages.

In fact, in many of the most fascinating conversations I have had with Christian theologians in recent years, they have spoken of the struggle that they have in using the John version of the passion and in framing it in such a way that it is not offensive to Jewish ears. I had thought that supercessionism was at an end, but apparently it has returned, or it never left.

Christianity came to believe that God was incarnate in a single human being. That belief was both its unique contribution to our understanding of God's revelation and, at the same time, its greatest vulnerability: the constant temptation to worship the image in place of God. Christ should take the believer beyond himself to God; if it blocks the way to God, it has become a golden calf – the ultimate sin.

Finally, what Giussani has accomplished superbly well is to present us with a powerful apologia for Christianity – apologia in the original and best sense of the term: a rigorous defense of the Christian faith. We must fully acknowledge the legitimacy – even the truth – of that claim for Christians. However, it is not my claim, nor is it my truth. I am convinced that no human being can possibly have access to God's truth in its purity; that's what makes us human and God, God. What we have is our individual and communal perceptions of God and of God's message for humanity. Judaism and Christianity share a good deal of that perception – but not all of it. It is precisely those differences in our perceptions that make theological exchange between our communities so necessary. We can thank Msgr Giussani for encouraging that debate.

## NOTES

1 L. Giussani, *The Religious Sense*, trans. John Zucchi (Montreal: McGill-Queen's University Press 1997); *At the Origin of the Christian Claim*, trans. Viviane Hewitt (Montreal: McGill-Queen's University Press 1998).
2 Ibid., 33.
3 See Giussani, *The Religious Sense*, 143.
4 Ibid., 143.
5 Giussani, *At the Origin of the Christian Claim*, 78.

# 17 Abraham and Liberty

## RAVAN FARHÂDI

I could never have imagined that in the United Nations, where I first presented a version of this chapter and where discussion of secular subjects limits anybody who would like to mention the name of God, I would have faced an audience of such distinguished personalities. I was very much impressed by what had been said before I spoke about a small but very dense book that takes a great deal of time and attention to read, Luigi Giussani's *At the Origin of the Christian Claim*.

All theologies face the following question: does human effort suffice as the source of faith, or, rather, does God make himself known to the human being? Answering this question would greatly contribute to situating the believer on the threshold of the third millennium. Msgr Giussani does offer an answer: in Christianity, he explains, the Mystery makes himself known by invading and dominating history. Giussani presents particularly remarkable quotations from the Christian Scriptures to validate his concept. He may be selective in choosing, but he succeeds in building a solid group of themes. There is no doubt that he addresses only intellectual Christians: he has written a book for very knowledgeable and intelligent readers.

Human beings are described in the book as discovering themselves in the presence of the Mystery, because they have already been invited and attracted by the hidden attendance of the mystery itself. Let us recognize that while Giussani writes within the Christian theological tradition, he proposes certain innovative modes of argument. There are interesting passages in the book, such as those explaining how human beings may proceed toward the path of exploitation instead of love. This path leads toward "human disorder."[1] The Christian tradition attributes this to a disorder human beings, because of their own faults, inherit "from the very origins of the human race" and that is "contrary to God's design … This is what the Christian tradition calls *original sin*."[2]

The eminent author points out that the Christian faithful have to welcome the message of salvation coming from Jesus. "This redemption [however] is not accomplished automatically." Jesus Christ has to be solicited and accepted by the faithful, who have "to collaborate actively … This happens through love that is free" and "freedom is love."[3] The author reminds us of the words of Jesus Christ quoted in the Gospel (Jn 8:31) "You know the truth and the truth will make you free."

Let us hope that the twenty-first century will be a century of dialogue. On 4 November 1988 the General Assembly of the United Nations unanimously adopted a resolution originally proposed by President Khatami of Iran to designate the year 2001 as the United Nations Year of Dialogue among civilizations. No doubt the dialogue between religions has an important place in this process. An Islamic symposium on the subject took place from 3 to 5 May 1999 in Teheran. Many Muslim scholars who had been invited by the Organization of Islamic Conference and who were guided by the noble Islamic teaching and values on human dignity and equality, tolerance, peace, and justice for mankind, were present. The symposium issued a statement of general principles favouring the promotion of the culture of dialogue.

Msgr Giussani refers to Abraham in many parts of his book and says that when Abraham is asked by God to sacrifice his son he "is a paradigm of the drama of man in his full stature."[4] In response to this statement, I would like to discuss of the place of Abraham in the Qur'an, a book that Muslims consider to be entirely revelation from God.

One of the recitations from the Qur'an, that is most often repeated during ritual Muslim prayers is the following:

Say: He is Allah, the One and Only;
Allah, the Eternal, Absolute;
He begets not, nor is He begotten;
And there is none like unto Him.[5]

God showed Abraham with certitude the glories behind the magnificent powers and laws of the physical universe and demonstrated to him the folly of worshiping the stars and other heavenly bodies.[6]

The Quoranic passage describing the readiness of Abraham to sacrifice his own son proves that the father and the son were both ready to submit to and to pass the trial.[7] To understand Abraham's place in Islam, one must remember that God commands the Muslim faithful:

O you who believe!
Bow down, prostrate yourselves,
And adore your Lord;
And do good;
That you may prosper.
He has chosen you,
And has imposed no difficulties on you in religion;
It is the cult of your father Abraham.[8]

Notice that God is calling here upon all those who believe, Arabs and non-Arabs. Therefore, Abraham is the spiritual father of all the Muslims in the world, whether they be Chinese, Nigerian, or of any other nationality. To the Arabs, Abraham is also a biological father, as he is for the Jews.

The Quoranic account of the life of Abraham (peace be upon him) has details of his life not only in Mesopotamia but also in Mecca, where, in accordance with the Islamic scripture, he raised, together with his son Ismael, the first building of the *Ka'ba* (a small stone building in the form of a cube). As part of the ritual of the *Hajj*, Muslims perform the circumambulation of the *Ka'ba* but also celebrate a special prayer on the area nearby, called the "standing point of Abraham."

God teaches in the Qur'an that the Abrahamic way is the superior one and says:

Who can be better in religion
Than one who submits his whole self to Allah,
Does good,
And follows the way of Abraham
The true in faith?
For Allah took Abraham for a friend.[9]

For Muslims, God describes the personality of Abraham. He deserves to be followed.

Abraham was indeed a model,
Devoutly obedient to Allah,
And true in faith,
And he did not join gods with Allah:
He showed his gratitude for the favors of Allah,
Who chose him,
And guided him to a Straight Way.
And We gave him Good in this world,
And he will be, in the Hereafter,

In the ranks of the Righteous.
So We have taught you the inspired message,
Follow the ways of Abraham,
The True in Faith,
And he did not join gods with Allah.[10]

Muslims read the praising of God by Abraham (peace be upon him) as recorded in the Qur'an. Abraham expresses his gratitude to the Creator, the Provider, the Bestower of health, the One Who causes death but Who also resuscitates, the One Who forgives the faithful:

The Lord and Cherisher of the Worlds;
Who created me ... it is He who guides me;
Who gives me food and drink,
And when I am ill, it is He Who cures me;
Who will cause me to die, and then to live (again);
And who, I hope, will forgive me my faults on the Day of Judgment.
O my Lord! bestow wisdom on me,
And join me with the righteous.[11]

When Abraham had no choice but to emigrate, his vision was inspired by the Lord, and he said: "I will go to my Lord! / He will surely guide me!."[12]

Mohammad (peace be upon him), the last messenger of God, has received the divine guidance to pronounce the following prayer:

Say: "Verily, my Lord has guided me
To a Way that is straight – a religion of right –
The Path trod by Abraham,
The true in faith,
And he, certainly, did not join gods with Allah."
Say: "Truly, my prayer and my service of sacrifice,
My life and my death,
Are all for Allah,
The Cherisher of the Worlds:
No partner has He:
This I am commanded,
And I am the first of those who bow to His Will.[13]

During the five daily ritual prayers at the end of the recitations, Muslims, while they are seated, recite an invocation asking for the blessing and the peace of God to be "bestowed upon Mohammad as it was bestowed upon Abraham." This is how practising Muslims pronounce the name of Abraham several times a day and during each ritual prayer.

Now I think I must also quote something about Moses (peace be upon him) from a passage of the Qur'an that proves how he was near to God, who says:

Also mention in the Book
The story of Moses:
For he was specially chosen,
And he was a Messenger
And a prophet.

And We called him
From the right side of Mount Sinai,
And made him draw near Us,
For mystic converse.[14]

The messengers of God are praised in the Qur'an:

We gave Moses the Book,
And followed him up with a succession of Messengers;
We gave Jesus the son of Mary clear Signs
And strengthened him with the holy spirit.[15]

Muslims also believe that Jesus, whose birth was miraculous, whose mother was virgin, spoke while he was in the cradle and gave his witness about his mission:

He said: "I am indeed a servant of Allah:
He has given me Revelation
And made me a prophet;
And He has made me blessed
Wheresoever I be,
And has enjoined on me Prayer and Charity
As long as I live;
He has made me kind to my mother,
And not overbearing or miserable;.
So Peace is on me,
The day I was born,
The day that I die,
And the day that I shall be raised up to life again![16]

NOTES

1 L. Giussani, *At the Origin of the Christian Claim*, trans. Viviane Hewitt (Montreal: McGill-Queen's University Press 1998), 95.
2 Ibid.
3 Ibid., 96.
4 Ibid., 9.
5 Q. 112:1–4. *The Qur'an*. Trans. Abdullah Yusuf Ali (New York: Tahrike Tarsile Qur'an 1998). Q. 112:1–4: 422–3.
6 Q. 6:74–9: 82.
7 Q. 37:3–113: 292–6.
8 Q. 22:77–8: 219.
9 Q. 4:125: 58.
10 Q. 16:120–3: 175.
11 Q. 26:77–83: 240.
12 Q. 37:99: 296.
13 Q. 6:161–3: 90.
14 Q. 19:51–2: 195.
15 Q. 2:87: 8.
16 Q. 19:30–3: 194.

# 18 Intercultural Dialogue

## SHINGEN TAKAGI

I first had the privilege of meeting Msgr Giussani ten years ago at Mount Koya, a sacred site in Japan. Mount Koya, or Koyasan, was established as the seat of Shingon Buddhism in the ninth century, nearly twelve hundred years ago, by the monk Kukai, or Kobo Daishi, as he is posthumously known. Kobo Daishi was also a renowned educator. In the year 828 he founded perhaps the first private college in the world, locating it in the capital of Japan of that time. The school, called the Shugeishuchiin, provided an ideal educational program for the common people. Msgr Giussani was especially interested in Kobo Daishi's educational philosophy.

I cannot go into great detail about the educational philosophy of Kobo Daishi, but to summarize, he believed in developing the full potential that all people are endowed with equally. Expressed in different terms, he believed in helping people to realize the true nature of the self. When this nature is recognized in oneself, it can also be recognized in others. In *Il rischio educativo* Giussani states that regardless of differences in culture or tradition, the minds of all persons are in their nature fundamentally equal.[1] The same idea is expressed by Kobo Daishi.

More particularly, Giussani's statement is in agreement with Kobo Daishi's philosophy of *San Shin Byodo*, or the identity of the three minds. The three minds are the mind of the self, the minds of all beings, and the minds of the Buddhas, who have perceived reality. There is no fundamental difference between these three. All are equal and identical. They comprise what is likened to a vast net that connects everything in the universe to everything else. All life is interconnected. This is known in Buddhism as *pratityasamutpada*, or conditioned origination.

Kobo Daishi identified the mind of the Buddha as the mind of compassion. Buddhism may alternatively be called the religion of compassion. More specifically, compassion consists of two aspects. There is *maitri*, which gives happiness to all beings, and *karuna*, which removes their suffering. Kobo Daishi stated that such happiness is to be given to beings regardless of our relationship with them. It must be given to all beings equally.

"Beings" in the broad sense, refers to all things existing throughout the universe. The mind of the Buddha, or the mind of compassion, has as its object not only humankind but everything occurring in nature, including animals and plants. *San Shin Byodo*, or the identity of the three minds, challenges us to rethink our idea of a universe centred on human beings.

A key feature of the twentieth and twenty-first centuries is the development of a world society based on technology. Unlike any civilization that has existed on the earth thus far, we are developing a civilization that is not based in a particular locality. It would seem that to be modern, it is necessary to participate in this civilization. But the industrialization that comes with it causes us to look no further than material pleasure and wordly delights. We are thus losing our ability to realize our true nature and are able to think only in terms of our smaller selves. Religion can help us to avoid this fate and recover our sense of our true nature, to express it in our daily lives, and to live up to our potential.

What will the twenty-first century hold for humanity? Along with the development of a world society, we can expect clashes between different cultures and polarization. The economic, political, and religious strife we see in the world now reflects this trend. However, Giussani's concept of *ecumenismo* (ecumenism) accepts other cultures in order to develop human potential and it provides a key to averting intercultural strife. At the root of this concept is the need for dialogue between different cultures and different religions. Of course, because different cultures and religions exist within totally different cultural frameworks, true dialogue is difficult to achieve. As the world becomes smaller every day, due to evolutionary developments in communication technology, we must seriously consider how to achieve meaningful communication that leads to mutual understanding.

When Giussani speaks of accepting other cultures, he suggests that cultural frameworks are not at all static. On the contrary, they contain an enormous amount of creative energy. By focusing this creative energy on dialogue, each culture can preserve its framework while progressing to a higher level of intellectual development. This is what Giussani means when he says that by accepting other cultures, we can develop the full human potential.

For his part, Kobo Daishi pointed to the need to discover deeper meanings in the teachings of the historical Buddha as they evolved; he emphasized the need to step out of fixed conventional categories. Kobo Daishi focused not on the structural frameworks of different religions but on the deepest meaning underlying them. In that deepest level of each framework he saw the truth.

It is clear that Giussani does not imply cultural uniformity when he speaks of accepting other cultures. While recognizing that different cultures and religions, possess their own original frameworks, he suggests that we must overcome low-level differences to cooperate and coexist at a higher level. Kobo Daishi calls this the world of the *Mandala*. The worldview of the *Mandala* is one of coexistence in harmony between different cultures and religions.

Through our deep meditation and prayer we realize our true nature; we realize that our true nature is linked to all beings and that we all share in the same life. At this point we transcend the frameworks that emphasize the differences between cultures and religions and that make dialogue so difficult. Meaningful dialogue and communication then become possible.

The history of the future will be written not through strife and opposition but through true dialogue. We must not forget that this dialogue will take place not solely between different cultures and religions but also between humans and nature itself. We must listen to the voice of nature, in which we can hear the voice of the divine.

What modern humans search for from technology is material and economic wealth or social convenience. The result is material wealth but spiritual poverty. What, then, do we truly need to search for? Let me tell you a little story. One dark evening when I was hurrying home, I came across a man looking for something under a street lamp. I asked him, "Are you looking for something?" He answered, "Yes, I'm looking for something I dropped. I dropped it over there in the dark, but it's brighter over here, so that's why I'm looking here." This is the story of modern men and women, searching under the street lamp. They are trying to find what they are looking for in the place they think it will be easy to find it, in material wealth or a better lifestyle. But they are looking in the wrong place for the answer they seek. The answer can be found in religion; through religion they can find the truth.

Kobo Daishi recommended isolated forests and mountains as the place to engage in religious practice. In our terms, he meant a natural environment. Human beings originally lived as an integral part of nature. But as they developed the idea that the natural world was there solely for their exploitation, they tried to control nature, and became alienated from it. In reality, they alienated themselves from their real nature. At that point, they lost the ability to hear the voice of nature and started living selfishly by their own cunning. They then started to destroy the natural world.

Kobo Daishi had this to say about the relationship between the human mind and the natural environment. The environment changes under the influence of mind. When the mind is impure, the environment will be soiled. The mind is also influenced by the environment. When the natural environment is calm, the mind is enriched. Our minds and the natural environment are closely bound; when we realize this bond our actions are naturally in accord with the Way. When we realize that the human mind and nature are bound together, we can hear the voice of nature. Another way to express this is to say that we can hear the voice of God.

NOTE

1 L. Giussani, *Il rischio educativo: Come creazione di personalità e storia* (Turin: SEI 1995); English edition: *The Risk of Education*, trans. R. M. Giammanco Frongia (New York: Crossroad 2001).

# 19 The Religious Sense and Modern Man

DAVID J. HOROWITZ

I am neither theologian nor philosopher, so I can speak about the religious sense and modern man only from my own experience. I am, after all, a modern man.

In 1997 I was privileged to participate at the Meeting in Rimini sponsored by the Catholic movement Communion and Liberation. Attending the Meeting meant that I had to prepare myself to speak about who I am and what I do, as well as to play my music for what I hoped would be an appreciative audience. In the process of writing my remarks, I found myself wanting to look at my life and my work in a deeper way. I began to wonder about the questions, Why? and How? What do I believe in? What do I stand for? What meaning does my life and work have for the world, for this audience? What meaning does it have for me? I was looking for words to describe those thoughts and feelings, which I was used to expressing only through the non-verbal medium of music. And in searching for these words, these answers, I found that I was turning inwards to confront the truth of my essential self, that fundamental core of memory and desire from which all spiritual journeys begin.

My first sense of religious identity was formed, and somehow lost, nearly half a century ago in an orthodox synagogue in Brooklyn. The congregation was made up of pious people, immigrants and sons of immigrants from Jewish communities in Eastern Europe. What I remember most vividly were the old men, the patriarchs of the community – the old men with their long gray beards, their prayer shawls, their endless swaying back and forth as they intoned the ancient words of the Hebrew service. They seemed to me of another place and time, representing an earlier, more primitive stage of human development. Was their old world more true somehow than the one in which they now found themselves? How could they inhabit the same place and time as the classrooms and playgrounds of my daily life? What was the meaning of the seemingly automatic nature of their mumbled prayers, the mysterious music rising and falling in great rhythmic waves? Was I, by virtue of birth and name, a part of this mystery?

I remember dreading the approach of my Bar Mitzvah, that Sabbath morning upon which I was to stand before these men to recite my portion of the Torah. I had seen them touch hands to lips, then reach out to touch the holy scrolls as they were brought down the aisles of the temple. Would I then be touched in the same way by merely reading from the scrolls, thereby taking the first step towards becoming one of them? Would I be initiated into the mysteries behind the murmuring, and become one with the hypnotic rhythm of their swaying, back and forth, back and forth?

The answer to these questions, I decided in my thirteen-year-old wisdom, was a resounding no: somewhere along the way, I had missed that first crucial turning, that special moment of understanding and faith that ushers a child into his religious heritage. And now I would never follow in the footsteps of my beloved grandfather Abraham, who had died shortly before my Bar Mitzvah. In fact, if God had denied him the joy of seeing me come of age, taking my rightful place beside him, swaying back and forth with him in perfect synchrony, intoning the sacred words like all the generations of Jews before us, well then, that God was no friend of mine. It was the confused logic of a child, and it sealed my thoughts about God and spirituality away in a safe place, far away from the grief and loss I felt.

When I finally had a family of my own, my wife would urge me to share my heritage with our children, so I would light the Hanukkah candles, feeling a bit of a fraud. I covered my head and murmured benedictions somehow remembered from long ago. And then I would feel a kind of warmth spreading through my body, find myself choking back tears. But tears of what? Of regret, of loss, of rage, of joy? I couldn't say, but the light in my own children's eyes meant more to me than anything else. I knew then that if I could break through the wall of silence that separated me from my own humanity, I could offer them and myself something worth cherishing.

But it was years before I began to deal with my personal identity issues, and then only after a particularly dark period in my life, one of clinical depression. Coming out of those shadows was truly a personal rebirth. I chose life over death, love over indifference, courage over fear. As I see it now, there is nothing more intrinsically human than the acknowledgment of a reality beyond ourselves, the promise of fulfillment of all the dreams that beckon us across the threshold of consciousness.

I write music: I am a composer. What I do is inextricably bound up with who I am. Music occupies the greatest portion of my waking life, and a great deal of my dream world as well. Making music draws upon the deep levels where my sense of humanity lies and provides a daily opportunity to share my human-ness with the world around me. In music, I can express the inexpressible. Music, which like all art (and religion) seeks to transcend the mundane by universalizing it, forces us to pay attention to meaning. I may have retreated from *religion* but never from a true religious sense, since music is a representation of the spiritual life of the composer made manifest for all to hear and experience, whether the composer feels aloof from or ignored by God or, at the other extreme, experiences a kind of religious rapture, as did Handel writing *The Messiah*. The results of the composer's labours, the music he has created, cause the listener to become engaged in the process, as a witness to the composer's thoughts and feelings on a level of consciousness that Wordsworth called "too deep for tears."

To write music is to bare one's soul. I speak to the world in this nonverbal language and people seem to understand precisely what I mean. For me, this is language directly from my heart, no matter what has occasioned its creation. For this reason I believe that the work that I do has meaning beyond its value as a marketable commodity. I am fortunate to have found a comfortable living by translating emotions into music. (I specialize in *nostalgia* and yearning, I'm not so good with "everyday contentment.") But it turns out that in music our inner conflicts provide an artistic tension, the compelling force, the humanity. I find that in music I speak my truth.

At the same time, I admit the irony of the fact that for years I have been writing tender, emotional music without understanding its source in my soul, wondering, as many composers have, just where the music comes from. Beethoven himself wondered the same thing; he said: "You may ask me where I obtain my ideas. I cannot answer this with any certainty; they come unbidden, spontaneously or unspontaneously. I may grasp them with my hands in the open air, while walking in the woods, in the stillness of night, at each morning. Stimulated by those moods which poets turn into words, I turn my ideas into tones which resound, roar and rage until at last they stand before me in the form of notes."[1]

But I would go a step further and say that the mystery of which Beethoven speaks, the origin of the creative act, derives from the artist's ability to confront the greatest mystery of all, what I have come to call the Ultimate Reality. And to live, as Beethoven did, in almost constant contact with this higher reality, this primal truth, is to be consumed by a quest for artistic perfection. The quest for the one true answer is never-ending. This state of being, as experienced by the greatest artists, leads inevitably to the creation of the greatest art, which is infused with a sacred spirit. And it is the supreme test of the artist's courage and dedication to continue the search, continue to produce great work, knowing that there is, ever beckoning, the promise of a perfect beauty to which s/he can aspire but seldom, if ever, achieve. This test has driven some artists to madness, like Schumann and Van Gogh. For myself, a musical composition is never simply a question of filling the air with notes; it is meeting a fundamental challenge of the soul. Stravinsky said, "The profound meaning of music and its essential aim … is to promote a communion, a union of man with his fellow man and with the Supreme Being." Through my own lifelong involvement with music, I have come to agree, to feel that even my music is an acknowledgment of a further reality of the human spirit, the potential of all we can be and feel, that which beckons us "from across the threshold of consciousness."[2]

It is both surprising and fitting that preparing to present my work at Rimini – the body of work which is in fact the expression of what I am and wish the world to know – should have led me to the life-affirming experience it proved to be. Making music is as natural to me as breathing and, I believe, a God-given gift of musical talent. I never expected it to lead me once again back to the mystery of those old men, with their long gray beards and prayer shawls. I was delighted to read the following passage in Msgr Giussani's *Religious Sense*: "The attraction of beauty follows a paradoxical trajectory: the more something is beautiful, the more it refers one on to something else. The greater the art (let us think of music) the more it flings wide open, does not confine, desire. It is a sign of something else."[3]

This "something else" is precisely what I wish to express, to acknowledge and to seek, in every aspect of my life. It is what I saw as a child, long ago, in that synagogue in Brooklyn. My heart has been brought full circle, back to spiritual matters. I begin to think that perhaps there is meaning for me there, still, in the mystery of the old men, murmuring prayers and fingering their shawls. In Rimini I met a great rabbi, David Rosen, who had come from Jerusalem to enjoy the energy and enthusiasm of the Meeting. After speaking with him for only a few minutes in the lobby of our hotel, the path back to my religious and cultural heritage seemed clearer.

If my reading of Giussani's book is correct, these are the appropriate issues for a human being: to recognize the transcendental nature of the human spirit – we all want to move beyond everyday reality, to push for engagement and community with our fellow human beings, and to remember that the religious sense is *the voyage of discovery* about self, meaning, and whatever truth we may come to know.

I feel very alive and full of the religious sense, and very much a work in progress. I would like to close by reading W.H. Auden's joyous poem "In Memory of William Butler Yeats":

Follow, poet, follow right
To the bottom of the night,
With your unconstraining voice
Still persuade us to rejoice;

With the farming of a verse
Make a vineyard of the curse,
Sing of human unsuccess
In rapture of distress;

In the deserts of the heart
Let the healing fountain start,
In the prison of his days
Teach the free man how to praise.[4]

## NOTES

1 From a written conversation with Louis Schlosser (1822 or 1823), quoted in S. Morgenstern, ed., *Composers on Music* (New York: Pantheon 1956)
2 Igor Stravinsky, *Poetics of Music* (New York: Vintage Books 1947)
3 L. Giussani, *The Religious Sense*, trans. John Zucchi (Montreal: McGill-Queen's University Press 1997).
4 From *Another Time* (New York: Random House 1940).

# 20 Educating in Reason

## GIORGIO FELICIANI

Like any university professor I have written a great deal over the course of my long academic career, but never has a text for publication involved me so personally as did the few pages that I wrote as a preface to the volume *Porta la speranza* by Luigi Giussani.[1] It did so because the author and his proposal for the Christian life enunciated in his first writings of were and still are decisive for my life. I am referring above all to the writings that were completed between 1959 and 1964 and collected in the first section of *Porta la speranza* under the title "Educare alla chiesa," because I can say of those years in which the great adventure of the Communion and Liberation movement began, "I was there."

I heard Giussani for the first time in 1957 at a meeting to prepare for the great Mission of Milan, promoted by the then Cardinal Montini, and I was favourably impressed by his personality, but with no immediate effect. Only several months later did I go to Giussani (I must confess without great expectations) for advice on a rather banal question. In my family and in school I had received a Catholic education, but I found myself without a communitarian context. Thus, I felt a desire for companionship and hoped to find it in a Catholic association, but among so many, I did not know which to choose. And when Giussani asked about my motivation, I could only say, "I want to do something Christian together with others." And he replied, "Well, then why don't you stay with us?" I immediately accepted the proposal, obviously without understanding anything but that it interested me. I could certainly not have imagined then that in that moment I had met the charism that, through this practically unknown priest, the Lord had prepared for me and that the acceptance of that specific invitation would in time determine my entire life.

Bit by bit, as I immersed myself in the life of Gioventù Studentesca (Student Youth), spending all my spare time there, I grew amazed with this life that I had not only never seen but had never even imagined could exist and that completely and unexpectedly answered the desires of my heart. In fact, Gioventù Studentesca provided a completely new experience in the Catholic world of the time. It was described by Giussani as a "movement," a term that is common today but at the time was almost, if not entirely, unknown. To the great scandal of various parish pastors and even of some eminent Catholic intellectuals, the movement presented itself in the schools with no mediation by the traditional ecclesiastical structures, uniting boys and girls, accepting anyone who wanted to be even partially involved without demanding that they become members, and operating with no set projects or programs. It was, in fact, animated by only one concern: to call people to Christ, making the most of the particular circumstances of the time and the people who became involved. This state of affairs was so new and original that Cardinal Montini himself confessed to Giussani that he did not understand his methods. However, this difficulty did not stop the great pastor of the Ambrosian Church from recognizing the considerable fruits of his priest's actions and encouraging him to go ahead.

In this short chapter it is not possible to present the experience of Gioventù Studentesca in all its richness and vivacity. It is already clearly and exhaustively described by its founder in the essays offered in *Porta la speranza*, and those who would like to know more on the subject can simply read it. However, I would like to underline how Giussani's decision to abandon the tranquility of his theological studies (some valuable and promising results of which are collected under the title "Prospettive sul protestantesimo e l'ortodossia" in the second section of the volume) arose from an exceptionally lucid judgment about the dramatic historical situation of the Church in Italy and in particular about the Christian presence, or better, absence, in the schools. As he wrote in passages that have, unfortunately, proven prophetic:

In the mid-1950s ... common opinion held that the Church was a staunch presence in Italian society ... but its weight and solidity were founded more than anything else on these two orders of motives: on the one hand the mass participation in the Catholic cult, often due to the force of inertia, and on the other hand – paradoxically – to a strictly political power, very badly used from the ecclesiastical point of view. In fact, neither the Church nor those party organisms which were its political manifestation showed any understanding of the importance of cultural creativity and thus of the problem of education ... [The Church was] still a staunch presence in Italian society ... but only as the outcome of a past which had not yet been overturned by an attack which every indication showed was being actively prepared in those forges of new men, of new society – the schools and universities. At the time it appeared clear to me that no tradition or, indeed, no human experience can challenge history and stand against the flow of time, except insofar as it comes to express and communicate itself in ways that posses cultural dignity."[2]

Thus it is not surprising that this concern characterized Gioventù Studentesca from the outset, to the point that culture, together with charity and mission, was identified as one of its fundamental dimensions. Giussani wrote in 1959 in the methodological directives for his movement that Culture must be able to offer the meaning of everything. The truly cultured person is one who has come at possessing the *nexus* that links one thing to another and all things among themselves ... If the person of Christ gives meaning to every person and to every thing, there is nothing in the world and in our life that can live for itself, that can avoid being invincibly linked to Him. Thus the true Christian cultural dimension is realized in *comparing* the truth of His person and our life in all its implications."[3] This comparison was also continually and systematically pursued and realized in Gioventù Studentesca through a multitude of initiatives in the most varied fields, such as history, philosophy, literature, music and theatre.

But in this context it is necessary at least to mention an essential aspect of the method of Giussani: education in reason. As he has taught for over twenty-five years and as he does not tire of repeating today, if reason constitutes the "distinctive characteristic of that level of nature that we call man, that is, the capacity to be aware of reality according to the totality of its factors ... this cognitive relation with the real must develop in a reasonable way; that is, the steps for establishing this relationship must be determined by adequate motives."[4] Evidently nothing can be excluded from this requirement, but it would be better to say that above all it appertains to faith in Christ and the Church. And, in fact, Giussani has documented the reasonableness of this faith in his *PerCorso*.

My purpose in this short contribution has been to speak of ideas and facts that began in the past but that continue to be so alive and present today that they determine my existence and that of many others. The proposal that Msgr Giussani advanced in the 1950s and 1960s is identical to what he presents today to his friends and to all those who want to listen to him or read what he continues to write. Anyone who, like me, has had the good fortune to follow him for forty years can attest, without fear of being contradicted, that Msgr Giussani has always said the same things! And the Gioventù Studentesca is anything but dead: like a child that grows it has developed into a movement present in eighty countries, with Giussani, going stronger than ever, continuing to lead with youthful boldness.


NOTES

Translated by Sheila Beatty

1 L. Giussani, *Porta la speranza* (Genoa: Marietti 1997).
2 L. Giussani, *Il Movimento di Comunione e Liberazione* (Milan: Jaca Book 1987), 13.
3 L. Giussani, "Gioventù Studentesca: riflessioni sopra un'esperienza," in *Il cammino al vero è un'esperienza* (Turin: SEI, 1995), 13.
4 L. Giussani, *The Religious Sense*, trans. John Zucchi (Montreal: McGill-Queen's University Press 1997), 12, 13.

# Contributors

LORENZO ALBACETE, Professor of Theology, St Joseph's Seminary, New York, former President of the Pontifical Catholic University of Puerto Rico

JORGE MARIO BERGOGLIO, Cardinal Archbishop of Buenos Aires

REMI BRAGUE, Professor of Philosophy, Université La Sorbonne, Paris 1

CARLO CAFFARRA, Archbishop of Ferrara-Comacchio, theologian

RALPH DEL COLLE, Professor of Theology, Marquette University, Milwaukee, Wisconsin

RAVAN FARHÂDI, Permanent Representative of Afghanistan to the United Nations

GIORGIO FELICIANI, Professor of Canon Law, Catholic University of the Sacred Heart, Milan. Chairman of the International Canonists Association

NEIL GILLMAN, Aaron Rabinowitz and Simon H. Rifkind Professor and Chairman of the Department of Jewish Philosophy at the Jewish Theological Seminary, New York

DAVID J. HOROWITZ, musician, Founder and Chairman of DHMA Incorporated, New York

RODNEY HOWSARE, Assistant Professor of Systematic Theology, DeSales University, Allentown, Pennsylvania

NIKOLAUS LOBKOWICZ, Director of Zimos (Central Institute for East-Central European Studies at the Catholic University of Eichstätt)

GILBERT MEILAENDER JR, Professor of Christian Ethics at Valparaiso University, Chile

JOHN O'CONNOR, Cardinal Archbishop of New York (d. 2000)

MARC OUELLET, P.S.S., Archbishop of Quebec

JAVIER PRADES, Professor of Theology, Theological Faculty, San Damaso, Madrid

DAVID L. SCHINDLER, F. Gagnon Professor of Fundamental Theology; Academic Dean, John Paul II Institute, Washington, DC

ANGELO SCOLA, Theologian, former Rector of Pontificia Università Lateranense, Patriarch of Venice

J. FRANCIS STAFFORD, Cardinal, President of Pontifical Council for the Laity

SHINGEN TAKAGI, Director of the Esoteric Buddhist Culture Research Institute and Professor of Buddhist Studies at Koyasan University, Japan

MICHAEL WALDSTEIN, President of the Internationales Theologisches Institut für Studien zu Ehe und Familie, Gaming, Austria

# Sources of Contributions

A STYLE OF THOUGHT
Angelo Scola

Lecture given at UNESCO, Paris, 21 January 1999, on the occasion of the publication of the French edition of *La coscienza religiosa dell'uomo moderno* (*La conscience religieuse de l'homme moderne*, Paris: Les Éditions du Cerf 1999). Published in *Realtà, ragione e fede nel pensiero di Luigi Giussani*, supplement to *Litterae Communionis – Tracce* 3 (March 1999).

CHRISTIANITY: A FACT IN HISTORY
Remi Brague

Lecture given at Unesco, Paris, 21 January 1999, on the occasion of the publication of the French edition of *La coscienza religiosa dell'uomo moderno* (*La conscience religieuse de l'homme moderne*, Paris: Les Éditions du Cerf 1999). Published in *Realtà, ragione e fede nel pensiero di Luigi Giussani*, supplement to *Litterae Communionis – Tracce* 3 (March 1999).

THE SPIRITUALITY OF LUIGI GIUSSANI
Lorenzo Albacete

Previously unpublished, written for this volume.

LIVING THE REAL INTENSELY
Michael Waldstein

Lecture given at the Augustinianum Institute, Rome, 26 November 1997, on the occasion of the publication of the Italian edition of *Il senso religioso* (Milan: Rizzoli 1997). Published in *The Religious Sense and Modern Man* (Milan: Coop. Edit. Nuovo Mondo 1998).

THE RELIGIOUS SENSE
J. Francis Stafford

Lecture given at The Religious Sense Symposium: Person, Meaning and Culture in America, Georgetown University Conference Center, Washington, DC, 10 September 1998. Published in *Communio* 25 (winter 1998): 663–78.

AN EXTRAORDINARY EDUCATOR
Marc Ouellet

Lecture given at The Religious Sense Symposium. Person, Meaning, and Culture in America, Georgetown University Conference Center, Washington, DC, 12 September 1998. Previously unpublished.

FOR MAN
Jorge Mario Bergoglio

Lecture given during the presentation of the Spanish edition of *Il senso religioso* (*El sentido religioso*, Buenos Aires and Madrid: Editorial Sudamericana – Ediciones Encuentro 1998), auditorium of Banco Rio, Buenos Aires, 16 October 1998. Published in *Litterae Communionis – Tracce* 4 (1999): 14–16.

THE RELIGIOUS SENSE AND AMERICAN CULTURE
David L. Schindler

Lecture given at The Religious Sense Symposium: Person, Meaning, and Culture in America, Georgetown University Conference Center, Washington, DC, 11 September 1998. Published in *Communio* 25 (winter 1998): 679–99.

MYSTERY INCARNATE
John O'Connor

Lecture given at the auditorium of the Dag Hammarskjöld Library, United Nations Headquarters, New York, 24 May 1999, on the occasion of the publication of the English edition of *At the Origin of the*

*Christian Claim.* Published in *The Believer at the Threshold of the Third Millennium*, suppl. to *Litterae Communionis – Tracce* 7 (1999).

THE CHRISTIAN, SUBJECT OF A NEW CULTURE
Javier Prades

Lecture given at a meeting of the Scientific Committee of the Centro di Studi sull'Ecumenismo, Milan, 6 February 1999. Previously unpublished.

TOWARD HUMAN FLOURISHING
Ralph Del Colle

Lecture given at the conference Toward Human Flourishing: Introduction to the Thought of Msgr Giussani, Marquette University, Milwaukee, Wisconsin, 14 November 2000. Previously unpublished.

AGAINST THE THEOLOGICAL PREJUDICES OF THE AGE
Rodney Howsare

Lecture given at the conference Toward Human Flourishing: Introduction to the Thought of Msgr Giussani, Marquette University, Milwaukee, Wisconsin, 14 November 2000. Previously unpublished.

THE ONLY POINT OF VIEW
Carlo Caffarra

Lecture given at the Aula Magna of the Catholic University of the Sacred Heart, Milan, 6 May 1998, on the occasion of the publication of *Porta la speranza. Primi scritti,* by Luigi Giussani. Published in *Alle radici di una storia*, insert in *Litterae Communionis – Tracce* 7 (1998).

ECUMENICAL BY ITS NATURE
Nikolaus Lobkowicz

Lecture given at the Aula Magna of the Catholic University of the Sacred Heart, Milan, 6 May 1998, on the occasion of the publication of *Porta la speranza: Primi scritti* by Luigi Giussani. Published in *Alle radici di una storia*, insert in *Litterae Communionis – Tracce* 7 (1998).

A PRESENCE THAT CAN BE TOUCHED
Gilbert Meilaender

Lecture given at the auditorium of the Dag Hammarskjöld Library, United Nations Headquarters, New York, 24 May 1999, on the occasion of the publication of the English edition of *At the Origin of the*

*Christian Claim.* Published in *The Believer at the Threshold of the Third Millennium*, suppl. to *Litterae Communionis – Tracce* 7 (1999).

## COMMON ROOT AND CHRISTIAN CLAIM
Neil Gillman

Lecture given at the auditorium of the Dag Hammarskjöld Library, United Nations Headquarters, New York, 24 May 1999, on the occasion of the publication of the English edition of *At the Origin of the Christian Claim.* Published in *The Believer at the Threshold of the Third Millennium*, suppl. to *Litterae Communionis – Tracce* 7 (1999).

## ABRAHAM AND LIBERTY
Ravan Farhâdi

Lecture given at the auditorium of the Dag Hammarskjöld Library, United Nations Headquarters, New York, 24 May 1999, on the occasion of the publication of the English edition of *At the Origin of the Christian Claim.* Published in *The Believer at the Threshold of the Third Millennium*, suppl. of *Litterae Communionis – Tracce* 7 (1999).

## INTERCULTURAL DIALOGUE
Shingen Takagi

Lecture given at the auditorium of the Dag Hammarskjold Library, United Nations Headquarters, New York, 11 December 1997, on the occasion of the publication of the English edition of *The Religious Sense.* Published in *The Religious Sense and Modern Man* (Milan: Coop. Edit. Nuovo Mondo 1998).

## THE RELIGIOUS SENSE AND MODERN MAN
David J. Horowitz

Lecture given at the auditorium of the Dag Hammarskjold Library, United Nations Headquarters, New York, 11 December 1997, on the occasion of the publication of the English edition of *The Religious Sense.* Published in *The Religious Sense and Modern Man* (Milan: Coop. Edit. Nuovo Mondo 1998).

## EDUCATING IN REASON
Giorgio Feliciani

Lecture given at the Aula Magna of the Catholic University of the Sacred Heart, Milan, 6 May 1998, on the occasion of the publication of *Porta la speranza: Primi scritti* by Luigi Giussani. Published in *Alle radici di una storia*, insert in *Litterae Communionis – Tracce* 7 (1998).

# Profile of Luigi Giussani

Luigi Giussani, born in 1922 in Desio (Milan, Italy), is one of the most influential thinkers and leaders in the Catholic world today. He lives near Milan and is the founder of the international Catholic lay movement, Communion and Liberation, which is present in about seventy countries across five continents, with a membership well in excess of one hundred thousand. In addition, hundreds of thousands of others have come into contact with him through his writings and the charitable, cultural, and social works of his movement.

At the age of ten, Giussani entered the Diocesan Seminary, where he studied under some of the more influential theologians of the time (Giovanni Colombo, future Archbishop of Milan; Carlo Colombo, one of Pope Paul VI's closest theologians; and Gaetano Corti, professor of the history of religion at the University of Trieste). After his ordination, he furthered his studies in Milan's Faculty of Theology, specialising in both American Protestant and Oriental theology (focusing upon the Slavophiles in particular). Eventually he joined the faculty. In his formative years he was especially interested in understanding the rational motives for faith and the individual's attachment to the Church. With marked sensitivity toward human and Christian experience, Giussani foresaw that Italian postwar society, although formally and apparently Catholic, had, in any case, begun to undergo a process of secularisation by which Christian faith was being gradually marginalised from social and cultural life.

Giussani shrewdly observed through chance conversations with high school students that this secular transformation was especially embedding itself in Italian youth, who not only looked upon Christianity with detachment and disdain but were no longer even aware of the nature or weight of the Christian proposal. This observation led him to his decision to leave seminary teaching in 1954 and to teach religion in the Liceo Classico Berchet, one of Milan's most important high schools. Giussani believed that it was imperative that the young people be able to rediscover faith as a present experience.

Many of the students he taught in the high school would become very influential in Italy and even abroad in later years. It did not take long for a deep friendship to develop between Giussani and his students, a friendship that grew into a movement called Gioventù Studentesca (Student Youth). Within a few years the movement had spread to other high schools in Milan and other Italian cities, and by the late 1960s, it included a few thousand students. In the early 1960s some of these students went abroad to Brazil and thus began the process of spreading the movement outside Italy. In 1964 Giussani joined the faculty of the Catholic University of the Sacred Heart in Milan, teaching introductory courses in theology. Soon these courses (Il senso religioso, Corso sulla Chiesa) became the most popular ones in the university, with over five hundred students and many auditors. He taught at the Catholic University until his retirement in 1990.

Soon after Giussani's arrival at the Catholic University, he and his movement came face to face with the raging European social crisis of 1968. In the ensuing ideological battles, student demonstrations, and debates, Giussani noted that the Catholic voice had been marginalised. Gioventù Studentesca too suffered a severe setback and was abandoned by many of its adherents during those years. Those who remained, however, became ever more aware of the meaning of their experience and presented themselves to the student world with a banner whose title summed up their proposal, Communion and Liberation: only a communion of those who gathered to keep the memory of Christ could lead to the true liberation of the human person. From that moment, Italian society witnessed the birth and spreading out of a new movement that through personal contacts moved quickly from the university into schools and factories and into the cultural and social mainstream of the country.

Communion and Liberation defined itself as a movement of education in a mature faith, that is, as personal self-awareness, freedom, and judgment. Such an education is "ecumenical" by its very nature, inasmuch as in deepening Christian truth, it makes one capable of recognising truth in anyone, regardless of its provenance. This missionary, and ultimately cultural, dimension of Msgr Giussani's charism, which has been transmitted to his entire movement, has led, in recent years, to the encounter with other non-Catholic religious experiences. This ecumenical openness has led to the flowering of numerous initiatives in the world of culture and education: schools at the elementary, junior high, and secondary levels; magazines and journals; cultural centres; research institutes; and in the most public gesture, the Meeting for Friendship among Peoples held in Rimini since 1980, with over half a million annual visitors.

Among the works generated by adults who belong to the movement that express commitment in the world of entrepreneurship, social assistance, and charity, the more significant undertakings are charitable work among the poor; Centres of Solidarity, to deal with the increasingly difficult labour market, especially unemployment among the poor; the creation of an international nongovernmental organization, AVSI; health complexes and hospitals, and special care for the needy, whether they are AIDS patients in Uganda or refugees in Rwanda.

One striking phenomenon in the history of Father Giussani's movement are the associations, recognised by the Pontifical Council for the Laity, through which people have formally dedicated themselves to Christ in a particular form, including the consecrated life. Over forty thousand adults from all paths of life and from many countries have been admitted into the lay association known as the Fraternity of Communion and Liberation. Over two thousand adults have entered Memores Domini, a lay consecrated life, and live "in the world" in "homes" on five continents. The Sisters of Charity of the Assumption, a female religious congregation founded in 1993, and the Priestly Fraternity of Saint Charles Borromeo, a missionary male fraternity of priests, have members dispersed in various parts of the world, including Novosibirsk (Russia), Montreal, Vienna, and Santiago. It is of great significance that at a time when vocations to the consecrated life are at a standstill, these various associations born of Father Giussani's movement are growing by leaps and bounds.

Many other individuals who are not part of the movement of Communion and Liberation have, nonetheless, maintained close ties to it, including the theologian Hans Urs von Balthasar, the playwright Eugène Ionesco, film director Andrey Tarkovsky, the writer Giovanni Testori, the painter W.G. Congdon, and Cardinal J. Ratzinger and John Paul II, who in 1982 officially recognized the Fraternity of Communion and Liberation.

Msgr Giussani is the author of numerous books that have provided the basis for the personal development of hundreds of thousands of young people and adults and have been translated into many languages. Since 1993 he has been the director of the series I libri dello spirito cristiano for the most important Italian publisher, Rizzoli RCS, and since 1997 he has been the director of the very successfull record series Spirto gentil.

In recognition of his enormous impact on contemporary society, Msgr Giussani was awarded the 1995 International Prize for Catholic Culture.

# Selected Works
# by Luigi Giussani

Luigi Giussani's writings cover a wide field, from theology to education, from pastoral care to cultural critique. His main works have been translated into many languages: English, French, Spanish, German, Russian, Polish, Portuguese, Bohemian, Slovak, Slovenian, Hungarian, Greek, and Albanian. For an up-to-date catalog of translations, see www.comunioneliberazione.org/storiatext/eng/book.htm. For a complete bibliography of books, articles, essays, and interviews to 1997, see L. Giussani, *Porta la speranza: Primi scritti* (Genoa: Marietti 1997). The following list records only the more recent of Giussani's main works, together with their English, French, and Spanish translations.

*La coscienza religiosa nell'uomo moderno: Note per cattolici impeganti.*
    Milan: Jaca Book 1985.
"Religious Awareness in Modern Man," *Communio: International Catholic
    Review* 25 (spring 1998): 104–40.
*La conciencia religiosa en el hombre moderno.* Madrid: Ediciones Encuentro
    1990.
*La coscience religieuse de l'homme moderne.* Paris: Les Éditions du Cerf 1999.

*Il senso religioso.* Vol. 1 of *PerCorso.* Milan: Jaca Book 1986.
*Il senso religioso.* Vol. 1 of *PerCorso.* Rev. ed. Milan: Rizzoli RCS 1997.
*The Religious Sense.* Montreal: McGill-Queen's University Press 1997.
*El sentido religioso.* Buenos Aires: Sudamericana/Ediciones Encuentro 1998.
*El sentido religioso.* Madrid: Ediciones Encuentro 1996.
*Le sens religieux.* Paris: Les Éditions du Cerf, 2003.

*Il movimento di Comunione e Liberazione: Conversazioni con Robi Ronza.* Milan: Jaca Book 1987.
*El movimiento de Comunión y Liberación.* Madrid: Ediciones Encuentro 1990.
*Le mouvement Communion et Libération.* Paris: Fayard 1988.

*All'origine della pretesa cristiana.* Vol. 2 of *PerCorso.* Milan: Jaca Book 1988.
*All'origine della pretesa cristiana.* Vol. 2 of *PerCorso.* Rev. ed. Milan: Rizzoli RCS 2001.
*Le défi de la foi chrétienne.* Paris: Fayard 1990.
*At the Origin of the Christian Claim.* Montreal: McGill-Queen's University Press 1998.
*Los orígenes de la pretensión cristiana.* Madrid: Ediciones Encuentro 1991.

*Perché la Chiesa*, Volume 1: *La pretesa permane.* Vol. 3 of *PerCorso.* Milan: Jaca Book 1990.
*Perché la Chiesa*, Volume 2: *Il segno efficace del divino nella storia.* Vol. 3 of *PerCorso.* Milan: Jaca Book 1992.
*Perché la Chiesa.* Volume 3 of *PerCorso.* Milan: Rizzoli 2003.
*Why the Church?* Montreal: McGill-Queen's University Press 2001.
*Por qué la Iglesia: La pretensión permanece.* Madrid: Ediciones Encuentro 1991.
*Por qué la Iglesia: El signo eficaz de lo divino en la historia.* Madrid: Ediciones Encuentro 1993.
*Pourquoi l'Eglise.* Paris: Fayard 1994.

*L'avvenimento cristiano.* Milan: Biblioteca Universale Rizzoli 1993.
*L'avvenimento cristiano.* Rev. ed. Milan: Biblioteca Universale Rizzoli 2003.

*Un avvenimento di vita cioè una storia.* Edited by C. Di Martino. Rome: Editoriale Italiana – Il Sabato 1993.

*Il senso di Dio e l'uomo moderno: La "questione umana" e la novità del Cristianesimo.* Milan: Biblioteca Universale Rizzoli 1994.

*Si può vivere così?* Milan: Biblioteca Universale Rizzoli 1994.
*¿Se puede vivir así?* Madrid: Ediciones Encuentro 1996.

*Realtà e giovinezza: La sfida.* Turin: SEI 1995.

*Alla ricerca del volto umano.* Milan: Rizzoli RCS 1995.
*El rostro del hombre.* Madrid: Ediciones Encuentro 1996.
*À la recherche du visage humain.* Paris: Fayard 1989.

*Il cammino al vero è un'esperienza.* Turin: SEI 1995.
*El camino a la verdad es una experiencia.* Madrid: Ediciones Encuentro 1997.

*Il rischio educativo: Come creazione di personalità e di storia.* Turin: SEI 1995.
*The Risk of Education.* New York: Crossroad 2001.
*Educar es un riesgo.* Madrid: Ediciones Encuentro 1991.
*Le risque éducatif.* Paris: Nouvelle Cité 1987.

*Il tempo e il tempio.* Milan: Biblioteca Universale Rizzoli 1995.
*El templo y el tiempo.* Madrid: Ediciones Encuentro 1995.

*Le mie letture.* Milan: Biblioteca Universale Rizzoli 1996.
*Mis lecturas.* Madrid: Ediciones Encuentro 1997.

*Si può (veramente?!) vivere così?* Milan: Biblioteca Universale Rizzoli 1996.

*Lettere di fede e di amicizia ad Angelo Majo.* Milan: San Paolo 1997.

*Porta la speranza: Primi scritti.* Ed. Elisa Buzzi. Genoa: Marietti 1997.
*Llevar la esperanza: Primeros escritos.* Madrid: Ediciones Encuentro 1998.

*"Tu" (o dell'amicizia).* Milan: Biblioteca Universale Rizzoli 1997.

*Generare tracce nella storia del mondo* (with Stefano Alberto and Javier
    Prades). Milan: Rizzoli RCS 1998.
*Crear huellas en la historia del mundo.* Madrid: Ediciones Encuentro 1999.

*Vivendo nella carne.* Milan: Biblioteca Universale Rizzoli 1998.

*L'attrattiva Gesù.* Milan: Biblioteca Universale Rizzoli 1999.

*Scuola di Religione.* Turin: SEI 1999.

*L'uomo e il suo destino: In cammino.* Genoa: Marietti 1999.

*L'autocoscienza del cosmo.* Milan: Biblioteca Universale Rizzoli 2000.

*Communion and Liberation: A Movement in the Church.* Ed. Davide Rondoni.
    Montreal: McGill-Queen's University Press 2000.

*Che cos'è l'uomo perché te ne curi?* Cinisello Balsamo, Italy: Ed. San Paolo 2000.

*L'io, il potere, le opere.* Genoa: Marietti 2000.

*El yo, el poder, las obras.* Madrid: Ediciones Encuentro 2001.

*Tutta la terra desidera il Tuo volto.* Cinisello Balsamo, Italy: Ed. San Paolo 2000.
*Toda la tierra desea ver tu rostro.* Madrid: Ediciones San Pablo 2000.

*Affezione e dimora.* Milan: Biblioteca Universale Rizzoli 2001.

*Avvenimento di libertà.* Genoa: Marietti 2002.

*Dal temperamento un metodo.* Milan: Biblioteca Universale Rizzoli 2002.

*Il miracolo dell' ospitalità.* Casale Monterrato: Piemme 2003.